SHOCK
FACTOR

ALSO BY JACK COUGHLIN

Shooter: The Autobiography of the Top-Ranked Marine Sniper
(with Capt. Casey Kuhlman and Donald A. Davis)

Kill Zone (with Donald A. Davis)

Dead Shot (with Donald A. Davis)

Clean Kill (with Donald A. Davis)

An Act of Treason (with Donald A. Davis)

Running the Maze (with Donald A. Davis)

Time to Kill (with Donald A. Davis)

On Scope (with Donald A. Davis)

The Night of the Cobra (with Donald A. Davis)

ALSO BY JOHN R. BRUNING

Level Zero Heroes (with Michael Golembesky)

The Trident: The Forging and Reforging of a Navy SEAL Leader
(with Jason Redman)

Outlaw Platoon (with Sean Parnell)

House to House (with David Bellavia)

Shadow of the Sword (with Jeremiah Workman)

Battle of the Bulge

Battle for the North Atlantic

Chasing Shadows (with Fred Burton)

The Devil's Sandbox

How to Break a Terrorist (with Matthew Alexander and Mark Bowden)

Bombs Away!

Heart for the Fight (with Brian Stann)

Ship Strike Pacific

Jungle Ace

Crimson Sky: The Air Battle for Korea

Luck of the Draw (with Ken Ruiz)

SHOCK FACTOR

AMERICAN SNIPERS IN THE WAR ON TERROR

Gunnery Sgt. Jack Coughlin, USMC (Ret.)

WITH

John R. Bruning

St. Martin's Griffin New York

www.stmartins.com

Designed by Omar Chapa

The Library of Congress has cataloged the hardcover edition as follows:

Coughlin, Jack.
    Shock factor : America's snipers in the War on Terror / Gunnery Sgt. Jack
Coughlin, USMC (Ret.) with John R. Bruning.
        p. cm.
    Includes index.
    ISBN 978-1-250-01655-3 (hardcover)
    ISBN 978-1-250-03837-1 (e-book)
    1. Iraq War, 2003–2011—Commando operations. 2. Snipers—United States—
History—21st century. 3. Snipers—Iraq—History—21st century. 4. Iraq War,
2003–2011—Campaigns. 5. Iraq War, 2003–2011—Atrocities. I. Bruning, John R.
II. Title.
    DS79.76.C6778 2014
    956.7044'342—dc23

                                                        2014025168

ISBN 978-1-250-07035-7 (trade paperback)

Our books may be purchased in bulk for promotional, educational, or business
use. Please contact your local bookseller or the Macmillan Corporate and
Premium Sales Department at (800) 221-7945, extension 5442, or by e-mail at
MacmillanSpecialMarkets@macmillan.com.

First St. Martin's Griffin Edition: November 2015

10 9 8 7 6 5 4 3 2 1

For Mark Evnin, one of the first snipers to fall during OIF I,
we will never forget you.

CONTENTS

Part III *Observations and Uprisings*

SHOCK FACTOR

PROLOGUE
Guardians

Shortly after I left the Marine Corps so I could provide a stable home for my two little girls, I flew to the Pacific Northwest to do an interview for *Shooter*, my first book, which detailed my experiences as a Marine sniper during the 2003 invasion of Iraq. I was scheduled to sit down with a local talk-show host of some renown. When I arrived in her studio, she welcomed me to her program, then asked, "So what's it feel like to be a murderer?"

Twenty years in the Corps taught me to expect anything and be ready for it, so this question didn't really surprise me. How I answered it surprised her.

"You don't really believe that," I said.

"What makes you say that?" she asked.

"Because if you really believed that I'm a murderer, you would not be sitting alone in this booth with me. And you'd already be dead."

The show's producer leapt to his feet, waving frantically for me to stop. The host's jaw dropped. She had no response.

Afterward, I thought about what she had said. I served my country as a Marine Corps sniper for two decades. I am a part of a community and a heritage that stretches back to the foundations of our Republic. We have been in every conflict and battle since Lexington and Concord—and not a few have turned in our country's favor as a result of our presence.

For two hundred years, others have called us murderers. To the

British officers we sniped off their horses during the American Revolution, we were ungentlemanly butchers. To our own troops in World War II, we were a scary, insulated community that stood apart from the line infantry. They called us "Ten Cent Killers," which was the cost of the .30 caliber rifle cartridge we used in our scoped Springfield 1903s. During Vietnam, the grunts called us "Murder Inc." or "Thirteen Cent Killers." Inflation made us more expensive, I guess.

Bottom line, being called a murderer comes with the territory. Over the years we have been the most misunderstood and marginalized community in the American military. Only in the past two decades has this really begun to change. And if those who wear the uniform don't get us, civilians certainly won't either. Yet the folks back home are the biggest beneficiaries of our work in combat—though they will never know it.

After that studio appearance in Seattle, I got to thinking about a shot I took in Somalia in 1993 that underscored a lot of the misperceptions about our community and who we snipers are.

My spotter and I were on the roof of a three-story building that sat astride one of Mogadishu's main roads, tasked with watching over a Marine reconnaissance platoon, about thirty men strong, that was out on a sweep. Their lieutenant had led them down into a brushy depression in an otherwise vast and open field. There was little cover, just a few tin shanties at the bottom of the draw, and another one at the far end of the open space just over nine hundred yards from our position. My spotter and I glassed (meaning searched through our optics) the area, alert for any of the clan members or bandits who had been taking potshots at our men and the UN's relief personnel. When my scan reached the shack at the far end of the field, I saw movement.

A man stepped into the doorway, his body at a forty-five-degree angle to me. He was holding an AK-47 assault rifle. He was only about three hundred yards from the recon platoon, well within the range of an AK-47 with iron sights.

As I watched him, he raised the AK to his shoulder. The barrel was pointed at my fellow Marines, who were unaware of his presence. All this had happened so quickly that we had not had time to radio a warning to the recon platoon.

I moved fast. Keeping my eye in the scope so I didn't lose sight of him, I factored in the wind speed, dialed in two minutes of windage, then took the shot. My M40 bolt-action rifle cracked and the report echoed through the city. Since I'd done the calculations on the fly, I was a little short. The 7.62mm round hit the ground in front of the gunman, skipped off a rock, and struck him in the right knee. He fell and his AK dropped.

I kept the scope on him, adjusting the crosshairs so they centered on his chin this time. A few seconds passed. The gunman seemed rooted in place, his weapon virtually forgotten. He didn't look like he was in pain, and he didn't act like the sudden shot had surprised him. Instead he remained motionless and continued to stare out at the Marines in the depression. I held my fire, waiting to see what he would do next, hoping that the wound I'd already inflicted would be enough to discourage him from doing anything further.

No such luck. He reached for his weapon. I pulled the trigger again. My second bullet hit his midsection. He flopped over on his back, his left leg twisted under him. I saw his wounded leg kick out, twitch, then go limp. By the time the Marines reached him, he was dead.

It was miraculous that my first bullet had hit him. Had it not skipped off the ground and knocked him off his feet, he would have been able to open fire on the recon platoon before I had had a chance to reload. He could have killed one of our Marines—one of my brothers. His death would have been traumatic enough, but what most books and movies won't show you is the effect that death would have had on his family, friends, community, and platoon. That moment would have forever scarred everyone in that Marine's life. With twenty years in the Corps, I've seen that happen many times. I've known widows who, decades after losing their Marine, were still adrift in their grief. I've met sons and daughters who never had the chance to know their fathers. I've seen parents whose grief has wrecked them. I've seen Marines blame themselves and never recover from the guilt of that loss.

I killed that gunman to save not just the Marine in his sights, but to spare everyone in his life the consequences of his death. Ask any military sniper why he does what he does and he will tell you, "To save lives." There is no way to tell how many Americans back home have had their worlds protected by our work. Since 9/11, I would venture to guess a majority of us have been silently affected in some way by our snipers. It is those shots we take that help keep those worlds intact.

Since I wrote *Shooter*, I've often been asked if I ever felt remorse for the lives I've taken. The answer is no.. I know what could have happened to our people if I had failed, and I will never regret doing all I could to protect them. The shots I didn't take are the ones I regret. They haunt me, because I know that there are evil men alive because of me who have most surely done my fellow Americans harm. The lives and worlds at home they've torn apart since my encounter with them . . . that weighs on my conscience. Other snipers will tell you the same thing.

A sniper team is one of the most powerful and multidimensional assets on a battlefield. We are the guardians of our brothers-in-arms and can perform that task in many ways, both with the triggers we pull and with the information we develop through stealth and guile. It has been that way since the American Revolution. In the pages to follow, you'll meet a dozen American snipers. You'll be immersed in their world and learn who they are and why they chose to join our community. You'll see them in action in missions both in Afghanistan and Iraq. You'll learn how they are the keepers of a heritage that began with the founding of our Republic. For all the changes in technology that have transformed our battlefields, the fundamentals of our community, established two centuries ago, remain the same.

We are a close-knit, tight-lipped community. Here, for the first, time, is a glimpse into our world and how we exist within it. We are proud of our profession and proud of the meaning our work has given us. We are life-takers when we have to be—usually as a last resort. But where we derive our value is not in the pull of the trigger, but in the lives we have saved and the families that have remained intact as a result of our precision, professionalism, and skill. That will always be our greatest contribution whenever our nation finds itself at war.

CHAPTER ONE
Messengers of Death

JANUARY 9, 1815

THE BATTLE OF NEW ORLEANS

The Shooter stood tall on the earthen rampart, his rifle at his side. His right hand held its barrel while his right foot backstopped the weapon's hand-carved stock. He wore buckskin leggings, a shirt and pants of woven linsey-woolsey, which gave him a tramplike appearance. A broad-brimmed felt hat shadowed his predator's eyes.

He stood alone, immune to the battle raging around him. The din had no parallel in his life—the crash of gunfire, the roar of cannon juxtaposed against distant bagpipes, and a New Orleans band belting out "Yankee Doodle." Around him, men died by the hundreds.

Across the battlefield, a group of British officers rode together. One, Lieutenant L. Walcott, sighted the Shooter and marveled at his poise. Suddenly, the Shooter moved. He shouldered his rifle and its barrel swung toward Walcott's party. The officers began to laugh. The American was over three hundred yards away, no way he could hit any of them. The gesture seemed ridiculous.

The Shooter pulled the trigger and shot one of the British officers right out of his saddle. His lifeless body flopped to the ground. The others in Walcott's group gaped at their dead comrade, shocked that one of their own could be killed so effortlessly at a distance that rendered their own weapons ineffective. Several long seconds later, they wrenched their attention back to the rampart. The Shooter had returned to his statuesque stance, rifle in hand, stock at his toes again. Beneath the brim of his hat, he tracked them and selected another target. The rifle came up and belched black smoke. The officer next to Lieutenant Walcott jerked back and fell off his horse.

Two shots, two kills. Walcott later recalled, "The cannon and the thousands of musket balls playing upon our ranks we cared not for; for there was a chance of escaping them . . . but to know that every time that rifle was leveled toward us . . . one must surely fall . . . that the messenger of death drove unerringly to its goal, to know this and still march on was awful."

The Shooter reloaded and resighted his weapon. Walcott and his surviving comrades exchanged terror-filled glances and wondered who would be the next of them to die.

Death on the battlefield is a random act. In the middle of a fight, a man can endure flying bullets and falling artillery because of their indiscriminate nature. The soldier in the heat of combat has built in psychological defenses to such incoming. *It can't hit me. The odds are with me. They aren't aiming at me.*

The Shooter stripped away those defenses, leaving Walcott naked to the primal fear aimed fire instills. For Walcott's group, there was no escape, and they realized it after the Shooter's second kill. Such a realization causes entire units to seize up in the midst of battle. Men who moments before were filled with courage or resolve will forget everything as their self-preservation instincts kick in. They will go to ground. They will cease advancing. They will lose control and run. Such elemental fear breeds panic, and in a test of arms, the ability to create panic wins battles. We call this the Shock Factor. It is a sniper's greatest weapon.

The Shooter's finger curled around the trigger, his rifle's front sight pinned on the officer riding beside Lieutenant Walcott. The Shooter had no scope, just his remarkable eyesight and a knack for gauging the wind and his bullet's drop. He took a breath, released half of it, and gently squeezed the trigger. Another of Walcott's friends was shot out of the saddle, probably dead before he even hit the ground.

Unlike his targets, the Shooter was not a professional officer. He was a frontiersman, born and raised in Tennessee or Kentucky, where a man's marksmanship determined the margin between life and death. His rifle was his most valued possession, precision-made by hand with loving care, its stock inlaid with ornate silver designs. It had probably been a family heirloom, handed down from one male member of the family to the next as part of his culture's rite of passage. Like his fellow "Dirty Shirt" frontiersmen, he joined this battle carrying his personal weapon. There were no government-issued guns waiting for him at the end of his passage south to face the British.

That was fine with him. His rifle was an extension of himself. In all likelihood, he'd been shooting it since he was a boy as he learned to hunt with his father or uncles. Bullets and powder did not come easily, so every shot counted in his world. In time, he developed such precision with his weapon that he could kill a squirrel by shooting the branch it was sitting on and sending wood shrapnel into the creature. That left the animal intact and edible. On the battlefield, such skill translated into deadly precision—and lots of headshots. He was an American rifleman; marksmanship was coded into his DNA. At New Orleans, future president Andrew Jackson had assembled the only sharpshooting army in United States history—and being on the receiving end of it must have been horrific.

Lieutenant Walcott was one of the lucky few British officers to survive the Battle of New Orleans. American rifleman killed or wounded virtually the entire British chain of command in less than twenty-five minutes of battle. The 93rd Highlanders, who marched toward our Shooter on the rampart with bagpipes blasting, went into the fight a thousand strong. Just short of the American lines, their regimental commander ordered his men to halt. Seconds later, an American rifleman killed him with a headshot. The rest of the regimental leadership went down before anyone could give an order. The 93rd stood there, shoulder to shoulder, its veteran soldiers completely at a loss for what to do next. They had never faced this sort of accurate fire before, and it paralyzed them. Not a man even returned fire.

The American dirty shirts poured it on. Six hundred Highlanders went down before the unit finally broke and ran. All across the battlefield, other British units did the same thing. Men who had never taken cover during a fight now sought any fold in the landscape that might offer respite from the deadly American bullets.

General Adair, commander of the Kentucky Riflemen, walked his line, pointing out targets to his men. He tapped one dirty shirt from behind and said, "See that officer on the gray horse?" The marksman nodded at the distant, moving target. Adair ordered, "Snuff his candle." The Kentuckian took aim and shot him right off his horse.

On the opposite side of the battle, a British colonel named Rennie led an assault on an isolated American redoubt emplaced ahead of the main rampart. He struck an impressive figure at the head of his men, coaxing them forward. The Americans in the redoubt abandoned their posts and scampered back to the main line. Rennie pressed forward and scaled the rear wall of the redoubt with two of his officers by his side. As he turned to urge his troops onward, several shooters from the New Orleans Rifles, a militia unit from the Big Easy, opened fire. All three officers went down. The leaderless British soldiers froze, then fell back pell-mell, their ranks savaged by the American fire.

Afterward an argument broke out among the New Orleans sharpshooters over who killed the British colonel. The best marksman in town, a merchant named Mr. Withers, flatly said, "If he isn't hit above the eyebrows, it wasn't my shot." After the battle, the New Orleans Rifles retrieved the colonel's body from a ditch—and found he'd been struck in the forehead. That settled the debate.

A half hour into the Battle of New Orleans and the British army had been reduced to panicked survivors cowering amongst heaps of their dead and dying comrades. Some sought to escape from the American shooters by low crawling. It didn't work. The Shooter on the rampart was joined by hundreds more who waited patiently until their quarries exposed legs, arms, or parts of their heads. The dirty shirts were used to bagging quail, squirrels, and hares on the run at seemingly impossible ranges; the British soldier who gave up even the tiniest part of his body paid the price. A flash, a report, and the target went down.

Others tried to flee the kill zone in quick rushes. The shooters were too adept for this to work. Those British soldiers died almost as soon as they stood up, except for one who proved particularly fleet-footed. He rose several hundred yards from the American ramparts and dashed like a rabbit toward the rear. Several shooters fired and missed him, which emboldened the Brit. He flopped to the ground, waited a few seconds, then stood up and mooned the Americans. Shouting obscenities, he sprinted rearward and took cover before anyone could kill him. Finally, the Americans brought forth one of their best sharpshooters. He eased into his stance, sighted his rifle, and waited. After a long pause, the Brit stood up, mooned the Americans again, and started to run. The American pulled the trigger and killed him with a shot to the spine, right between his shoulder blades. Mercy was absent that day.

For most of those soldiers trapped in the American kill zone, there would be no escape. One by one, the frontiersmen picked them off. Terror-filled cries rang out. Calls for help went unheeded. When the last shot had been fired, over fifteen hundred corpses littered the battlefield. Sixty Americans had died, almost all to artillery fire at the start of the fighting.

New Orleans is a case study in how precision marksmanship can destroy a numerically superior foe's will to fight. Despite having better weapons, better supplies, veteran troops and leaders, the British stood no chance in the face of the dirty shirts and their stunning accuracy. In minutes, that accuracy shredded their officer corps and left the foot soldiers leaderless and panicked in the kill zone. When they started to break and run, they received no respite. The British army came apart in a welter of blood and terror, victim of the Shock Factor applied on a macro scale.

I witnessed the Shock Factor firsthand many times during my

career. During one fight in Iraq in the 2003 invasion, I spotted a two-man Iraqi machine-gun team in a window of a building while I was scanning for targets from the hatch of one of our Amtracs—an amphibious armored personnel carrier. The two men were so close together, I couldn't tell who was the loader and who was the gunner. I drew a bead on them just as they swung their weapon toward another Amtrac not fifty yards from their building.

I pulled the trigger once. My M40 barked, and the loader vanished from the window. The gunner was so stunned by his comrade's death that he couldn't move. This surprise and fear-borne paralysis is a significant way we snipers psychologically dominate our battlefields. I racked my M40 rifle's bolt and killed the frozen gunner with my second shot.

When an enemy force advances into a sniper's zone of control, one well-placed bullet can stop the assault in its tracks. As soon as the enemy troops realize they are under precision sniper fire, they will often seek cover and stay there until the sniper either leaves or is taken out—no easy task. Often, the Shock Factor causes strange reactions. The death of one of their own, combined with the sound of only a single shot, acts like a reset button on the neural circuitry of the men nearby. They'll dive for cover, only to pick totally exposed places. They'll freeze up, as the Iraqi gunner did; they'll run in odd directions or return fire randomly. Some will flee. Some will cower. Some will babble nonsensical orders. A very few will actually continue to function and search for the sniper's position. They are the ones we usually make priority targets.

In Somalia, I learned that a sniper doesn't even need to kill an enemy to create the Shock Factor and psychologically dominate him. My spotter and I had just climbed atop the Spaghetti Factory, a tall building in the heart of Mogadishu that provided a good vantage point of the city. While a platoon of our men conducted a patrol a few hundred yards to our left, we started to scan the area. The first thing we saw was a group of teenaged boys huddled together. On previous missions into the city, we'd seen these sorts of human clusters and learned to recognize that they usually meant the kids involved were up to no good. They were usually smuggling something the huddle was designed to conceal, like drugs or ammunition or weapons. We call behavior like this a tell, or a target indicator.

This time, they were circled around a fourteen- or fifteen-year-old boy who held an American-made M1 Garand rifle that dated back to the Second World War. I centered my scope on the kid and saw he wore cut-off jeans and flip-flops. Like the other kids, he was shirtless and super-model skinny. We checked the wind. Three to five miles an hour—not a factor at the distance between my rifle's barrel and the kid, who was one hundred sixty-eight yards away.

The gaggle of kids began to move toward our patrolling Marines. The boy with the rifle looked like he was psyching himself up to take a shot. I watched through my scope, reporting everything I saw while praying that he'd lose heart. I could not let him shoot a Marine and tear worlds apart back home, but I could not stand the thought of killing a child.

He and his pals kept moving toward the platoon. Soon, they'd be in a position to open fire. My mind raced, searching for options.

Inspiration struck. I adjusted the crosshairs and pinned them on the M1 Garand's stock. The boy was carrying it low with one hand wrapped around its receiver. The stock jutted out behind him as he walked.

I pulled the trigger. The stock splintered. The stunned children scattered as the boy dropped the Garand. I scanned their faces and saw shock on all of them. They stopped running a few seconds later, then looked around as if they'd been witness to some sort of super-natural event. I hoped this would convince them to go on home, but teenage bravado prevailed. The boy in the cut-offs and flip-flops steeled himself and returned to his weapon. As he bent down, I put a round right into the dirt next to the Garand. It kicked up a cloud of dust and the rifle jerked. The boy leapt backwards, as if the gun were possessed. The other boys scattered again.

Long seconds passed. The boys approached the Garand one more time like kids goading themselves through a cemetery at midnight. When they tried one more time to retrieve the weapon, I put another bullet beside it. That did it. The boys scampered off and left the weapon in the dirt. I later retrieved it and took it home as a souvenir.

Without taking a killing shot, my accuracy destroyed the boy's will to fight. That is significant power, and no other element on the battlefield has it.

In the years since the Shooter killed Lieutenant Walcott's brother officers at New Orleans, the technology and science of long-range precision marksmanship has undergone multiple revolutions. They have served to widen the kill zone for us, which in turn has magnified our psychological power. Today, we snipers are more flexible. Night is no longer an obstacle. Neither is weather. But even as we adapted the latest hi-tech gadgets, the basic skill sets the Shooter used in 1815 have remained the same. They are the same principles I learned when I became a sniper some one hundred seventy years after the Battle of New Orleans.

More than once our community has been disbanded. Wars end and snipers are the first to be trimmed from peacetime military budgets. We've paid the price for those mistakes when we've found ourselves in another conflict and had to build a sniper program on the fly. In World War I, our shooters were given less than two weeks extra training before being sent into the trenches to fight Germans with years of sniping experience. The same thing happened in World War II. The Army's snipers received a nine-day course in theater before entering combat. They suffered an eighty-five percent casualty rate as a result.

Marine snipers had better equipment and better training, but even after they more than proved their worth on the island battlefields of the Pacific, the entire program was dismantled after Japan's surrender. When Korea kicked off five years later, the cycle repeated itself, and both services had to scramble to rebuild sniper programs from scratch.

When Korea ended in 1953, it happened again. The courses were abandoned and the snipers sent to other duties. It took Vietnam to break this pattern at last. Both the Army and the Corps established schools in country. The 2nd Marine Division kick-started the effort, closely followed by the 3rd. Both units built ranges around Da Nang and culled through the records to find expert marksmen or aging competitive shooters who had once been part of sniper units. They found shooters in unlikely places, like supply offices and desk jobs. Carlos Hathcock, one of our most successful snipers, had been an MP before he was pulled into the new program. It took time to rebuild and relearn the field craft and skills the Shooter of New Orleans possessed a century before. But when it all came together, our snipers set a fresh standard for effectiveness. Men like Carlos Hathcock and Chuck Mawhinney established the new legacy and became our role models in the years ahead.

Vietnam ended in 1975, and fortunately this time the community was not disbanded. Since Grenada, we have rolled into every battle with an increasing level of professional acumen and expertise. Gone are the days where our raw recruits were born on the frontier and raised with a rifle in hand. While more snipers hail from urban backgrounds, our classes and schools have expanded in scope and depth to hone their skills to a razor's edge. Today's American sniper has no peer in training, skill, and support. Despite this, we still face friction within our own chain of command over how we should be used on the battlefield.

This is an old problem that dates back to the Revolution. The best officers grasp the Shock Factor and find ways to apply it, but most have no understanding of the psychological power we possess. Those men historically have reverted to their default knowledge base. We've ended up being used like regular line infantry too many times to count, and it only serves to increase friendly casualties.

Part of the problem we face is that the Shock Factor cannot be replicated in a clean, analytical training environment. It is a phenomenon reserved only for combat, and the reaction to it cannot be quantified. Nor can it be fully understood unless experienced or witnessed. As a result, our capacity to influence a battle has almost always been underestimated. Until the War on Terror, New Orleans was the exception, not the rule.

During my career, I only glimpsed the Shock Factor once in training during a 2000 multinational field exercise. One phase of the training included an assault in urban terrain. As we planned how this would look, I suggested we deploy a few of my sniper teams to hold the objective town against a battalion-level infantry assault. I had no doubt we could keep the enemy at bay for as long as necessary, provided we were allowed to use all our skills in stealth and concealment. The leaders running the exercise refused to believe this, and my commander did not want to put two of his men out on an island without support. Even in training, our officers are often casualty-averse. Of course, this is usually a good thing, but when it comes to snipers, this level of caution stems from a failure to understand our capabilities.

After an intense discussion, I finally convinced them to let us give it a try. We were using simunitions—short-ranged projectiles that sting like paintballs when they hit a man—so I knew we would have to rely on stealth and concealment instead of stand-off distance. The result? Our two-man sniper team held up seven hundred Marines for an entire morning. We used surprise and precision to stop every assault, and our red force never even located us.

To our delight, the surprise and mild pain the simunitions inflicted actually created a mild form of the Shock Factor. It was the closest we ever came to replicating it in a peacetime setting. Unfortunately, our leadership did not appreciate our success. They pulled us out of the action so the assault battalion could finish its mission and complete its training objectives. We were seen as hindering the training process, not enhancing it. For the rest of the exercise, we sat on the sidelines feeling like the Corps' bastard redheaded stepchildren. The psychological power we had demonstrated was all but ignored.

Fortunately, since 9/11 this attitude has started to change. Our officers now undergo sniper employment courses, taught by snipers, before they take over battalion-level commands. Since most of the

Corps has seen extensive combat over the past decade, our officers are more familiar with the Shock Factor than ever before. They've seen it in the field during firefights with an enemy who wears no uniform and often fights us amongst innocent civilians. They've seen how threats come at our soldiers and Marines from every compass point, and they've learned the value of having a sniper team on their shoulder, watching over them for just such surprise attacks.

In this perilous environment, we snipers are in our element. As the war has dragged on, our role on the battlefield has expanded. Our leaders have recognized the value of our psychological power and surgical accuracy in a fight that is as much for the hearts and minds of the locals as it is to destroy the enemy. Without a sniper's precision, we would have to rely on firepower to take out our enemies. Laser-guided bombs and artillery destroys neighborhoods and kills civilians—side effects that generate bad press, complicate our efforts politically, and spawns fresh recruits to the insurgent cause. A post-Vietnam study found that it required ten thousand bullets for a conventional unit to kill a single Viet Cong. It took a sniper three and a half. We shooters can find, fix, and eliminate the enemy without endangering local populations, all while leaving property undamaged. Our psychological power can crush an attack before the enemy has a chance to launch it.

This is our kind of fight. As Lieutenant Walcott wrote, we are messengers of death. If a sniper is stalking you, his bullet is not *To Whom It May Concern*, but a very direct and personal *Special Delivery* to you. That personal aspect makes us more than messengers of death. We are deliverers of fear.

PART I

SPECIAL OPERATIONS

CHAPTER TWO
Night Assault

YOUSSIFIYAH, IRAQ
THE HEART OF THE SUNNI TRIANGLE
JUNE 16, 2006

For months, the tide of war in Iraq had been turning against the Coalition. Thanks to the cunning strategy employed by al-Qaida Iraq's commander, Musab al-Zarqawi, the country had fallen into a brutal civil war drawn along ethnic and religious lines. Using foreign volunteers as suicide bombers, Zarqawi had unleashed a wave of terror not on American forces, but on the Shia majority within Iraq. His minions blew up markets, mosques, and local councils and assassinated Shia officials, all in a bid to destabilize Iraq so completely that the American effort in the nation would be swamped by violence and doomed to defeat.

That spring, the strategy was working. Zarqawi's cells had killed thousands of innocent Shia, who in turn had formed local militias that retaliated against their Sunni countrymen in night raids full of shocking levels of brutality. The war devolved into a bloody street-by-street battle for control of all of Iraq's major cities. Where once Sunni and Shia lived together in harmony, by 2006 they were ruthlessly purging their neighborhoods and carving out enclaves as the sectarian murders left scores, if not hundreds, of dead every night.

Caught in the middle trying to control this Arab versus Arab bloodletting was the American occupation force in Iraq. Both sides carried out attacks against U.S. troops whenever it suited them. The Shia, led by Moqtada al-Sadr's Mahdi Militia, had launched two major rebellions in 2004, followed by periodic upticks of violence in 2005 and early 2006. Meanwhile, the Sunni population, under attack by increasingly reckless and barbaric Shia militias, turned to al-Qaida in Iraq for protection and help. In Sunni-dominated areas, such as the districts south of Baghdad, the Sunni insurgents virtually controlled the countryside. Known as the Sunni Triangle, the area around Youssifiyah became one of the most dangerous places in Iraq. Here, sixteen miles southwest of Baghdad, hundreds of Coalition soldiers died fighting in the town and its environs, mostly to the roadside bombs the Sunni cells had so craftily perfected. From October 2005 through June 2006, the American units around Youssifiyah were attacked 2,296 times. The insurgents had detonated over 1,600 roadside bombs during those attacks.

The legendary 101st Airborne Division joined the fight around Youssifiyah in the late fall of 2005. From their first missions, the Screaming Eagles encountered fearsome opposition as these young Americans were on the receiving end of most of those twenty-two hundred attacks. The 2005–2006 deployment became a hellish slugfest of roadside bombs, sudden ambushes, and betrayals by traitorous Iraqi "allies." The 101st's 1st Battalion, 502nd Parachute Infantry Regiment suffered twenty-one killed in action during this deployment, along with scores more wounded from an original force of about seven hundred.

For the men of the 1/502, each day began and ended with uncertainty. Spread dangerously thin across checkpoints and forward operating bases, they had little support available when the enemy struck at them. As the losses mounted, morale plummeted. For some of the soldiers, the enemy became all Iraqis, not just the al-Qaida-armed and -financed insurgents. What followed was a descent into one of the worst chapters of the Iraq War.

2000 HOURS
JUNE 16, 2006

Specialist David Babineau should not have been on bridge duty that night. At twenty-five, he'd done his eight years in the Army and had been ready to get out the previous fall. But as his platoon readied for a second Iraq deployment, he'd been stop-lossed. Instead of serving out the end of his contract and hanging up his uniform, the father of three found his service extended until after this tour in the Middle East.

He never grumbled about that. Rather, he'd always exhibited leadership skills and had a knack of getting along with everyone. At times officers took note and asked him why he didn't push to make sergeant. Truth was, he didn't care about rank. He was happy where he was, and looked forward to leaving the Army when 1/502nd returned home later in the fall of 2006.

On the night of June 16, Babineau was detached from his platoon with two other soldiers, Private Thomas Tucker and Private Kristian Menchaca, to guard a bridge over a canal outside of Youssifiyah. The original bridge had been destroyed at some point earlier in the war. Now an armored engineer vehicle rested in its place. Called an AVLB, for armored vehicle-launched bridge, the massive vehicle carried a metal temporary bridge on its back that could be unfolded to cross such a divide as the canal. With it in place, the Coalition needed to guard it, lest it be destroyed or even stolen by the local insurgents.

For weeks, Bravo Company, 1/502 had parceled out men and Humvees to guard a series of checkpoints around Youssifiyah. The nearest one from the AVLB was almost a mile away and out of visual sight. With so many losses—Bravo had taken ten casualties by June 16—and with many of the men on leave, by mid-June the company was running at about two-thirds normal strength. Without the resources to properly man all the checkpoints, 1st Platoon, Bravo Company was reduced to guarding the bridge with a single Humvee and three soldiers.

It was a threadbare way to wage a war, and the men in the Humvee that night were bone tired and jaded.

Menchaca, a Texas-born Hispanic with an easy grin and fun-loving personality, had gone on leave only a few weeks before. His family back in south Texas was shocked at the twenty-three-year-old's gaunt appearance and nervousness. He chained-smoked—something he had not done before the deployment, and spoke of how his base had burned down in a fire, leaving some of the men of 1st Platoon without any clothes save the uniforms on their backs. They received no influx of supplies, no additional clothes. Before he departed for Iraq at the end of his leave, he asked his family to send him some basics—soap, baby wipes, plus Oreo cookies. He always had a weak spot for them. He returned to his brothers in 1st Platoon, where his resolve and devotion never failed, even in the worst moments. On the sixteenth of June, he volunteered for the AVLB guard detail so another soldier could stay behind and enjoy his birthday.

Thomas Tucker, a twenty-five-year-old from tiny Madras, Oregon, had been equally weary, but he'd done his best to hide from his family the daily reality he faced. Before he'd headed out, he left a voice mail message back home explaining he was going on a little vacation and he'd be back soon.

A tough kid from the hardscrabble eastern Oregon high desert, Tucker grew up hunting and fishing like most rural Oregon boys. He loved to work on old pickup trucks, and his sense of humor had a knack of drawing people to him. When friends dug a little deeper, they found beyond his small-town crust a talented artistic soul. He loved music, played in the high school band, and had a penchant for sketching and drawing.

Another time, just before he went into battle, he left another message for his mother, "Be proud of me, Mom. I'm defending my country." At his core, Thomas Tucker was an old-school American patriot.

The three men hunkered down beside the engineer vehicle and bridge and did their best to combat the boredom they would face for the next twenty-four hours. The company's thin ranks forced the platoons to change shifts at the checkpoints once a day, instead of every four to eight hours. The men endured hour after hour of mind-numbing nothingness, parked beside the canal in the darkness of a steaming hot Iraqi night.

They did not know al-Qaida was watching them.

Babineau had seen firsthand how insidious al-Qaida's operatives could be at times. A few months before, Babineau had been at another checkpoint when an Iraqi civilian came through it. The man was well known by the men of 1st Platoon. Always friendly to Americans, he had given the battalion tips on enemy activity in the past. This time, as he walked through the checkpoint, Babineau's friend, Sergeant Ken Casica, approached the man to chat with him. Casica, who had tattooed his daughter's name on his arm before the deployment, said something to the Iraqi. The man spun around and pulled a 9mm pistol from his waistband. He shot Casica in the neck, then turned his weapon on Staff Sergeant Travis Nelson, a forty-one-year-old Alabama native. Nelson had been facing the other way, and the Iraqi's first shot caught him in the back of the head. Babineau dove for cover behind a Humvee as the gunman fired at him, then tried to kill the soldier in the turret of the vehicle. He missed, and a second later, a short burst from the turret gunner's M240 Bravo machine gun blew the Iraqi's head off.

After that incident, the men of 1st Platoon treated every approaching Iraqi as a potential threat.

But on this night, not a soul stirred—at least not that the three men at the bridge could see. But in the darkness, hiding in the shadows, was a well-trained team of devoted Jihadists. Silently, they watched their target, waiting for the moment to strike.

Al-Qaida's spies had long since noticed the Americans left only one Humvee's worth of troops to guard the engineer bridge. In Baghdad proper, it had become standard Army procedure as early as 2004 to never leave the wire with less than three vehicles. Here in the heart of al-Qaida Iraq's stronghold, the lone Humvee was terribly vulnerable, and the insurgents knew it. They watched the shifts change every day, and they plotted an attack. They knew the nearest American reinforcements were almost a mile away, so they devised a way to delay their response. That left only a nearby Iraqi Army outpost as the only possible source of help for the three Americans. The Iraqi troops were poorly trained and undermotivated. Either al-Qaida convinced them to stay out of the fight, or they had no stomach for it. Whichever the case, the insurgent force knew it would not be impeded by America's Coalition partner.

The hours dragged by that night. Tucker, Babineau, and Menchaca let their guard down as the darkness offered nothing but emptiness and boredom. Exhaustion set in. Almost twenty-four hours into their shift, they retreated into the Humvee, closed the armored doors, and pulled off their heavy Kevlar helmets. One of them tossed a pack of Skittles into his helmet.

The eyes on them had seen this happen before. In early June, the assault team had rehearsed their attack for two straight days as part of their final preparations.

Now was their moment. Sweeping out of the darkness, AK-47s blazing, they charged the Humvee. The soldiers bailed out of their vehicle, but they stood no chance. Before any of them could fire a shot, the enemy probably wounded Tucker and Menchaca. Babineau, in a desperate bid to escape the onslaught, bolted down the bank of the canal. Behind him, the al-Qaida assault team opened fire, raking his back and head with bullets. He fell dead into the reeds and shallow water at the edge of the canal.

The soldiers at the nearest checkpoint heard the gunfire and tried to radio the men at the engineer bridge. When they received no response, they climbed into a Humvee to go investigate. The vehicle refused to start—its battery was dead. Sick with worry, the soldiers dismounted and ran to their only other ride, an ancient, Vietnam-era M-113 armored personnel carrier. The track spun onto the road and rumbled toward the bridge, only to encounter two large objects blocking the route ahead. The driver stopped, worried that there might be a roadside bomb.

Time ticked by. The four men in back grew almost frantic. Finally, they piled out and decided to run the rest of the distance on foot. The M-113 and its crew remained behind for an hour and a half, stalled by a couple of oil drums the insurgents had placed across the road.

Fifteen minutes after they'd heard gunfire, the four men from 1st Platoon reached the engineer bridge. The Humvee appeared intact, its

M240 Bravo machine gun still in the turret. Both doors on the right side were lying open. Spent shell cases littered the Iraqi dirt. At first they found no sign of their brothers. Then, beside the Humvee, they encountered a pool of blood. Then another. Thirty yards from the Humvee, they found Babineau's body.

Thomas Tucker and Kristian Menchaca were nowhere to be found.

With dawning horror, the soldiers who first responded to the scene realized their brothers had been captured. There was no worse fate for an American in Iraq. Everyone had seen the al-Qaida torture videos. They knew that if they couldn't find Tucker and Menchaca quickly, the worst would happen.

The platoon converged on the scene. They went to every nearby house and dwelling, interrogating the inhabitants and demanding to know what they'd seen. If anyone resisted, or seemed to know more than they were letting on, the men unleashed cold fury on them.

When the Screaming Eagles went to find out what the Iraqi Army troops had seen, they listened in stunned disbelief as their Coalition allies professed ignorance. They told the Americans they hadn't heard or seen a thing. The lies were outrageous—everyone in the area heard hundreds of gunshots from AK-47s being fired full auto. The Iraqi Army reaction only stoked 1st Platoon's rage.

First platoon searched for their captured men for sixteen hours straight, even as the division began to flood the area with more troops. The 4th Infantry Division sent reinforcements into the area as well. An Air Force parajumper team arrived, as did specialized dive units. Drones, helicopters, and jet fighters soon buzzed overhead.

The search soon focused on a nearby village and a power plant. At the entrance to the plant, an American discovered blood smeared on a bridge handrail. Blood trails and drag marks led from the road into the facility. All through the following morning, American troops searched every inch of the power station. They found a chunk of American body armor, and an abandoned white truck with congealing blood pooled in its bed.

The search continued. Hundreds, then thousands of American troops and Iraqi commandos descended on the area. They searched villages, conducted air assaults, interrogated detainees. All through the seventeenth, the insurgents emerged from concealed positions to launch hit-and-run attacks on the search teams. Mortar fire rained down on the Americans. The fighting killed one Coalition soldier and wounded a dozen more. Thirty-six insurgents were captured and two al-Qaida operatives killed. The area was laced with roadside bombs, twelve of which went off and destroyed or damaged eight vehicles.

Through the explosions, mortar fire, and AK-47 ambushes, the Americans pressed on in search of their lost soldiers. Finally, on the afternoon of Sunday, June 18, a sweep through the village of Rushdi Mullah netted two prisoners who told their interrogators where Tucker and Menchaca could be found.

Two miles northeast of the power plant, American troops located their mutilated bodies. Al-Qaida had mined the road around them with bombs, and had booby-trapped their remains. It took twelve hours for specialized engineers to defuse the bombs and clear a path to the bodies. When the Americans finally reached them, they discovered Menchaca and Tucker had been tortured. Postmortem, Tucker had been decapitated. Both had been eviscerated, then dismembered.

The Mujahideen Shura Council of Iraq, one of the al-Qaida front groups in country, later released a video showing Jihadists defiling the bodies. One jubilant terrorist held Thomas Tucker's head up for the camera. The four-minute, thirty-nine-second video extolled the greatness of the holy fighters responsible for the mutilation, and announced that Abu Ayyub al-Masri, al-Zarqawi's replacement as head of al-Qaida Iraq (Zarqawi had been killed by U.S. forces earlier in June), had personally killed both men.

The U.S. Army vowed to track down those responsible and mete out justice. In the meantime, the bodies of the three Screaming Eagles were returned to the States. In Madras, the memorial service for Thomas Tucker drew thousands of people. The procession to the cemetery where he was laid to rest was eight miles long—longer than

Madras itself. Late into the evening that night, hundreds of residents protectively ringed the Tucker residence, keeping outsiders and reporters at bay as they consoled the family.

Back in Iraq, American intelligence concluded that al-Qaida had lied about al-Masri killing the two soldiers personally. Although Zarqawi had been filmed slowly decapitating an American contractor in 2003, the claim that al-Masri was involved in the murders was seen as a bid by al-Qaida to build up their new commander after Zarqawi's death.

But who had planned and carried out the attack? And who had killed Tucker and Menchaca once the al-Qaida assault force had seized them?

Months passed seemingly without any progress in finding those responsible. Finally, in 2008, the U.S. Army developed enough evidence against three men to hand them over to an Iraqi court. DNA evidence convinced the court that one of the men had been in the truck used to drag the bodies. He received a death sentence for his role. The other two were acquitted.

Back home, pundits railed against this meager response. Where was justice for the families? One man out of the entire team was convicted? It seemed a pathetic effort compared to the barbarity that befell these two warriors. Bloggers howled at our apparent impotence, one even went so far as to say President Bush should have personally announced he would have every man responsible hunted down, much as Russian president Vladimir Putin had done after a terrorist attack in his country.

In the shadows, another story developed, far away from the media's prying eyes. Unknown to the American public, the Iraq War's most deadly sniper had been put on al-Qaida's trail.

CHAPTER THREE
Al Shatan

That June, sixty miles northwest of where al-Qaida captured and killed Thomas Tucker, Kristian Menchaca, and David Babineau, one of the pivotal battles of the Iraq War was raging. After the second Battle of Fallujah in November 2004, much of the surviving insurgent leadership retreated to Ramadi, a city of about 500,000 people that sprawls for dozens of miles along the banks of the Euphrates River. It had long served as the capital of Al Anbar Province, which made control of it both strategic and symbolic. Despite every Coalition effort, in the spring of 2006 the city remained a hornet's nest. Daily, American patrols trying to secure Ramadi's streets ran into fierce firefights or roadside bombs. Iraqi police who dared to take a stand against the insurgents had their families threatened or killed. Some were captured and beheaded by al-Qaida zealots. Others simply walked off the job, or did al-Qaida's bidding, which inflicted major setbacks on the Coalition's effort to establish Iraqi control of security in the area.

In early June, just after Musab al-Zarqawi, the head of al-Qaida Iraq, was killed by USAF bombs, the Coalition began to concentrate troops around Ramadi. Its citizens learned of this development and, fearing a second Fallujah, began to leave in droves. A big battle was in the offing, and both sides prepared for another brutal urban slugfest.

The Americans assembled a joint force that included parts of the Army's legendary 1st Armored Division and the 8th Marine Regiment. Instead of assaulting the city directly, the Americans threw a cordon around Ramadi, using outposts to choke off the flow of supplies and reinforcements to the insurgents hiding within the labyrinth of streets and alleyways.

Al-Qaida's legions did not sit quietly as they were surrounded. Using teams of up to a hundred men, they assaulted many of the newly established American combat outposts and tried to overrun the troops there. Pitched small-unit battles raged around these key positions, but the Americans held firm and drove off the attackers.

Meanwhile, instead of launching a full-scale assault into the city, the Americans moved in one block at a time. Hoping to keep the damage to the city to a minimum, artillery and air strikes were used only as a last resort. Without such firepower, sniper teams became the best way to help support the patrols pushing into the city. Both sides deployed some of the most deadly snipers of the war, and Ramadi became fertile hunting ground for these shooters.

Rumors swirled through the American ranks that an Iraqi Olympics sharpshooter had been brought into Ramadi to help beat back the Coalition offensive. Known only as "Mustafa," there is some doubt as to whether he was a concoction of al-Qaida propaganda or an actual person. Either way, the effect on American morale was significant, especially when the insurgent shooters began killing Marines and GI's with devastating, long-range shots. Like our snipers, the enemy's favored high ground. They took to using the local children's hospital for hide sites, which prompted the staff there to evacuate the kids to the lower levels of the facility. Ramadi's main hospital, a towering structure with a commanding view, also became a key sniper position, one from which the enemy sharpshooters claimed many Coalition lives.

As the battle slowly developed, SEAL Team Three deployed to Ramadi to assist with the offensive that spring. Arriving a short time after the majority of the team reached the area was thirty-two-year-old Chris Kyle. He'd been held up Stateside due to illness while his team settled into Al Anbar Province, but was eager to link up with his brother SEALs and get into the fight. Unfortunately, the military's transportation system made this difficult, and after he flew into Baghdad, the Navy sniper could not find a ride out to Ramadi. Finally, he convinced a corpsman to help him out. The corpsman triaged Chris and an Army Ranger stuck in the same situation, and ordered both men medevac'd into Ramadi.

Despite the belated and backdoor arrival into the inferno raging around the city, Chris Kyle soon made a name for himself. A veteran SEAL who had already seen combat during the drive on Baghdad in 2003, Petty Officer Chris Kyle had a passion for all things gun—not surprising given his Texas upbringing.

Born and raised on an Odessa-area cattle ranch, he worked as a cowboy for seven years before joining the Navy. Through his college years, he roped calves and broke colts for four hundred dollars a month and a cot in the bunkhouse of a twelve-thousand-acre ranch. Horses became a passion of his. In '92, he turned pro on the rodeo circuit, but his budding career came to a crashing halt when a bronco flipped over and crushed him in the chute before a round. Trapped, unconscious, beneath the terrified animal, Kyle suffered severe injuries while his friends struggled to get to him. When the chute gate was opened, the horse bolted. Kyle's foot was stuck in one stirrup, and he was dragged into the arena, which inflicted even more injuries to his body. When he was finally freed and taken to the hospital, the doctors discovered he had broken ribs, a shattered wrist, bruised lungs and kidneys, two badly injured knees, and a severe concussion.

He spent one night in the hospital and walked out the next morning. His wrist subsequently required multiple surgeries to fix, and eventually the bones had to be stabilized with permanent metal pins. The accident destroyed his rodeo career, so he decided to try and join the Army, Marine Corps, and Navy. His wrist disqualified him for service.

So he returned to the cowboy life. He ate lunch from a chuck wagon and spent his days riding among hundreds of head of cattle. Seven years passed, and then his recruiter called to tell him the entry requirements had changed. He could now join the Corps with his stabilized wrist. Instead of the Corps, Kyle joined the Navy with the intent of becoming a Navy SEAL. He had heard the SEALs were the best of the best, and he wanted to roll with that crowd.

In 2003 he took part in the invasion of Iraq, riding into combat aboard three-man dune buggies and manning the rig's Mark 48 machine gun. When he came home from that first combat deployment, he spent a week with his family before shipping out to SEAL sniper school.

Like so many great American shooters, Kyle learned to shoot from his father, who gifted him a 30-06 as his first rifle. On their North Texas ranch, Kyle and his father stalked white-tailed deer, wild turkey, pheasants, and quail. Between hunting excursions, his dad showed him the finer points of marksmanship, and soon Chris was zeroing, or sighting in, all the families' firearms on the back forty.

When he was about ten years old, he was out with his dad, stalking deer while armed with a lever-action 30/30. He crept up to a canyon and discovered his quarry about three hundred yards away and perhaps ninety feet below him. The elevation threw him off, and it took him six tries before he finally brought the deer down. His father told him afterward, "Chris, you've got to learn shot placement." He worked for hours, patiently showing his son how to do this until Chris could routinely kill a turkey with a headshot or bring a buck down at three hundred yards with a bullet to its heart.

In 2003 SEAL sniper school took that raw, backwoods talent and gave Kyle the sophisticated understanding of the long-range precision marksmanship needed to be able to take out targets well over a thousand meters away. The first two weeks of the school taught him how to use photography on the battlefield to provide real-time imagery to his commanders. He learned to take photos through his scope then upload them to headquarters via satellite radios and computers. After that, he went through a four-week-long stalking phase before transitioning to six weeks of shooting. He emerged from the course a master of all four sniper rifles employed by the SEALs. Those included the Mark 11, the Mark 12, the .300 Win Mag (for Winchester Magnum), and the Barrett .50 cal.

In 2004 Kyle served in combat again during Operation Iraqi Freedom, where he took part in the Battle of Najaf that August, then the Second Battle of Fallujah in November. He accounted for forty enemy KIA during the latter campaign.

It did not take Chris Kyle long to make an impact in Ramadi. After arriving at the main base outside the city, Chris learned that most of SEAL Team Three was busy operating on the other side of town. While he waited for a way to get out to his unit, he received permission to climb into one of the base's guard towers and search for targets. Insurgents had been launching hit-and-run attacks against the perimeter armed with AKs and RPGs (rocket-propelled grenades), and Chris thought he might be able to help out with that situation.

In quick succession, he detected, tracked, and smoke-checked two enemy fighters who were trying to maneuver onto the base and spray the towers with AK fire.

Not long after, he went out with a small team to take up position about two hundred yards forward of a small Marine outpost inside the city. He and the other four men with him climbed a battered and abandoned seven-story office building that overlooked some of the main roads in town. Throughout the day, they saw only a few insurgents moving on the streets below. They would dart from corner to corner, moving like wraiths. Chris killed several of them with well-placed shots.

After sunset, the Jihadists launched an assault at the Marine outpost, just as they had at other isolated Coalition bases scattered in and around the city. This time they advanced right into Chris Kyle's field of fire. He quickly killed three RPG gunners as the two M60 machine gunners with him opened up as well. The attack slowed momentarily, then the insurgents figured out where Chris and the rest of the team were hiding. They returned fire, and it grew so intense that the Marines at the outpost ordered them to collapse back to the safety of their walls. Two of the men made it, but Chris, an officer, and one of the machine gunners stayed behind to cover their withdrawal. Before they could get out, the enemy had surrounded their building, cutting off their escape route.

As the fighting intensified, the Marines sent out a quick reaction force, or QRF, to fight their way on foot to the building. As they fought through the two hundred yards of urban jungle to Chris's building, a cagey insurgent lurked in an alleyway and let the patrol pass him by. As soon as the Marines had their backs to him, he swept out of his position, weapon ready. Kyle spotted him and dropped him with a single shot. He was so close to the Marines that Chris's fellow Americans thought they were taking insurgent sniper fire.

Later, after the Marine QRF had extracted Chris and the rest of the men, an officer approached him and thanked him for saving his life. Apparently, the insurgent who had moved in behind the patrol had been drawing a bead on him when Chris's bullet ended the threat.

In the days and weeks that followed, Chris took part in dozens of patrols and missions. He killed two enemy sharpshooters during countersniper missions in support of the 8th Marines as they sought to increase the size of their footprint in the city. In other actions, he and Team Three worked with Army units and National Guard troops. They conducted joint patrols, provided overwatch for Marine units, and went after insurgent leaders in kill or capture missions. Through all the fighting around Ramadi, Chris Kyle's coolness under fire and incredible accuracy had become almost mythic to his fellow Navy SEALs, who nicknamed him "The Legend." Around Ramadi, as Chris's kills mounted, the insurgents came to know who he was, too. They dubbed him Al Shatan, or "The Devil." The Sunni terrorists grew so desperate to stop him that they put a twenty-thousand-dollar bounty on his head. Though he was blown up in IED (improvised explosive devise) attacks seven times and wounded by gunfire on six other occasions during his ten-year career as a SEAL, no insurgent ever collected that bounty.

•   •   •

Meanwhile, as the fighting raged in Ramadi and around Youssifiyah, American intelligence picked up the trail of the men who had murdered Thomas Tucker, Kristian Menchaca, and David Babineau.

In early July, the insurgents released a second video that showed terrorists dragging Tucker's and Menchaca's bodies through a street while a crowd looked on and cheered. They then set the bodies afire, and kicked Thomas Tucker's head around as if it were a soccer ball.

These were the images the Mujahideen Shura Council showed the world. But there was another video that American intelligence captured that proved the insurgents were lying about who actually killed the two 101st Airborne troopers. The Mujahideen council had announced that al-Masri, the new leader of al-Qaida Iraq, had personally executed the men. The video showed that another high-level al-Qaida leader had actually been the perpetrator. Dubbed "Muhammad" by the Americans, he had used a large knife to behead the helpless prisoners. It was reminiscent of the murder of American civilian Nicholas Berg, which was personally carried out by al-Qaida's leader in Iraq, Musab al-Zarqawi.

Zarqawi had been killed only ten days before Tucker and Menchaca were captured. The truth was that al-Qaida's senior command structure in Iraq had suffered a staggering blow, and the organization was struggling to recover with al-Masri now at the controls. American intelligence believed that Muhammad had been in the running to be al-Zarqawi's replacement, at least for a short time. He had been a highly successful bomb maker for years. Personally killing two American airborne soldiers was part of his power play within al-Qaida.

Muhammad was a dead man walking, he just didn't know it. There was no way he and the rest of those responsible for these savage killings would escape American justice. Our intel types thirsted for revenge, eager to get Muhammad in the sights of a kill or capture mission. That was no easy task. He was elusive, cagey, and well protected. Our intelligence assets pursued every lead and angle they could develop to find a way to get him.

This wasn't just a matter of vengeance. Muhammad stood poised to seize an even more important role for himself within al-Qaida. If we could eliminate him, the terrorist command structure in Iraq would take another significant hit. Take out these al-Qaida-sponsored or controlled networks and Iraq had a chance at stability again.

That job fell to our special operations task forces and their interrogation teams. Throughout the country, the special operators were knocking big holes in al-Qaida's local networks. Here and there, a valuable nugget of information was culled from some of the detainees grabbed on these missions.

In one case, a Special Forces team found an adolescent boy whose father had been a key player in an Anbar Province suicide-bomb cell. The team surprised the boy's dad and several suicide bombers inside their apartment. The cell had been about to initiate an attack, and as the Americans entered the building, the suicide bombers detonated themselves. The boy and his mentally retarded brother were the only survivors.

The boy had been steeped in Jihadist propaganda. He proudly told American interrogators how the network functioned, where they kept their weapons and ammo, and pointed out all the safe houses his father had taken him to over the past several months. He was completely unaware that his bragging to the "American infidels" caused the downfall of his dad's node in the al-Qaida network.

Such strokes of luck played out all over Iraq that summer, dealing further body blows to the terrorists wreaking havoc among the nation's citizenry. Finally, Intel picked up a few tidbits about Muhammad. We learned that he used two safe houses outside of Ramadi and was known to frequent both several times a month. We also discovered that he traveled in a Chevy Suburban sport utility vehicle.

Based on this intel, plus photos we had acquired of Muhammad, SEAL Team Three was ordered to kill or capture him. To the team, there was no question of capturing Muhammad. They'd seen too many murderous terrorists released from Iraqi prisons after risking their lives to detain them to allow Muhammad a chance to escape justice.

SEAL Team Three was uniquely suited for the mission. Consisting of eight sixteen-man platoons, the team had been operating around Ramadi for months and had already been through multiple seven-month deployments in Iraq and Afghanistan. They knew Anbar Province and the areas around Muhammad's safe house very well already. And, of course, SEAL Team Three included one of the most lethal snipers in American history: Petty Officer Chris Kyle.

Given Kyle's record, he was a natural for the mission against Muhammad. The plan called for Kyle's platoon to establish a hide site overlooking the primary safe house. If their target failed to show up after a week, they would switch to the secondary safe house and wait for him there. A CH-53 Super Stallion Marine helicopter would insert them into both locations at night, and the team would take enough food and supplies for a week at each position.

The team consisted of four snipers, four AWs (automatic weapons gunners using Mark 48 machine guns) and twelve riflemen. The snipers selected a mix of SR-25s, a .50 caliber MacMillan, and Kyle's Winchester .300 Win Mag bolt-action rifle. Kyle settled on the Win Mag as, beyond a thousand yards, it was the most accurate of the available weapons. Should they have to take a long-range shot, Kyle and his rifle would handle it.

Rounding out the team would be several "straphangers"—specialists who work with SEAL teams. This included an interpreter, a master-at-arms (Navy military policeman), a SEAL spook with sophisticated signals intelligence gathering equipment that would enable them to listen to enemy radio and cell phone conversations, plus several techs who were experts at exploiting intelligence on the battlefield, such as DNA from the men the SEALs killed.

Before departure, the plan hit a snag. Everyone wanted a piece of this mission. Menchaca's and Tucker's brutal murders left everyone in Special Operations Command full of rage and a desire to be in on the payback. From the original sixteen men, the team grew to over thirty, far too many than were necessary.

In early July, the Super Stallion inserted the team at the first hide site, which was a walled compound not far from Muhammad's safe house. For a week they waited for Muhammad to show up in his American-built SUV. But his Suburban never came bouncing down the rutted dirt road to the farm that served as his hideout. The men grew bored and restless. Day after day they took three-hour watches behind their weapons and tried to remain alert. When off duty, they slept or dined on Meals Ready to Eat (MREs). Some of the men had brought books or magazines.

The magazine selection led to a lot of banter and teasing. When one SEAL noticed that his buddies were reading back issues of *Men's Health*, he shook his head sadly. That prompted a long back and forth on the quality of the porn the SEALs had brought along. *Playboy* was always excluded from such hide sites as it was considered far too tame. *Cherry* and *Hustler* were favorites. *Military History* was also a staple, and the SEALs sat in their Iraqi hide site reading accounts of the Alamo, Normandy, and Waterloo as they waited for their quarry to show up.

The first hide site turned out to be a bust. At the end of the first week, the team got permission to switch to the secondary target house. The CH-53 picked them up and moved them to the alternate hide site, which was a walled farmhouse about three hundred yards from the target area.

Their new hide had been long abandoned. Surrounded by a brown-gray outside wall, the house had no running water and only bare, dirty floors. The kitchen was empty and little furniture remained. The SEALs found a single table on the first floor, which Kyle carried upstairs and positioned in the back of one room with a window that overlooked Muhammad's crash pad. Then he and another sniper pulled a door off its hinges and laid it atop the table. That gave the men a stable firing platform, set back away from the window so that anyone outside would be unable to see the shooter and the weapon.

Part of the team, including the machine gunners, took station on the second floor in rooms on either side of Kyle's. The rest of the

SEALs found good spots on the first floor or on the roof. The men on the roof would be their fail-safe. Their job was to stay hidden. If the firefight threatened to get out of hand and the SEALs needed additional weapons in action, they would either knock loopholes in the three-foot parapet that skirted the roof, or, in a dire situation, just come up over the wall and start shooting.

The snipers established fields of fire and handed out assigned sectors to search and target. Once all of that had been worked out, the men settled back into all the boredom of a Stateside police stakeout.

Halfway through the second week, the SEALs grew convinced that the Intel guys had blown this one. Though the team never let its guard down, and the men standing watch were always hypervigilant, the mood in the hide grew more relaxed. The scene took on the trappings of a camping trip with a gaggle of old pals. The bloated size of the team led to everyone being more cramped than usual, and living atop one another created its own stress and internal dynamics.

Then one afternoon a dust trail appeared in the distance. Three vehicles approached from a rutted dirt road, and as the snipers scanned the rigs, they could see that the middle rig was a candy apple Chevy Suburban with tinted windows.

Muhammad had arrived.

"Check this guy out," somebody said. "He's got to be driving the only candy apple red Suburban in Iraq."

"Arrogant bastard," somebody else muttered.

Given how his vehicle stood out, Kyle wondered how it had taken so long to track the al-Qaida leader down.

Muhammad's convoy was coming from a different direction than the Intel guys expected, and the SEALs would not have the shot they had prepared for as a result. The original plan had called for the snipers to take Muhammad out as soon as he dismounted from his SUV and was positively identified. Now they realized that, thanks to the direction Muhammad was coming from, by the time his Suburban reached the farmhouse, he'd be on the wrong side of the rig for an easy kill shot. He would dismount and have the vehicle between him and the American snipers.

No plan survives first contact, and the SEALs adeptly switched gears. Instead of taking Muhammad out with sniper fire alone, they decided to use every rifle and machine gun to flay the enemy convoy with gunfire once they parked. They'd kill everyone, then get back aboard the CH-53.

The three vehicles rolled up to the safe house. The lead and trail rigs were Toyota HiLux pickup trucks, each with members of Muhammad's personal security detail. Altogether, the SEALs counted seven tangos plus their primary target.

The Mark 48 gunners fingered their triggers and waited. Before anyone could open fire, the team had to be absolutely certain they were going to kill the right people. This would entail a delay that could cost them a shot, but it had to be done.

The three rigs stopped near the safe house's front gate and the drivers shut their engines off. A passenger in Muhammad's Suburban dismounted and walked around to open the door for his commander.

The SEALs only had seconds now. Chances were, Muhammad would get out and walk straight through the front gate and disappear behind the nine-foot wall that surrounded the safe house.

The door opened. A dim figure wearing a Western-style jogging suit could be seen inside. He looked to be the right size and build for what they knew of Muhammad, but his face wasn't visible.

Both Toyota drivers popped their doors and stepped outside. They held AK-47s at the ready and began scanning the area with a professionalism the SEALs did not usually see from these terrorists. This bunch had been well trained.

The figure inside the Suburban moved. His face slipped into the afternoon sunlight as he climbed out of the SUV. It gave the SEALs the glimpse they needed. No doubt, the man in the jogging suit was Muhammad. As the snipers reported the positive ID, Muhammad's feet hit the dirt and he disappeared behind the Suburban. Their window to take him out had vanished that quickly.

The passengers in both Toyotas cracked their doors. Soon, the SEALs would face a tricky tactical challenge of having to take out all eight targets simultaneously before their quarry could take cover or return fire. No doubt the team's firepower could overwhelm Muhammad's security detail, but nobody wanted to suffer casualties from whatever return fire the enemy could muster. The trick was to bring everyone down before they could even get a shot off.

The Mark 48s thundered to life. All four gunners walked their fire through the vehicles at chest-height. One of the Toyota drivers went down, a fan of blood spraying across his vehicle. The other bolted, but managed only a few steps before the SEALs killed him. He tumbled and lay still, arms and legs sprawled, less than six feet from the lead pickup.

Short, accurate machine-gun bursts ripped into the trucks. The passengers in both Toyotas were torn apart where they sat. The man who had opened the door for Muhammad froze as his comrades died horribly all around him. Then Mark 48s caught him cold. More blood splattered the SUV and streaked down its custom candy apple clearcoat paint job as his lifeless body sank into the powdery dirt.

In seconds, the SEALs killed seven of the eight terrorists. Only Muhammad had survived. When the shooting started, he dove prone on the far side of the Suburban and nobody could see him well enough to get shots off. The Mark 48 gunners laid on their triggers, walking their fire back and forth until each man had burned through an entire two-hundred-round belt.

And then, an eerie silence descended on the scene. From his firing platform atop the table, Kyle scanned the SUV and could not see Muhammad. Taking out his security detail would serve little purpose if they couldn't kill him, too. The mission would be a failure; Tucker and Menchaca would go unavenged.

The Americans waited for Muhammad to make a move. The minutes ticked by. The snipers quartered off the SUV to ensure somebody would have a shot no matter which way he moved should he spring to his feet and make a break for it. Whatever happened, they could not allow him to go through that gate. He would be able to get inside the safe house unhindered, and the SEALs did not know if there were weapons in there. They would have to assault the house and hunt for him room to room, and that ran a substantial risk of taking casualties.

The SEALs stayed glued to their sights. Could Muhammad have been hit? Is that why he hadn't moved? The Mark 48s had sent eight hundred rounds downrange. The Suburban looked like bloody Swiss cheese. The Toyotas were riddled with bullet gashes. The convoy was a ghoulish scene. So perhaps their target had been hit. They couldn't be sure.

An hour passed with no movement. Something had to be done to end the impasse, but sweeping the target area with part of the team was deemed too risky. Intel had warned them that Muhammad's security detail all wore bomb vests. That information did not appear to be accurate, but the SEALs couldn't be sure. Perhaps Muhammad himself wore one, just in case he faced capture, so he could take a few Americans with him as he punched his own ticket to Allah.

There had to be an alternative to risking lives in such a move.

Inspiration struck the SEAL commander. Perhaps they could put one over on Muhammad if he was still alive. The team called in the CH-53 and they would stage a false extraction. A few minutes later, the bird arrived and set down behind the hide site. A third of the team rushed from the house and flowed over the helicopter's ramp to settle down inside. In seconds, the Super Stallion was back in the air, seemingly heading for home.

Kyle and the other snipers remained in the hide, waiting to see if Muhammad would react. It turned into a battle of patience. The SEALs relaxed, this was their sort of game. Kyle lay on the door, covering down on the nearest approach route between the SUV and the safe house's front gate. As they waited, the men bantered back and forth over who might get the shot. The machine gunners squared off against the snipers and challenged them. It was on now, and the friendly competition kept everyone alert and at their best.

An hour later, Muhammad's head prairie-dogged over the Suburban's hood. Just his eyes appeared as he took a quick look around. The SEALs held their fire. He ducked back down. A moment later, he reappeared and studied the hide site. He vanished, thought things over, and concluded that the Americans really had left.

He stood up, right in Kyle's field of view and sprinted for the gate. Kyle knew the range: three hundred yards, well within the Win Mag's capabilities. Long ago, his father had taught him to use a slow, steady pull on the trigger. He mirrored that lesson as he laid the crosshairs on his running target. Muhammad was moving laterally across Kyle's field of view, an almost ninety-degree angle. In novels and movies, this seems like a piece of cake. Pull the trigger and the target drops.

Baloney. Kyle faced a significant challenge by Muhammad's sudden bolt to freedom. Here's why:

Hollywood aside, shooting a moving target is no easy feat for a sniper no matter the range. There are two ways to do it: tracking and ambush. The tracking method requires following the target and keeping your crosshairs on him. To do it, you need to know your range to the target, the speed of the target, and the angle at which he is moving to your barrel. Then you set the crosshairs not on him, but in front of him. We call that "mil lead"

Mil lead is one of the quirky things about long-range precision marksmanship that makes it both an art and a science. Every sniper's mil lead is different. Even if the target is moving at the same speed and angle, no two snipers will need the same amount of lead to hit him.

When we train to hit moving targets, we keep detailed notes in our data books. The more we practice, the more data we develop and the better we can pinpoint the mil lead we need. It is a repetitive, sometimes frustrating task that is complicated by a couple of additional factors.

First, in the field we will never know exactly how fast a target is moving. So, for humans, we have three types of leads we practice based on average speed sets. The first is a "walking lead." Every human walks at a different pace, but that pace is within a speed range that we can use to guesstimate our lead.

A "jogging lead" is used against men who are walking unusually fast or loping. This requires a little more lead. The last we call the "run lead," which we employ against men sprinting on the battlefield.

Through training and dedicated data mining, each sniper figures out how much lead he will need for each speed. We know those calculations off the top of our heads, so in combat we don't need cheat sheets for this type of shot. Though I've been out of the game since 2005, I can still remember my run lead is two and three-quarter mils at three hundred yards. These are things we snipers never forget.

Complex enough? We're only halfway there. Speed is only one part of the equation. The other is the angle of the target's line of movement to your rifle. Let's say our target is running across a street within our field of view. He's moving perpendicular to our sniper team. That's the most acute angle we have to deal with and because of that it will require the most lead. My run lead is two and three-quarter mils at three hundred yards only if the target is moving ninety degrees from me across my field of view.

If your target is moving diagonally from you, or toward you, that requires smaller mil leads. The less acute the angle, the less mils you'll need to get on your target. The lead also changes depending on whether the target is moving toward your rifle or away from it.

In combat, there's no way to tell exactly what the angle of our targets are. This is why training is so crucial. The more we practice, the better we get at guesstimating the angle, and the more accurate we become. We write everything down and memorize it, so that in combat we have instant recall and can calculate our shot placement as accurately as possible.

There's another complication to this equation. Right-handed snipers use their right eye in the scope. Their leads are different if the target is moving left to right versus right to left. The phenomenon is the opposite for left-handed shooters. I've never really figured out why this is the case, but it is a universal truth. Not only does each sniper have to learn the mil lead he needs, but he must to do so for both directions of movement.

Movement speed, angle, and lead all need to be calculated on top of wind, range, weather, and elevation. Once you factor all those elements into the shot, it becomes obvious that tracking and firing at a moving target is one of the most technically demanding types of shots for us snipers. To do it well requires significant investments in training, time, data entry, and memorization. The next time you see a Hollywood film where snipers are smoke-checking running targets left and right, remember all the background math and physics that goes into every trigger pull.

There is one other way to take down a running man; we call it the ambush method. In this scenario, we anticipate the enemy's movement and figure out a point along his projected path that will give us the clearest possible shot at him. Then we place the crosshairs on that point and wait. When our running enemy reaches our mil lead, we pull the trigger. The target literally runs into the shot. It is a slightly easier technique for taking out a moving target, but it can only be done if you know where the enemy is going. If you don't know that, tracking is the only way to kill him.

There are some advanced ways to get around the uncertainty of what an enemy will do. If a sniper team has been watching a particular place for an extended period of time, he and his partner will study the terrain and tactical situation. Based on that study, they will assign areas of responsibility to each other. Then, within those areas, they will create their preplanned ambush points based on possible routes of movement the enemy might use. From there, the team can build a decision tree that covers all possible enemy behaviors. This is called Planning the Target Zone.

Let's say our sniper team is covering a street with a couple of doorways and alleys in their areas of responsibility. Each man will select ambush points between the alleys and doorways to ensure that any enemy entering the area can be taken out with this method.

The downside to this, of course, is the enemy can either do something unexpected or the snipers don't have time to work through all the possible scenarios. In that case, they have to switch to tracking their targets.

When Muhammad made his run for it, Chris Kyle had been covering his area of responsibility to the right of the vehicle. In a split second, Kyle had to judge how fast his target was running, the angle he was to the SEAL's rifle, and his probable path. It was clear Muhammad was trying to get to the front door. Kyle had planned his target zone carefully. He shifted his reticle to one of his preplanned ambush points. Muhammad moved into his scope, sprinting flat out now. Running lead, left to right, adjusting for low wind (0–3 mph). He'd already fed proper DOPE (data on previous engagement) into his scope, so he didn't need to factor in temperature and drop. He had a good zero.

When Muhammad reached the mil lead threshold, Kyle pulled the trigger. The Win Mag's heavy bullet punched through Muhammad's rib cage, knocking him off his feet.

It was a remarkable shot. Kyle had hit a moving target's profile exactly center mass. The target area on Muhammad's body was probably less than eight by eight inches. It was a wound that no man could survive, the sort of shot Chris had learned to make with his father while out hunting deer on the family spread back in Texas. Shot placement was everything.

The bullet did its work. Muhammad died in seconds, his body splayed on the ground only a few steps short of the front gate.

Justice served, SEAL style. The team called for extraction. The Marine Super Stallion reappeared and touched down near the hide site. Kyle and the rest of the team rushed aboard. As they choppered their way back to base, the SEALs broke out celebratory cigars. Mission accomplished. And this one felt good.

There were at least four al-Qaida operatives involved in the executions of our soldiers. Other special operations teams killed two of them. Seal Team Three took care of the other two. It was a clean sweep. In September 2001 President George Bush had told the American people, "Americans should not expect one battle, but a lengthy campaign unlike any other we have ever seen. It may include dramatic strikes visible on TV and covert operations secret even in success." Kyle's bullet scored one of those secret successes. The country did not learn that the men responsible for murdering Menchaca and Tucker had been hunted down and killed. There was no closure for the families back in Oregon and Texas as a result. But behind the scenes, the SEALs made sure the executioners faced a reckoning—a far more permanent one than the driver of the truck that carried the bodies received in 2008.

Chris Kyle retired from the U.S. Navy in 2009 with two hundred fifty-five confirmed kills to his credit, more than any other sniper in American history. His service during eight years of combat in some of the heaviest fighting in Iraq and Afghanistan earned him two Silver Stars and five Bronze Stars for Valor. He was wounded in action repeatedly, but never received a single Purple Heart. Just before one firefight he had been talking to his wife on a sat phone. When the bullets started flying, he dropped it and picked up his rifle. Moments later, he and several members of his team were wounded, and his wife heard him shout "I'm hit!" before the sat phone cut out. For three days she waited for word, terrified that she'd heard her husband's final words.

When Kyle came home from his final deployment, he saw what eight years of combat had done to his wife. He made the decision to retire from the Navy to devote himself to his family. He returned to his beloved state of Texas, where he now ran a company that trains law enforcement and military snipers. But for Kyle the future wasn't in the corporate rat race. He dreamed of a day he could throw his cell phone away, put on a pair of boots, and ride among his own herd of cattle on a north Texas prairie he could call his own.

In 2010, his best-selling book, *American Sniper*, was released. Chris gave most of the book's proceeds to the families of fallen SEALs he had served with during his time in combat. He spent his days running his consulting business and reaching out to veterans with disabilities.

After serving as guardian angel for countless Marines around Ramadi in 2006, Chris and his business partner were murdered on February 2, 2013, by a Marine veteran suffering from an acute case of post-traumatic stress disorder. After a furious law enforcement chase, the Marine drove Chris's pickup into a police car and was captured. His motives for the murder were unclear.

Chris Kyle's memorial service was held at the Dallas Cowboys football stadium. Thousands of mourners lined the streets and filled the stands to pay their final respects to an American icon whose life had been devoted to protecting his fellow Americans. That he was slain by one of those very men in a fit of senseless violence after he had done so much for his country remains one of the most painful ironies of the War on Terror.

CHAPTER FOUR
The Playground of Snipers

Ramadi in the late summer of 2006 was a city in its death throes. Unlike Fallujah, this battle was drawn out, a slow-motion car wreck that consumed Ramadi in a way not seen in military history since the Battle of Stalingrad in 1942–1943. While the U.S. forces showed restraint and only used such firepower as aerial bombs, rockets, or the main gun on an M1 Abrams tank as an absolute last resort, the insurgents were under no such limitations.

Enemy car bomb factories hidden in warehouses in or around the city churned out dump trucks filled with thousands of pounds of ammonium nitrate. Foreign volunteers, whom al-Qaida cell leaders leg-cuffed in place should they have any second thoughts about martyrdom, drove the trucks into Iraqi Police checkpoints or Coalition combat outposts. The massive blasts from these deadly weapons took down buildings and left the streets heaped with burned debris and human remains. Through some freak of physics, the drivers were usually blown straight up into the air. Their bodies would come apart, but the head was almost always found intact. During the cleanup after these attacks, it fell to American and Iraqi troops to locate the driver's head, photograph it, and conduct a retinal scan to identify the terrorist if his eyes remained in their sockets.

Each bomb factory had specific tells picked up by U.S. military forensics experts. Some set up fail-safes, or "chicken switches," so that if the driver tried to opt out at the last minute, the vehicle could be detonated remotely by observers watching from a safe distance. Others tore down vehicles to their bare frames, welded modifications and explosives in place, then rebuilt the rig so it looked like any other on the streets. Some of these were so cunningly constructed that even a detailed search by Iraqi security forces missed the threat concealed within them. Al-Qaida's factories grew so sophisticated that they were able to produce tractor-trailer rigs loaded with six to eight thousand pounds of explosives. Such infernal devices took down entire city blocks when they went off.

Sometimes the bomb makers improvised even deadlier ways to attack the Coalition. On August 21, 2006, al-Qaida operatives drove a dump truck filled with fuel up to a Coalition outpost on the edge of town and successfully detonated it. The blast drenched the base in flaming fuel, killing three Iraqi police officers and horribly burning eight American soldiers.

The truck and car bomb menace grew so severe that summer that three or four bombs a week were blowing up in and around the city. Finding the factories became a key priority, as these attacks almost always inflicted military and civilian casualties. But finding them required venturing into the heart of the city, where al-Qaida's legions had seeded the streets and alleys with thousands of IEDs. In some places, so many had been emplaced that they resembled urban minefields, and some of the bombs were so powerful they could (and did) destroy M1 Abrams tanks and M2 Bradley Fighting Vehicles.

When the troops tried to move off the streets and into businesses and homes, they faced another threat—building contained IEDs. Al-Qaida would wire a dwelling with propane tanks, explosives, or artillery rounds left over from the Saddam era. Once a door was opened and a wire or infrared beam was broken, the entire building would explode and come down around the patrol. Dozens of these BCIEDs detonated around the city that summer, leaving entire blocks in ruins.

Piles of concrete and rebar heaped on either side of garbage-strewn roads littered with the burned-out carcasses of cars and tire-less, bullet-riddled trucks became the indelible image of Ramadi for countless American soldiers who struggled to defeat al-Qaida. Water mains were ruptured by IEDs and flooded the streets. Sewage lines, never Iraq's strong point, clogged up or broke and added a foul stench to the ruins. Severed power lines hung limply across sidewalks, festooned trees and walls, and lay in tangles in the streets. Animals caught in cross fires lay rotting in the rubble, as nobody was willing to risk removing them since al-Qaida had been known to plant bombs around or inside their corpses. On one wall deep in the city, the enemy had spray-painted in Arabic "This is the graveyard of Americans."

It was a graveyard. The soccer stadium, controlled that summer by al-Qaida, became a dumping ground for corpses. The enemy dug up the field and turned it into a mass grave. Civilians they'd tortured and killed were laid to rest there atop Jihadists and foreign fighters alike.

All the while, the civilians trapped within their devastated neighborhoods sought any means to survive. With shops closed and the economy destroyed, for many men the only way to feed their families was to do al-Qaida's dirty work. The terrorists hired children to be lookouts, or to scout locations for IEDs. They paid adults to plant the bombs or to assist in their construction. Others received a bounty for the Americans they killed.

There were even contract snipers working for al-Qaida. One used a van as a mobile sniper hide. Concealed in back behind a curtain, he killed a U.S. soldier with a shot to the head, only to be overrun and captured a short time later. When he was interrogated and identified, the Americans discovered the gunman was a teacher at a nearby vocational school for women. For extra money, he moonlighted as a sniper for al-Qaida.

The Anbar Provincial Government was located in downtown Ramadi. It was a sole enclave in a sea of hostility. The governor and his staff were frequent targets of assassination attempts, and they lived under siege surrounded by a protective cordon of Marines. Anytime the governor tried to go anywhere, he and his security detail almost always came under attack. In such a situation, the government had no hope of functioning. The governor controlled nothing beyond the rifle barrels of the Marines keeping him alive.

Day after day, the fighting demolished Ramadi a little at a time. Where Fallujah had been a full-on onslaught, a set-piece battle that ended after two months of fighting, Ramadi was the battle without end. It became the Guadalcanal of the Iraq War, a brutal struggle of attrition that wore away the souls of the Americans caught in its vortex of violence and misery.

Every time an American patrol left an outpost, they were sure to encounter some sort of opposition. The threats were everywhere—bombs buried under the asphalt in the streets they used, buildings wired to blow. Random gunmen lurked in the shadows to spray AK fire and run. Zealots wearing suicide vests, grenades, and mortar fire launched from tubes mounted in the beds of flatbed "bongo" trucks so they could keep mobile were just a few of the threats the Americans faced every day. On average, any patrol in the city that summer would get attacked within eight minutes of heading out the front gate.

Despite the lethality of IEDs and suicide bombers, al-Qaida's snipers were the threat American troops feared the most. In an IED environment, slow movement is the best way for a foot patrol to detect that sort of threat. But with al-Qaida snipers lurking in the shadows of broken buildings, atop minarets and mosques, slow movement was a death sentence. Marines and soldiers alike took to sudden rushes from one concealed position to another. They dashed down streets in one-hundred-thirty-eight-degree heat, laden with eighty pounds of gear or more, hoping the speed and sudden changes of direction would throw off the aim of any marksman who had them in his crosshairs.

Though IEDs killed more Americans in Ramadi, the sniper shots were the ones that affected the troops the most. In three months, 2nd Battalion, 8th Marines (2/8) suffered eight casualties to enemy snipers. Two journalists embedded with 1/506th Parachute Infantry at Camp Corregidor (located just outside Ramadi) also fell wounded to sniper rounds.

On June 21, 2006, Lance Corporal Nicholas Whyte prepared to

depart from a forward outpost on a foot patrol through a Ramadi neighborhood. Whyte, who was two days shy of his twenty-second birthday, had served in Fallujah and had done an earlier tour in Haiti before his company from 3rd Battalion, 8th Marines joined the central battle of the Iraq War. He'd been raised in Brooklyn, New York, in a tough neighborhood near East Flatbush, graduating from James Madison High School in 2002. After a year of college, he volunteered for the Marine Corps.

As he and his fellow mortarmen finished gearing up, they laughed and joked about playing multiplayer Diablo II together when they returned from the mission.

A few minutes beyond the wire, a sniper's shot rang out. Nicholas Whyte fell dead. His stunned platoon scanned the streets, the scores of doorways and dark, glassless windows overlooking their position as they worked to evacuate their fallen brother. The moment underscored the reality of the Ramadi campaign: no matter the countermeasures taken, snipers in the city would always have the advantage. There were simply too many places to hide, too many windows, too many darkened corners of shattered buildings within which al-Qaida shooters could hide. Every time an American or Iraqi patrol moved through the streets, they were vulnerable from dozens of places at once. Even the best eyes and the most alert men in a squad or platoon could not possibly cover down on every potential threat.

Worse, when a sniper did take a shot, a platoon was often in the grimmest of situations: under fire from an unknown location with no hope of finding the source of the shooting. Al-Qaida's snipers were masters of concealment and adopted many of the tactics they'd seen American snipers use against them, including hiding deep inside a room with a window overlooking a key street. Concealed in the darkness, they were all but invisible. Others drilled holes behind car taillights so they could fire from the trunk of a nondescript sedan. Still others used mosques and hospitals for their hide sites, believing the Americans would not fire at such places.

The foot patrols tried a variety of countermeasures to foil enemy snipers. They popped smoke grenades everywhere they ran, making it harder for the shooters to see them. They began bringing shotguns out on patrols so they could shoot locks off of gates and doors quickly as they ran from point to point. They tried moving at night, or with armored vehicles in support. Even the presence of M1 tanks or M2 Bradleys failed to deter the al-Qaida gunmen, who took to targeting the crews of such vehicles.

Private Kelly Youngblood was a nineteen-year-old M1 Abrams driver from Mesa, Arizona. A year removed from basic training, he'd deployed to Ramadi in February 2007. In a letter home to his sister, he wrote, "I'm afraid to leave the building to go to the tank because there are snipers everywhere."

On one of his first patrols, his tank came under RPG fire and a rocket exploded right beside his tank. Just before that mission, another rocket had detonated at his combat outpost, killing one of Kelly's friends and narrowly missing him.

Sixteen days after he arrived in Ramadi, he was shot in the head by an al-Qaida sniper as he climbed out of the driver's hatch of his tank after a long shift within the vehicle. His brothers got him to the medics, who tried for over an hour to save him.

The sniper who killed Private Kelly had waited for hours for a tiny window of opportunity. Those shots and others made the Americans utterly paranoid. Said one Marine to a reporter, "It just feels like someone's always watching you. It really messes with your head."

Al-Qaida snipers overwatched every Coalition outpost in the city and its environs. It became so dangerous that a vehicle stopping at the gates of a combat outpost (COP) ran the risk of taking precision fire. Drivers learned to keep their vehicles moving, even when they had to stay in a specific area. Back and forth, back and forth, they'd switch gears repeatedly to throw off the aim of RPG teams.

At one Iraqi checkpoint, a sniper shot an Iraqi soldier. He went down in the open, and one of his comrades rushed to his aid. That act of supreme bravery cost the second soldier his life—another crack from a Dragunov rifle and another Coalition casualty.

Into this chaos and death stepped American snipers—Marines, Army, and Navy SEALs. They did their best to protect the Joes on the ground as they tried to secure the streets. From overwatch positions all around the city, they built hides and hunted al-Qaida.

One of the earliest, and best, sniper locations was the ruins of a hotel. Dubbed the "Ramadi Inn" by the snipers who established hides in it, the four-story building held a commanding view of the city and afforded the Americans excellent fields of fire along Route Michigan. Early on, they fortified the place with sandbags up to shoulder height. But the level of incoming small-arms fire showed that to be inadequate. Rounds would pass above the sandbags to ricochet around the concrete walls, and several Americans were wounded that way. Afterward, the men built the sandbag walls up to the ceilings in every room they used. There were so many in the building that the Inn was sometimes called "OP Sandbag."

The snipers there built elaborate hides set back from the windows with narrow vision slits built into the sandbag walls. From the street, they were virtually undetectable. Yet the enemy knew the Americans held the building, and they kept up a steady rain of rockets, mortars, and small-arms fire on the place that took its toll. The snipers reverently wrote the names of all their fallen brothers on the walls under the words "Never Forgotten."

Others scrawled motivational graffiti in their hide sites. One group of snipers wrote "Kill them all" and "Kill like you mean it" on their walls. Somebody else later added a quote attributed to Senator John McCain, "America is great not because of what she has done for herself but because of what she has done for others."

OP Sandbag became one of the great sniping sites of the War on Terror. Hundreds of al-Qaida fighters fell to the men behind the M24s, M82 Barrett and Marine M40s concealed there. In 2005–2006, the scout-sniper platoon from the 3rd Infantry Division's 2/69 Armored set the gold bar standard in Ramadi. The sniper element of the platoon was only ten men. Calling themselves "Shadow Team," the section was led by Staff Sergeant Jim Gilliland. They soon earned a fearsome reputation as one of the best precision-shooting units in Iraq. Over the course of their deployment, the ten men of Shadow Team killed well over two hundred enemy fighters. They did it through careful observation, an understanding of enemy tactics, and a few surprising moments where luck and skill came together.

On one early mission, Shadow Team had set up in two hides overlooking an auto repair shop suspected of being an insurgent ammo resupply point. For eighteen hours, they watched an unusual amount of traffic come and go in the place, but could not positively identify any hostiles. They saw no weapons or IEDs, and so they remained silently in place, observing the facility hour after hour.

To combat the boredom, Gilliland quietly game-boarded potential scenarios with the men around him. How would they handle multiple targets at once? Who would have what area of responsibility? They envisioned every type of engagement they could dream up, then walked through how they would handle them until each member of the team knew his role intimately. Gilliland's men functioned as a true team. The media's image of the lone sniper shooting targets with one shot, one kill was nowhere in evidence within Gilliland's section. They worked together, and in the process multiplied their effect on the battlefield.

But no matter how you plan and prepare, the enemy can still throw curveballs your way.

Eighteen hours into their overwatch mission, a four-door sedan suddenly roared into the street below Gilliland's hide site. The car screeched to a halt less than sixty yards from their rifles.

Gilliland and the three men with him gaped in astonishment as an insurgent popped out of one of the rear doors and walked around the fender to the trunk where he retrieved a 155mm artillery shell prepped with plastic explosives in the fuse well—a classic, ready-made IED. A couple of his pals jumped out and helped emplace it. The Americans watching them could see them joking and laughing amongst themselves until one went back and sat in the front side passenger seat. They were casual and blasé, despite the nature of their mission.

Shadow Team had already seen this once before. On one of their first missions, they saw a couple of insurgents get out of a car on a busy street and carry a 155mm artillery shell across traffic to emplace it. The civilian cars stopped and waited for them to cross. Even as the fighting destroyed the city around them, its citizens tried to carve a life out of the ruins. And part of that required traveling farther and farther through the war zone just to get basic survival supplies such as water, food, and fuel. Watching two al-Qaida terrorists seed their streets with bombs was nothing new. It was business as usual in Ramadi.

At least it was until Gilliland's men drilled both insurgents with well-placed shots from their M24s. Both terrorists fell dead before the shocked Iraqi commuters waiting to continue on their way.

This time the terrorists had blundered. Gilliland and his men were so close to where the sedan stopped that they didn't have a good shot from their hide. Rather than use their bolt-action M24s, the men quickly grabbed their M4 carbines and rushed onto the roof of their building. Four M4s, four targets. The men took aim and unleashed a fusillade of 5.56mm bullets into the street at point-blank range from an elevated position. The first rounds tore through the driver's side windshield, killing him before he could even move. The terrorist riding shotgun tried to bail out, but one of Gilliland's sharpshooters stitched him as well. He slumped over, dead, half-in and half-out of the vehicle, its passenger-side door hanging open.

The men kept up the barrage. The car caught fire. A third insurgent went down as he stood in front of it after emplacing the IED. The last one was hit as well. He fell to the street, wounded, and began to crawl away from the burning car. At that point, Gilliland's men had been spotted on the roof. Without any cover atop it, they elected to withdraw back downstairs to their hide site. By the time they got back, the fourth insurgent had dragged himself out of their field of view.

Such attacks and others knocked the casualness out of al-Qaida. They grew cautious and cunning. They hired kids to find American sniper hides, and when they did they would set up subtle signals for their al-Qaida masters. Usually the kids would pile pebbles in front of a building being used as a hide site. Other times they would signal by hanging towels in certain ways nearby.

It was hard to move around the city undetected as a result. But that did not diminish the effectiveness of the American sniper teams. The days of casually planting IEDs ended. As the snipers took a steady toll of the terrorists, they began using subtle methods to get the bombs in place. Usually, this started with a quick recon of a previous IED crater. A kid or a hired local adult would walk down the street and peer into the hole to make sure it was clear and could be used again.

The kids sometimes made passes on bicycles. They'd ride around the crater then speed off back down the street, weaving through the debris and trash to report what they'd seen. Next, a car would make several passes down the street as a second reconnaissance of the area. On each pass, the car would slow down as it went by the potential bomb site. If al-Qaida was satisfied with the spot, they'd send in the emplacement team. There were many variations on this, but usually the team consisted of two cars, one with the bomb in the trunk and the other to pull security. A van or larger sedan would follow and linger behind the other two. That one served as their casualty evacuation vehicle should anyone get hit and wounded.

They'd roll up to the site and the section assigned to planting the IED would dismount, carry the bomb to the selected location, prep it, and pull out. They did this as quickly as possible to minimize the chance of a sniper kill while they were exposed in the street.

Before American snipers began to have an effect on al-Qaida's operations in the city, the enemy would frequently use acid to melt the asphalt in the street, then scoop it away to plant an IED. With the bomb in the roadbed, they'd bury it with the melted asphalt, then scatter trash atop the site before bugging out. Such bombs were almost impossible to detect and took a heavy toll of American vehicles. They also became impossible in much of the city where our snipers had eyes on the scene.

If al-Qaida's sharpshooters affected our men and messed with their heads, American snipers had a profound effect on the enemy's psychology as well. Intercepted radio and cell phone communications between cells and their commanders revealed a growing rift between what al-Qaida's leadership wanted and what its front-line fighters were willing to attempt. More than once, a cell received orders to emplace IEDs in a particular location. The cell commander flat-out refused, telling his superiors that if he and his men did that, they would be killed by American snipers.

For both sides, killing the enemy's snipers became a critical aspect of operations in Ramadi. Al-Qaida had the edge at first, as the locals actively assisted them and the Americans rarely moved around undetected in the city. The terrorists used such knowledge to deadly effect more than once. One of their earliest coups came in June 2004 when they caught a four-man Marine sniper team by surprise on a rooftop and killed them all. They videotaped the scene and celebrated in front of the camera around the dead Marines—images that were later posted on Jihadi websites—before making off with two M40 rifles, a thermal scope, night vision, and other gear.

One of the al-Qaida snipers around Ramadi used one of those M40s for two years. On June 20, 2006, the scout snipers from 3rd Battalion, 5th Marines (3/5) spotted a car parked suspiciously on a road near Habbaniyah, about forty kiloyards outside of Ramadi. As they watched it, they saw the driver pick up a video camera to film a passing Marine convoy of amphibious tracks. Zooming in on the vehicle, one of the Marine snipers spotted the butt of a rifle inside the car. They watched it carefully until the driver pulled it into his lap, making as if to use it against the column of vehicles passing by his position. That was enough. The Americans opened fire and killed the driver. A few minutes later, another man showed up and slid into the passenger seat, unaware that his buddy had been killed. He looked over and saw the driver and froze—the Shock Factor at work. Suddenly, he broke free from his paralysis, jumped out of the car, and ran around to the driver's side. He threw open the door and was trying to pull the driver out so he could use the vehicle to get away. He wasn't thinking clearly. If he had been, he'd have realized that by doing this, he'd exposed himself to the snipers who had just shot his friend. This is another aspect of the Shock Factor—irrational behavior. They don't think; they just act. And sometimes they do things that seal their fate.

Sergeant Kevin Homestead, a member of 3/5's scout sniper platoon, shot him dead with three shots from his M4 before the insurgent could get the car into gear. When a patrol from Kilo Company, 3/5 went to secure the car, they discovered the rifle inside it was one of the M40s taken off the Marines killed in Ramadi in 2004. The enemy sniper had dumped the expensive Unertl scope the rifle originally carried, replacing it with a cheap Tasco. Other than that, the weapon was intact.

Countersniper operations consumed both sides as the struggle for Ramadi unfolded. Jim Gilliland scored the most impressive countersniper kill in Ramadi, and quite possibly the Iraq War. The previous September, as his Shadow Team occupied the Ramadi Inn, an al-Qaida sniper killed one of Gilliland's friends and fellow NCOs from the 2/69 as he helped lead a patrol. With the men in the street pinned down by the enemy gunman, they radioed for help, telling Jim that the sharpshooter was using a hospital for his hide. Gilliland was 1,250 yards from the hospital—technically out of the M24s performance envelope. Yet desperate times call for extreme measures. He glassed the hospital and found the enemy sniper lurking in the shadows of a fourth-floor room. He was partially concealed, giving the American only a waist-up shot.

Gilliland was using a Leupold scope accurate to a thousand yards, and his weapon was considered accurate out to seven hundred. To kill the sniper, he had to make a rough series of calculations in his head. Gilliland's M24 was the only one the team possessed that hadn't been painted. As a result, the men called it the "Black Gun." This was the sort of shot the M82 Barrett would have been more suited to take, but Gilliland had the Black Gun already against his shoulder and he didn't want to expend critical time maneuvering the heavier .50 cal into place. In that interim, the enemy sniper could kill another American.

He took aim at a point twelve feet above the sniper's lair, then pulled the trigger. The 7.62mm bullet arced across the city and struck the insurgent in the chest. He grimaced and fell over out of sight. A subsequent patrol found him dead, the single 7.62 bullet center mass his only wound.

At the time, Gilliland's shot was the longest 7.62 kill of the Iraq War. It did nothing to deaden the pain of losing Staff Sargeant Jason Benford, the al-Qaida sniper's victim and close friend of many in Shadow Team.

Layered into countersniper operations in Ramadi were raids conducted on known al-Qaida hideouts. American intelligence developed information on where some of these snipers hunkered down between missions, and U.S. patrols went after them in their lairs. In one attack, an al-Qaida sniper was killed in a safe house northeast of Ramadi. When the Americans searched his dwelling, they discovered a pile of videotapes documenting all the shots he'd taken on Coalition troops.

The enemy also made a point of going after American snipers. In September 2006, Chris Kyle's sister platoon from SEAL Team Three had kicked out a four-man sniper element to overwatch a section of Ramadi. In the morning of the twenty-ninth, the element's snipers killed two insurgents. The enemy made a concerted effort to drive the SEALs off the rooftop. The Americans came under heavy small-arms fire, and an RPG narrowly missed them. Mike Monsoor, a machine gunner with the platoon, took up a firing position between the two snipers and returned fire.

Suddenly, a grenade sailed over the parapet, thrown by an insurgent who had carefully crept toward the SEALs position until he was virtually beneath it. The grenade hit Mike in the chest and bounced to the roof between his brother SEALs. Shouting a warning, he dove on the grenade as it detonated, shielding his teammates from its blast with his body. He died thirty minutes later. President George W. Bush later awarded Mike Monsoor the Medal of Honor for his supreme, selfless act of bravery.

Mike was Team Three's second casualty in a matter of weeks. On August 2, 2006, part of Charlie Platoon had sortied into central Ramadi to provide overwatch support for an Iraqi Army sweep of a particularly dangerous neighborhood. Chris Kyle was part of that element, which bounded forward to establish a position in a battered apartment complex. Moments after getting on the roof, Chris and his fellow SEALs came under accurate small-arms fire. As they scrambled for cover, an al-Qaida sniper fired a shot at Chris's friend Ryan Job. Job was manning a machine gun that morning. The sniper's bullet struck the Mark 48s upper receiver and fragmented. Parts of it ricocheted into Ryan's right eye and cheek, knocking him over. The SEALs quickly administered aid and evacuated their wounded brother.

Ryan lost his right eye and the vision in his left. Though blinded by the al-Qaida gunman, he returned to the States determined to live life to the utmost. He learned to hunt again and bagged an elk on one outing. In 2009 he climbed Mount Rainier, one of the most technical and difficult mountains in the United States. He became an inspiration to thousands of wounded warriors, only to die at the hands of a nurse during his final surgery to reconstruct his face. In post-op, a nurse administered an overdose of painkillers, taking the life of one of America's most beloved SEALs.

Through 2004 and 2005, the fighting in Ramadi had simmered and smoldered. When the American slow-motion offensive to capture the city once and for all began in June 2006, the fighting flared into full-scale kinetic warfare. There was no attempt at winning the hearts and minds here, it was a straight-up slugfest with the snipers on both sides shaping the nature of the fight and the tactics employed. In the months ahead, the Iraq War would be won or lost within the streets of the Al Anbar capital.

And at this critical junction, SEAL Team Three rotated home after a long, bloody, and successful tour of duty. Replacing them in the city would be SEAL Team Five, an experienced unit whose ranks included legendary SEAL Marcus Luttrell, as well as a backwoods country-boy-turned-elite-sniper Adam Downs.

CHAPTER FIVE
The Pigeon Flipper

SEAL Team Five arrived in Ramadi starting in late September 2006, set to replace Mike Monsoor's Team Three. Composed of a solid backbone of veterans of both Afghanistan and Iraq, Team Five included perhaps the best-known SEAL in the Navy, Marcus Luttrell. Marcus had been severely wounded in Afghanistan during Operation Red Wings when the four-man reconnaissance team he was with was attacked by hundreds of enemy fighters. The other three operators assigned to the recon element were killed, along with eight more SEALs and eight air crew who died when an RPG struck their CH-47 Chinook helicopter. Thirty years old, standing six foot five, Marcus returned to duty with Team Five after only partially recovering from his wounds. He would endure agonizing pain throughout his Ramadi deployment, though he never let it stop him from getting back out in the field with his brothers.

In Team Five, Marcus was reunited with one of his close friends from earlier in his Navy career. Adam Downs met Marcus when they attended a SEAL training school together. Though Marcus was raised in Houston, Texas, and Adam grew up in backwoods Illinois, the two formed a close friendship based on their mutual love of the outdoors and hunting.

Adam prided himself on being a good ol' boy, and the men in his platoon called him the "Redneck Mujahideen." Rock-solid in a fight, devoted to his brother SEALs and to the mission, he'd gained a reputation for fierce loyalty and reliability on the battlefield during his first combat deployment to Iraq the year before. With Team Five, he could usually be found with a cigar in his *mouth and a half-chewed old stogie stuffed away somewhere in his kit. He told Marcus and the other guys in the platoon that his old unit had not taken a single casualty when he carried that old cigar with him. It became his good-luck talisman, and he made a point of never leaving the wire without it in Ramadi.*

Though both Adam and Marcus were combat veterans, nothing they'd ever experienced approached the ongoing mental and physical grind they encountered in the killing ground of Ramadi.

OCTOBER 2006
RAMADI, IRAQ

SEAL Team Five's Alpha Platoon slipped through the gate at COP Firecracker and plunged into the darkened streets. It was after midnight: vampire hours for the men of Naval Special Warfare. The men wore their unit patch, a kicking bull, on their right shoulders. *Mess with the bull, get the horns.*

Tonight, they would seize a building in south-central Ramadi that had been picked as the site of the Marine's next COP. With ten snipers, Alpha Platoon's mission would be to reach out and touch anyone who tried to interfere with the COP's construction.

The building selected had been an Iraqi Army facility at some point. Before that it had housed a small college before the war forced its abandonment. Most recently, it had served as a base of operations for al-Qaida in this section of the city. Surrounded by an oval stretch of road, it looked like a typical concrete government building in the middle of a traffic circle, which the Americans had dubbed "the racetrack."

Adam Downs loped along with the rest of his squad. They kept about twenty yards spacing between each man—just in case somebody triggered an IED or the element suddenly took automatic weapon's fire.

This was Adam's first mission as a sniper. He'd been a machine gunner and a medic with his first platoon in 2004. He'd spent that deployment protecting Iraqi politicians, which he and the rest of his team hated. Politicians were bad enough, but the Iraqi ones were a particular brand of self-serving, loathsome cowards, and the SEALs came to detest their charges.

At the end of their deployment, Adam's platoon was finally unchained from protecting "public servants" and turned loose on direct-action missions in northern Iraq around Mosul. Those ops lead to his first firefights.

On this night, Adam had done what a lot of rookie NFL players do before their first game: they'll overload themselves. They put on way too many pads and get so armored up that they lose the agility that attracted their coaches in the first place. Easy to do. In Adam's case, he'd taken too much gear along. He was a jack-of-all-trades for Alpha Platoon, a sniper, a qualified and experienced breacher, as well as a combat medic. Each specialization required specialized gear, and on his first time out in all three roles, Adam tried to carry *everything*. His utility belt sported more gizmos than Batman's, including two breaching explosive charges, an emergency airway kit, six tourniquets, and a radio.

He'd slung his .300 Win Mag bolt-action rifle over his back, then strapped his assault pack over it. The pack was full of more gear—40mm He rounds for the M203 grenade launcher mounted under the barrel of his M4 carbine, more medical stuff, batteries, his ghilly suit, the olive drab screens he planned to use to camouflage his hide, plus MREs and a single bottle of water. "I didn't want to look like a pussy," he later recalled about the minimal amount of water he carried.

"But I did have a Satanic amount of ammunition—something like eleven or twelve magazines." Altogether, with his body armor, helmet, Rhodesian vest (or chest rig) that held his spare ammunition, and two weapons, Adam probably lugged close to ninety pounds into the city that night.

Marcus Luttrell, who was his team's acting chief, checked on him. The two had been friends for years, and had come together in Team Five after Marcus became the Lone Survivor of a Seal Team Ten fire team from Operation Red Wings in Afghanistan the previous year.

They'd gone through 18 Delta Combat Medic school together, and Adam always credited Marcus with getting him to graduation. "Marcus," Adam later said, "taught me how to study. He pulled me through all those classes."

"How ya holdin' up?" Luttrell asked him.

Another thousand yards and I'll be ready to turn a gun on myself.

No way was he going to complain or show weakness. Marcus was setting the standard for toughness within the platoon. He was a walking case study of ground-pounder injuries—his back was jacked up, his thumb and wrist and knees were all in various states of agony. While some guys would be content with Med Hold, or a desk gig, Marcus sucked it up, never bitched, and stayed at the tip of the spear.

Adam exhaled sharply and whispered, "I'm good to go."

Next mission, he was going to prioritize all this shit. It felt like his spine was compressing.

Gunfire rang out in the distance. Through his night vision, Adam could see the greenish flares of fires burning somewhere in the city. They cast an eerie glow over the man-made horizons of the buildings that flanked this battle-damaged avenue.

As they approached the target building, the platoon peeled off into a narrow alley. They'd come at it from an unexpected quarter— unfortunately this meant scaling a wall. The SEALs climbed over it one at a time. When Adam hauled himself over it, all the extra weight caused him to lose his balance. He slipped and fell hard against his assault pack—and the .300 Winchester Magnum rifle beneath it.

Fuck this Ninja shit.

He picked himself up and kept moving as he cursed under his breath. He hoped his Win Mag and its Nightforce scope were okay.

This section of the city had once been a ramshackle slum. Trash lay everywhere in stinking heaps, and abandoned, half-ruined dwellings lined the alley.

They reached the racetrack and stacked up on the target building. A moment later, at an unspoken command, Alpha Platoon poured inside.

The place had been a carnival of horrors, a base where al-Qaida abused the locals who had dared oppose them. Some were perhaps unfortunates who violated the Shuria Law al-Qaida had implemented in 'hoods they controlled. Caught smoking? Al-Qaida's adherents would sometimes kill the offender on the spot. Other times they'd cut off his smoking fingers. Those who were beardless, or violated the dictates of al-Qaida's dress code, would find themselves abducted off the street and tortured in a place like this one.

The SEALs went from room to room, finding blood splatters on walls, dried blood pooled on floors, and more splashed across tables. Steel spikes, rusty iron rods, pliers and knives provided testimony to what had been happening here.

Sickened by what they'd found, the men secured the building and began to establish overwatch positions on the fourth floor. Adam began to construct his hide in the back of what had been a science classroom of some sort. Bottles and bunsen burners, sinks and rows of work spaces dominated the room. The windows had long since been shot out or shattered, leaving an unobstructed field of fire to the south. This was the most likely avenue of approach the enemy would use should they try to stop construction of the new COP, and Adam relished the opportunity to take the fight to them. Mike Monsoor and Marc Lee had died only two months before; in Naval Special Warfare, the community was so small everyone either knew each other, or knew their reputation. Team Five had arrived in Ramadi eager to avenge the loss of Team Three's beloved brothers.

Adam set up his olive drab screens between the windows and the back of the classroom. Then he found some relatively undamaged—and nonbloodstained—tables that he dragged over to the far corner. He put two together and hefted a third atop them. Then he found a bench and slid that up there as well. When he climbed into his hide, he noted with satisfaction that he had a great view of the street and nearby buildings.

He settled into his spot and began his turn behind the Win Mag. Before he'd left the COP for this mission, he'd covered his face with cami paint, a ritual that dated back to his days in southern Illinois hunting with his best friend Justin and his father, Dale. Now he pressed his eye into the Nightforce and glassed the street. No movement yet, but the hour was still early.

He settled down and fell into his hunter's zone: a combination of patience and alertness. He'd learned both in tree stands around Elko as a teenager. When he was ten, Dale had selected a Ben Pearson compound bow for Adam that Adam's father then purchased as a Christmas gift for him. He and Justin spent hours sending arrows into paper plates taped to hay bales. Later, they went to archery tournaments— Justin was one of the best archers in his age group. Dale mentored both boys, and after they turned fourteen, he began to take them bow hunting.

For Adam, sitting in a hide in Ramadi in his zone brought back the best moments of his childhood. Those tree stands. Hours and hours of nothing but quiet waiting and camaraderie. Except this time, instead of waiting for a buck to come by, he was keeping watch over young Americans and trying to keep them safe.

The Army's combat engineers showed up with all the material needed for the construction of the new outpost. They'd gotten so good at this that the troops referred to it as "COP in a Box."

Seize, hold, expand. That was the strategy, and each COP pushed al-Qaida that much further into a corner from which its fighters could not escape. Their days of operating at will within the city were numbered. The insurgents realized it, and the fight had become increasingly tenacious.

The sun rose, and the new day began. People began moving around the city, and the insurgents were certainly reconning the new American position. Around the racetrack the engineers worked furiously against the clock to fortify the COP before the first attack inevitably came. Adam and "Dave" watched them work as Marine patrols arrived to provide extra security. They dismounted and moved out with a Humvee or two in support.

Look at those guys down there. Half of 'em were dating the prom queen this time last year. Now they're just trying to stay alive in this fucked-up place.

This mission had meaning. In a war where orders often made no sense, and so much waste was evident everywhere, this moment, this place, had purpose. With his Win Mag, he could keep those Americans below alive. That was if the Rules of Engagement, the ROEs, didn't get in the way. Even if they did, he'd pull the trigger and let the administrative chips fall where they may later if it meant saving an American life.

He shifted his scope and searched for activity on the rooftops down the street. Nothing of interest, but it got Adam thinking about some of the things he'd learned during the urban warfare section of sniper school back in Indiana.

The avenue stretching south had two visible cross streets. One was about two hundred yards away. These side roads channeled wind, and because of the dynamic currents in an urban environment, the wind can blow in different directions and speeds from block to block.

Take a shot at a bad guy three blocks up a street, and a sniper might have to deal with three different wind factors in the shooting equation. This can make shooting at a distance in cityscapes a significant challenge.

Another challenge is the nature of engagements in urban terrain. In rural areas, or open terrain, the range between friend and foe is usually a lot farther away than in urban areas. This makes things easier on the sniper, as he can take a Win Mag or an M40 or a .50 cal and know the general distance at which he'll be shooting targets. In Afghanistan, MARSOC snipers routinely opened fire at Taliban fighters twelve hundred yards away or more.

In places like Ramadi, the enemy can be anywhere. Firefights will range from farther than a thousand yards down to point-blank with sudden, surprise attacks like the one that killed Mike Monsoor. Snipers have to fulfill multiple roles in a city fight, which requires multiple weapons—an operator cannot effectively clear a room with a Win Mag. Trying to shoot a target at close range with a ten-power scope presents all manner of problems as well, so the snipers in Ramadi carried M4s as well as their sniper rifle.

On the fourth floor of the new 17th Street COP, Adam had a better field of fire than usual. He could see out to perhaps eight hundred yards down the street. The buildings were not uniform in size and shape, more of a mishmash that created corners and dead spaces between the alleys and side streets. This made for lots of places for insurgents to lurk. Adam scanned each one, then started back on the rooftops.

Right away, he spotted an Iraqi male atop a building a few hundred yards away. A quick examination of the man revealed that he had no weapon in his outstretched arms, but he was holding something small cupped in his palms. He walked to the edge of the roof and flung something into the air.

It took a moment for Adam to register what he'd just seen. The man had tossed a pigeon. The bird began flying around as the Iraqi disappeared from view. He returned and released another one. Within a few minutes, he had a whole feathered squadron loitering overhead. He began to whistle and clap at them, which prompted the pigeons to do aerial front-flips. They spun and tumbled around him while Adam watched with interest.

What kind of a person played with pigeons in the middle of a combat zone?

A memory welled from his mind. A movie from a few years back . . . what was it?

Tom Berenger.

Denzel Washington.

This Iraqi reminded him of a scene from that movie. It was in some American urban ghetto. As Denzel's character approaches a neighborhood, they saw the same thing. What did they call it?

Flipping pigeons.

That's right. *Training Day.* The gangbangers used the birds as a way to signal impending danger.

Could this guy be doing the same thing?

Adam watched him more closely now. He was a male of military age. Bearded, like everyone else. No weapons, of that he was certain.

Where did this fit into the ROEs? Every time an America sniper pulled a trigger in Ramadi, the military made him fill out a shooter's statement and the incident was investigated to make sure the shot didn't violate procedures or the current ROEs.

He reported what the Iraqi was doing to his commander, who told Adam to keep an eye on the pigeon flipper.

A moment later, Dave called out the arrival of several military-aged males in the street, about a hundred thirty yards away. Just as he did, the pigeon flipper vanished. Adam checked the street. In the nearest intersection a group of men were gathering. They were laughing and smiling, like they were meeting at a park back home for a soccer game or something.

Laughter in Ramadi was not a common commodity.

What the hell was going on?

Adam looked over the crowd and saw one of the males gesture toward the COP. He was wearing a big, baggy brown sweater, the sort you might see a merchant seaman wear. It looked like it hadn't been washed in years. In Ramadi, nothing had.

Brown Sweater abruptly stopped and looked directly at the fourth floor. He seemed to be staring right at Adam.

Okay, asshole. Maybe you know where I am. Fine. Bring it. Let's get this on.

"Boss, can we pull on these motherfuckers?" Adam asked his commanding officer.

"Any weapons?"

"None visible."

"Negative."

Something did not feel right here. The gagglefuck in the street looked like nothing more than a cover for surveillance of the new COP. No sneak and peak here. They knew the ROEs and knew the SEALs could not engage them. They were exploiting the Coalition's own rules to get a handle on the best way to launch an attack.

Adam sat there, watching them laugh and felt cold rage.

This kind of bullshit will lose you a war.

A few of the men drifted away down the side street. The remaining ones stayed only a short time longer before walking casually away. After they left, Adam pulled his eye from the scope and looked down over his rifle. The street was empty, at least for the moment.

He was about to go back to glassing the rooftops when he noticed a scuff mark on the windage adjustment dial on the side of his Nightforce.

Oh shit.

He'd zeroed his rifle to seven hundred yards before the start of the mission. The scuff hadn't been there. With a sinking feeling he realized he must have struck it when he fell off the wall during the infil.

Was his zero off?

There was no way to tell. He couldn't take a shot without revealing his position. Besides, if he fired randomly in the city, surely somebody would have his ass for that.

The uncertainty fed his rage.

He stared down into the now-empty street, wondering if he should swap out with Dave or another sniper whose zero was certain on his rifle.

That might be the professional thing to do.

He considered it for another moment. Each sniper's weapon was tailored and zeroed specifically to his eye, grip, and cheek placement. He couldn't just take another rifle and settle back down. He would have to either switch out, or make it work and compensate for any movement on the dial after he saw where his initial shot went.

Adam watched as a Marine patrol dashed into his field of view. They crossed through the second intersection a few hundred yards further down the street, their Humvees rumbling through the rubble and trash while their gunners held their heavy weapons and scanned the rooftops. The column vanished from view a moment later.

He wasn't going to leave; no way. He'd just gotten to this shithole, and he was determined to help those Americans below in the street.

Right then, an explosion tore through the neighborhood. Dirt and debris fluttered down from the ceiling as the shock wave shook the building. The platoon radio filled with chatter. One of the Marine patrols had just taken an IED strike.

Adam gritted his teeth and seethed. There wasn't anyone in his field of view, not even any civilians. They'd cleared the area, probably having known in advance the attack was coming.

Another explosion rocked the school. More grit filtered down from the ceiling, peppering the snipers with dust and grime. Probably asbestos, too.

The snipers had no eyes on the blast, and there was speculation as to what it was. An IED? A heavy mortar—say a 120mm? Maybe a rocket strike? Whatever the case, the enemy had just made it clear they would not let this COP go up without a fight.

A few minutes passed without any further activity. The street remained empty until a wrecker turned a corner and came down toward the COP, towing one of the Marine Humvees. The whole front clip had been blown apart by the IED hit. The wheels were mangled, the tires burned. The hood was gone, the windshield spiderwebbed with cracks, and the engine was a tangled mess of broken metal and hoses.

A burst of automatic weapons fire rang out a few blocks away. Again, Adam had no visual on it. An American machine gun rattled off a long series of replies. The exchange reminded him of his first tour as a Mark 48 automatic weapons gunner and his first firefight.

His platoon had established an overwatch position in Mosul. The unit's snipers had set up hides on the top floor of the building while Adam and the rest of the guys pulled security on the ground floor. For hours, they kept their eyes on a fractious, hostile neighborhood until a sedan sped around a corner and screeched to a halt right in front of their building. Four insurgents with AK-47s bailed out of the vehicle, while several more came out from a doorway across the street.

It was a classic case of a sudden, point-blank situation with the enemy in an urban environment. The enemy had no idea they'd just parked in front of a SEAL Team, which made things easy. The snipers opened fire first, dropping several Muj before Adam could even pull the trigger on his 7.62mm machine gun.

Adam's burst raked right through a window, blowing out the glass and sending shards flying into the street. He laid on the trigger and caught one of the insurgents still standing by the sedan as he wielded his AK-47. The man went down, riddled with bullets.

The enemy tried to maneuver on the SEALs' position, but the team killed them all or drove them off.

Adam kept that fight in the back of his mind as he watched the street and listened to the sporadic gunfire erupting around the school. In an urban environment, you can't take anything for granted. One minute you can be watching an intersection eight hundred yards away. The next you're locked in a battle at near hand-to-hand range. Relax only at your peril.

He scanned the street again, looking for any Muj trying to sneak up on the building. Then he worked his way forward, his crosshairs passing through the first intersection. Nothing so far. He began to work on the rooftops. And that's when he saw him.

The pigeon flipper was back on the roof.

CHAPTER SIX
The Bull's Horns

"Boss, can I engage this guy?" Adam asked as he watched the pigeon flipper. The man had sent his birds into the air over his building again, and they busily executed somersaults at his command.

If you have to ask, you probably shouldn't take the shot.

Adam thought of the paperwork required after every trigger pull. Some JAG guy second-guessing his every move, passing judgment on whether he should have fired his weapon in the middle of a war zone. His maternal grandfather had served in Europe during World War II. What would have happened if they had these ROEs then?

The team's officer in charge told Adam that if it becomes obvious the pigeon flipper was signaling enemy forces, he could take him out.

Who plays with birds when running gunfights have broken out all over your neighborhood?

The sun was to the man's back as it rose over the buildings to Adam's left. The classroom grew increasingly bright, making the Illinois native worry again that his hide could be seen from the street.

The pigeon flipper disappeared again, and the birds all landed somewhere out of sight. This gave Adam a chance to take stock. He pulled his eye from his Win Mag's Nightforce and glanced around the room. Sunlight streamed through the glassless windows and soon there would be no shadows concealing their position. Behind him, somebody had covered the wall with camouflaged paper. It was the same woodland pattern he wore when hunting in Illinois. Against it, his hide stood out. Maybe Brown Sweater had already made his location. If not, whatever eyes were out there watching him would surely have him and Dave when the sun rose a little higher.

At least if anyone started shooting at him, he could return fire without having to worry about a prison sentence. Plus, he knew he was a better shot than al-Qaida's warriors were.

Fine. Bring it.

He settled back into his stance and brought his eyeball to the scope. At the closest intersection, the gaggle of military-aged men returned. They were laughing and joking again, but this time, several broke into spontaneous dances. A few pointed at the school and made mocking gestures.

They were celebrating. Right there in the street, right under the eyes of the enemy they'd just hammered. Smack in the middle was Brown Sweater, slapping backs and high-fiving like some immature athlete.

Dave was watching them, too. Adam heard him say, "They're rubbing our faces in it."

"Yep."

There were eight to ten in the middle of the intersection now. The celebrating died down, and they went into a tight huddle. Every few seconds, one of them would stick their head up out of the huddle and stare over at a particular part of the school. He'd nod, then drop back down into the huddle. It seemed as if they were calling their next play against the new COP.

Street football, Ramadi style. You fire the RPG at the gate, we'll sweep left and emplace an IED.

"Can we pull on these motherfuckers?" Adam asked. But as soon as he did, he knew the answer.

"Can't man. Can't do it. We're not inside the ROEs."

ROEs the enemy clearly understood.

Adam scanned for weapons, though he knew they'd be unarmed. He checked Brown Sweater thoroughly, looking for a pistol in his waistband, or perhaps in his pocket. Nothing.

Brown Sweater's head rose above the huddle. He looked straight up at the school's fourth floor. From his scope, Adam could see his dark eyes seemingly boring into his.

He sees me. I know he sees me.

Snipers spend so much time watching other people who don't know they're being watched that they can tell who is up to no good, and who's just a passerby pretty easily after a while. Little details—facial expressions, body movement, the way somebody walks or stands—they telegraph tension, or fear, or anticipation.

Brown Sweater's eyes were full of hate. Adam had no doubt of that.

But he knew he could not take the shot. Even if he didn't get prosecuted, there could be a media circus. Those vultures were always circling, looking for another Haditha story, or Abu Ghraib. Even if it escaped the notice of the press, there were other drastic measures that could be taken against a sniper who'd strayed from the ROEs. A Trident Board could be convened by Naval Special Warfare, and the sniper could be kicked out of the teams. For Adam, after ten plus years, to get booted back to the fleet as a medic was a fate worse than death.

The huddle broke as the men dispersed again. Some ran across the intersection and disappeared to the east. Some exited to the west. A silence fell across the neighborhood, broken only by a few stray AK reports in the distance. A few more minutes passed. The snipers scanned and searched to no avail.

A third explosion shattered the calm. Another IED, but this time nobody was hurt and the targeted Humvee was not damaged.

A few minutes later, the pigeon flipper reappeared on the roof. His feathered pals began their aerial acrobatics. Adam reported it, and observed him long enough to make a decision.

Okay, that's it. This guy is definitely signaling somebody. He needs to die.

Before Adam could take aim, though, he ducked out of sight again. Adam vowed to dump the son of a bitch the next time he showed his face.

Sure enough, the birds had just landed back at their roosts when the gagglefuck returned to the intersection. The same ten, scruffy-looking males. This time, they stood close together, as if hiding from view something going on in the middle of the huddle. Adam couldn't get a fix on what they were doing. Neither could Dave.

Once again, Brown Sweater was right there in the mix. Greasy hair combed forward over his forehead. Long enough that his bangs almost touched his eyebrows. Cold eyes.

Adam reported what was going on again. This time, the officer in charge, the OIC, had had enough. "Hey fellas, you see anything suspicious, drop the hammer. I've had enough of this shit."

So had everyone else. Everything going on since sunup had been hanky. Now it was game on, bad guys.

As if they sensed it, the gagglefuck broke up again. Brown Sweater trotted off, exit stage right. The street grew quiet again. The pattern had been established, and it was getting old. Time to throw something new at these sons of bitches.

A car rolled up one of the side alleys and pulled to a stop. Brown Sweater got out and walked into the street Adam was overwatching perhaps forty yards farther down from the first intersection.

He walked along the right side of the street to a doorway. It was set back a ways from the street, and the corner of a building partially obscured Adam's view of it. Nonetheless, he had a good enough view. He watched Brown Sweater through his Nightforce as Danny called out the range.

"Hundred ninety-three yards."

Adam stole a quick look at the intersection to make sure the wind hadn't picked up there. In these moments, he looked for any indicators of a breeze—a fluttering towel, a passerby's shirt riffling, paper or trash cartwheeling as it rode the wind. Anything to get an idea of the dope to dial into the scope.

The morning was still. Nothing moved in the intersection. If Brown Sweater did anything to merit dropping the hammer on him, this would be a straightforward shot. Except the Win Mag had been zeroed at more than twice the engagement distance. Adam made a mental note to adjust for that by aiming a little lower.

But what if the fall knocked the scope out of alignment? What if the dope had been messed up when the dial got scuffed?

Brown Sweater knocked on the door. It opened, but neither Dave nor Adam could see who was inside. A hand reached out toward Brown Sweater to pass him something. For an instant, Adam had a clear view of the tailpipe of an RPG. Brown Sweater gripped it.

A bolt of adrenaline struck Adam, the same way he'd get juiced when a buck appeared in front of his blind back home when he and Justin and Dale would bow hunt. All morning, these bastards had been mocking the Americans, but not anymore. Brown Sweater finally made a mistake.

And signed his death warrant.

Adam reached up with his left hand and set his dope to a hundred yards without ever taking his eye out of the scope. The Win Mag fired a one-hundred-ninety-grain cartridge at a flat trajectory with a velocity of twenty-five hundred yards per second. At this range, if he hit him, it would be like using a sledgehammer to drive a finishing nail.

Adam forced himself to relax. Brown Sweater secured the RPG and stuffed it under his clothes.

Adam centered his crosshairs just below the man's heart. He was standing with his right side angled toward the school, with just enough of his chest visible for Adam to get a good target picture.

He slid his index finger into the trigger guard. Brown Sweater hadn't moved, but he wasn't going to stay there all day. This was the moment. Adam pulled through and felt the trigger break. A split second later, the Win Mag kicked against his shoulder.

Shit! I didn't breathe through the shot!

The 7.62mm round streaked downrange, leaving a faint vapor trail in its wake that some snipers can detect. The bullet struck Brown Sweater just above his heart, probably right in the breast bone.

Damn. Too high. Was going for his pump house.

Seemingly, in slow motion, Brown Sweater turned and looked up at the school's fourth floor. It felt to Adam as if the two made eye contact again. This time, the anger and malice and cold hate radiating in those dark eyes were gone, replaced by a mix of surprise and utter despair. His eyebrows drooped, and his mouth opened.

Then he toppled over a few feet from the door.

Adam racked his Win Mag's bolt. The spent casing spun out of the rifle and tinged off the desk before rolling off the edge and coming to rest on the floor below his hide. He slid the bolt back in place, jacking a fresh round into the chamber. The smell of gunpowder filled the room.

Adam watched Brown Sweater as he lay in front of the door. Whoever had been inside was nowhere in sight now, leaving his insurgent buddy to bleed out on his front porch. He was down, but had he killed him? Adam wasn't sure. He thought about taking a second shot to finish Brown Sweater, but realized that was a revenge impulse born from all the rage and frustration the morning had brought.

Be professional. Keep it to that one shot.

A flurry of moment caught his eye. From across the street to Adam's left, another insurgent sprinted from the cover of an alleyway. He was going straight for Brown Sweater, AK-47 in hand. He wasn't fast—in fact the man was pudgy and overweight. But he had courage to run after his downed comrade across an open street, something his pal in the doorway most certainly did not. As he ran, Adam recognized him as another one from the intersection gaggle.

After shooting high with his first shot, Adam adjusted his aim slightly and put the crosshairs a little lower on the running man's body. He tracked the insurgent as he reached the other side of the street and stopped beside Brown Sweater's bloody, twitching body.

The minute the pudgy Muj halted, Adam had him cold. He pulled the trigger, felt the Win Mag's kick. An instant later the bullet punched through the Muj's right side. It broke the man's ribs and probably clipped a lung. Adam had hit him just below the mid-axillary line. Was it enough to kill him? The sniper wasn't sure.

Damn. Too low. Just a little too low this time.

The second Muj dropped his AK and tumbled to the ground. Part of the building that jutted out toward the street blocked Adam's view of where he fell so he couldn't tell if his target was still alive or not.

Movement in the doorway wrested Adam's attention away from Brown Sweater and where his pal might have fallen. He shifted the scope slightly just in time to see a woman step outside. She saw Brown Sweater and began wailing. Even from his position almost two hundred yards away, Adam could hear her cries of anguish.

She bent down and grabbed Brown Sweater's now-still body, her own form wracked by her sobs. She pulled him toward the doorway, leaving a bloody streak on the ground in his wake. With a furious tug, she dragged him through the door. The last thing Adam saw were the man's shoes vanish into the darkness beyond the doorway.

A few minutes later, she stepped outside again to dump a bucket of soapy water onto what amounted to her front porch. The soap bubbles turned crimson as the water mingled with the blood drying there. She stood alone, staring down at the mess, still sobbing. Then she turned and went back inside, closing the door on all the violence that had gripped her neighborhood for months now.

Who was Brown Sweater to her? Husband? Son? Brother? No way to tell. The Marines had their hands full all over the sector that morning and a squad could not be spared to investigate. Whoever he was, he'd been trying to kill the Americans in the streets around the new COP. No doubts there, and Adam would spare no sympathy for him. By dropping Brown Sweater, he knew he'd saved American lives.

His life for saving some of ours.

The sniper's cold equation.

Shouldn't have been doing that, buddy.

Adam and the rest of his platoon never saw what happened to the second Muj he'd shot. After he fell out of his field of view, the man was probably dragged off as well. Did he survive? Not likely. If he had, he would have had a long recovery ahead of him.

After Adam took those two shots, the gaggle never returned. Neither did the pigeon flipper. Message received. You mess with the bulls of Team Five, you get the horns.

There were four attacks against the COP that day, though. Several Marines were wounded; fortunately nobody was killed. All day long, the insurgents harassed the Americans with hit-and-run small-arms-fire attacks. They shot at the Humvee patrols with machine guns and rocket-propelled grenades. Other attacks were designed to draw attention away from teams of dedicated IED emplacers. Team Five learned that day how al-Qaida would do anything, use anyone to get those bombs in position.

At one point, Marcus Luttrell, who had been hunkered down in a nearby room, spotted three terrified women pushing a handcart with an oil drum stashed inside it. Behind the women, a single armed Muj male moved with them, shielding his body with those of the women. Adam's fellow snipers put a round into the oil drum, and one between two of the women that struck the ground directly under the Muj.

The Shock Factor worked to the letter here. Precision fire, even when not fatal, can destroy an enemy's morale. The three women froze, then panicked and ran back down the street. Their panic infected their Muj captor, and he bolted back into enemy territory as well, his flip-flops flying off his feet as he fled. The Marines investigated the oil drum and discovered an IED within it. Two shots from Team Five's snipers served to foil what could have been a fatal attack.

The SEAL platoon stayed at the 17th Street COP for five days. Altogether, they killed four insurgents, while one Marine on the roof of the building took a bullet in the back that passed down his leg and exited out at his knee. Adam was credited with the team's first kill of the Ramadi deployment.

The 17th Street COP gave the Americans a foothold in the Qatana District. For two years, the Qatana neighborhood had been a backbone of al-Qaida's presence in Ramadi. Now the Coalition had just stuck a knife in it. But gaining the foothold was one thing—seizing control of the neighborhood would be a totally different challenge, one that would come at a heavy cost to Team Five and Adam's circle of friends.

CHAPTER SEVEN
Sniper with a Rocket Launcher

NOVEMBER 19, 2006

RAMADI, IRAQ

Heroic restraint.

That's what they called the courage needed to stay within the ROEs. With the new counterinsurgency doctrine now fully adopted, our strategy in Iraq had changed from one of overwhelming firepower to a kindler, gentler type of fighting that looked more like neighborhood law enforcement with heavy weapons than a military operation. It took guts not to shoot on sight anything that resembled a legitimate target in a city where threats lurked around every corner, hid in every alley. Bombs, snipers, mortar barrages—the enemy practiced no heroic restraint, just suicide attacks, hit-and-run raids, and massive assaults on the forward COPs.

Every time SEAL Team Five's snipers pulled their triggers, the shooter reports had to be filed, investigations carried out. The men got to the point where they hated those things, and hated the sight of the JAG officers seemingly ready to second-guess every battlefield decision. After his first report, Adam told his OIC, "Boss, I suck at paperwork. Hell, I wouldn't even know how to write my own name if it wasn't stenciled on my gear."

The reports and ever-present reminders that one wrong move in combat could destroy a career, or even land a sniper in prison, affected Adam and everyone else whenever they went into the city. They grew cautious on the trigger, and at times males they were almost certain were enemies escaped their wrath simply because whatever they were doing did not fall into the narrow range of the ROEs.

As difficult as these restrictions were for the SEALs and frontline troops, there was a point to heroic restraint. The civilians caught in the middle were the key to this fight, and the change of strategy began to make a difference to them. In one neighborhood, al-Qaida drove truck-mounted mortars into the streets almost every day to fire a few harassing rounds at the Coalition outposts nearby. The Coalition sometimes launched counterbarrages if the trucks could be pinpointed before they broke contact and sped away. The destruction the counterbombardment did to the neighborhood actually turned the locals against al-Qaida, not the Coalition. They rose up and tried to stop the enemy from launching their attacks from their neighborhood.

Al-Qaida did not take kindly to such a rebellion. They stormed into the neighborhood and burned the sheik's house down. They caught a sixteen-year-old boy, beheaded him, and delivered his head to one of the sheik's police units. Then, in a wave of terror, they grabbed locals, trussed them up and tied them behind their vehicles. Shouting Jihadist slogans, they drove around the neighborhood with impunity, dragging their victims sometimes to their deaths.

After al-Qaida beheaded more children, the local imam used the neighborhood's mosque to declare holy war against the holy warriors. The sheik went to the Americans and solidified an alliance with the Coalition. American troops, with the help of the locals, swept the neighborhood and captured numerous insurgents. After that, al-Qaida entered that part of Ramadi only at their extreme peril.

After that, more and more neighborhoods followed suit. They raised their own militias, their tribal leaders sent men to join the Iraqi Police (IP). More stations were established, and though the IPs left a lot to be desired with their professionalism and resistance toward graft, they started to show courage and heart. Dozens were killed manning checkpoints designed to foil vehicle-borne IED (VBIED) attacks in the city.

As the Iraqi policemen died to protect their neighborhoods and the population slowly began to turn on al-Qaida, the flow of intelligence to American forces increased. This played to SEAL Team Five's strengths as a surgical force, and the operators soon had plenty of specific individuals to hunt down on kill or capture direct-action missions.

Adam volunteered for missions with both elements of the platoon. As long as he was in the city, he wanted to contribute as much as possible. During direct-action missions, he usually functioned as the team's breacher, blowing doors with small strip-charges. He'd carried out many such missions in Mosul during his previous deployment, where he had learned never to assume what lay on the other side of the door. The bad guys they encountered inside these houses never offered serious resistance. The team caught them asleep, or overwhelmed them with sheer violence of action before they could find a weapon. But at times, as they were being detained, those they captured would take a swing at an operator. That never ended well for the insurgent, who usually ended up bruised and battered, facedown, and zip-cuffed.

During one direct-action mission in Ramadi, the platoon hit a house harboring a known IED specialist. Taking out these bomb makers was one of the team's top priorities, so the men were juiced for this mission. Adam breached the door, the operators flowed inside—only to find their man was not at home.

Fair enough. In Ramadi, the Americans had to think on their feet and improvise. The operators faked an extraction, leaving behind a small contingent that included Adam. While he and a few others hunkered down in the house, one of the SEALs hid inside the family's outhouse. Thinking all was clear, the bomb maker slipped into the courtyard sometime before dawn and decided to go relieve himself before he entered the house.

He opened the outhouse door to find the barrel of a SIG Sauer pistol pointed at his forehead.

Game over, Fucker.

Except he didn't know it. As one of the operators tried to zip-cuff him, the bomb maker bit him on the hand. Adam and a couple others came over to help, but the man refused to go quietly. He fought and struggled until the SEALs knocked him off his feet and kneed him in the face. After that, compliance was his watchword.

Between the direct-action missions, Team Five's snipers played a key role in expanding the Coalition's hold on Ramadi. They covered the construction of new outposts and kept watch over Army and Marine patrols as they swept into hostile neighborhoods. Such missions helped take the pressure off the forward COPs and push the Coalition's presence deeper into al-Qaida-held territory. These were risky missions, and the team faced new threats from a cunning and capable enemy who knew the terrain and had eyes everywhere.

In the early hours of November 19, 2006, SEAL Team Five's two platoons moved into the city to support an upcoming major Coalition operation in the Second Officers quarter of Ramadi. Nicknamed by the operators as the "P-Sectors" for the designations on their maps, the Seconds Officers quarter included the Al Iskan and Al Andols districts—both firmly controlled by al-Qaida.

The plan called for Marine and Army elements, supported by Iraqi troops and police, to surge into the P-Sectors and root out the enemy by going house to house in search of weapons caches, intel, and insurgents. The mission was aggressive and would strike at the heart of a key al-Qaida stronghold in the city. The SEALs knew they would be in for a fight.

Team Five's platoon at Camp Corregidor was assigned to protect the eastern flank of the Marine units involved in the operation. Staging out of COP Eagle's Nest, they were to take fifty men (SEALs, specialists, and their Iraqi Jundis, or soldiers) and set up three mutually supporting sniper overwatch positions before dawn.

In the meantime, Adam's platoon at Camp Lee would stage out

of COP Iron and cover the patrols from two hide sites in the Al Iskan District. They'd be rolling out light that morning, having only a dozen operators and specialists, plus five Jundis to protect the Army's flank.

The Camp Corregidor SEALs reached their assigned buildings without incident, only to discover they couldn't see enough of the neighborhood from two of them. The nature of the buildings and streets in Ramadi were such that the high ground that provided good, unobstructed views was difficult to find. This made the three-hundred-sixty-degree protection of any site they did pick very difficult. Most every building would have blind spots—ones that the enemy frequently had already identified and knew how to exploit.

The special operations snipers flexed and found two new positions that gave them better visibility on the neighborhood. They secured them, finding the families inside sullen and hostile—characteristics of areas long in al-Qaida's control. But as the snipers set up their hides, they discovered that the teams could not see each other's positions. There were too many buildings and obstacles between them. The original idea had been to pick three sites that could cover each other in case of attack. Now, each hide would be out on its own little island.

Across the quarter, Adam and his platoon departed from COP Iron at about 0200. They moved through the city on foot for over a kilometer and a half before reaching their two selected sites. The first, a three-story house, had already been secured by a squad of 1st Armored Division soldiers, which made things easy for the SEALs. Adam went up to the roof with his spotter and the team's JTAC (joint terminal attack controller), whom everyone had nicknamed "Fizbo." He was a Navy fighter-bomber pilot, and had already earned the SEALs respect for his dedication, professionalism, and repeated attempts to get bombs on enemy fighters during skirmishes with the enemy. Each time their chain of command had denied the request, but Fizbo's persistence impressed the operators.

The Camp Lee element's other sniper team set up in a house

about a block away from the initial hide. They had good visibility from both positions and could support each other easily, as only a ruined building stood between them.

Adam built his hide on the third floor and started the morning spotting for "Mark," another one of the team's snipers. Adam had volunteered to go out with the Gold element of the Camp Lee–based platoon, as they were short-handed that morning, so he was working with operators he knew well but had not gone out into the city with many times yet.

Mark had steadied his match-grade SPR .223 caliber rifle with a shooting stick instead of a bipod. This looks just like a big "Y" and the barrel of the weapon rests in its crook. Adam hunkered down beside him with a pair of binoculars. Together, they started mapping out their assigned sector, lasing the key features so they knew the ranges to them.

Three hundred yards from their hide, the road dead-ended at a T-intersection. They couldn't see much beyond the buildings on the south side of it, so that became the limit of their field of view to the south that morning.

After sunrise, some of the other SEALs caught sight of numerous unarmed military-aged males. Some strolled around the street, trying without success to look casual and not like they were looking for where the Americans had set up shop. A few were even less subtle. They peeked out from around corners, or lurked in the alleyways where they stared at the rooftops. Adam and Mark listened to the chatter as their brothers reported what was going on, but they didn't see any of this themselves. At least not at first.

A few hours after dawn, a military-aged male ran into the intersection clutching an AK-47 at the low ready. He looked a little like Elmer Fudd hunting Bugs Bunny, only with Fudd in a dead sprint.

Adam called him out to Mark. The insurgent was three hundred yards away, but moving quickly perpendicular to their position, and they had only about a twenty-yard-wide field of view at the intersection. It would be a tough shot to make on the fly like this.

Mark swung his rifle back to the intersection and found the target in his Leupold scope just a split second before he vanished out of their line of sight at the edge of the intersection.

"Fuck! Can't get the shot!" the SEAL sniper said.

Frustrated, they considered options.

"Let's go up on the roof and see if we can get eyes on him," Adam suggested.

Mark agreed and they climbed out of their hide and headed up onto the roof where another team was already set up and overwatching another sector. They reached the roof and crawled to the south-side parapet. Mark stayed low while Adam popped his head over the edge to try to catch a glimpse of the insurgent.

A quick sweep revealed a limited field of view again, only marginally better than the third-floor hide. He ducked low and waited a few seconds before taking a second look. Nothing. No sign of the insurgent, or anyone else at that intersection.

Adam studied the buildings around the T. No movement. It was mid-morning by now, and the neighborhood looked as empty as the set from *28 Days Later*. He'd had his head above the parapet for about thirty seconds when a single round impacted three inches below his chin. The bullet ricocheted and pelted Adam with concrete fragments. A split second later, Adam heard the rifle's report.

Sniper!

Adam dropped to the roof, heart pounding. He looked over at Mark and the two exchanged a few quick expletives.

Wasn't checking my flank. The fucking shot came from my right.

Adam stayed low and moved off the roof to report what had just happened. He found the OIC downstairs and let him know there was an enemy sharpshooter somewhere out to the southeast.

"Are you okay?" the OIC asked.

"Hell yeah!" Adam replied. "I'm still here talking to ya, aren't I?"

More than anything, the shot pissed Adam off. That son of a bitch who almost took his head off was still out there in some dingy hide, looking for Americans to kill. No way was Adam going to stay in the relative safety of the house while that threat loomed over the Army patrols now filtering through the streets around them.

Fuck it. Let's do this.

Adam went back to the roof and settled down beside Mark, ready to see if he could find the enemy sharpshooter. But only a minute or so had passed when Fizbo, the team's JTAC, called out trouble.

He'd been talking to a Marine F/A-18 Super Hornet pilot orbiting overhead. The aviator had his sensors trained on the neighborhood to the south, and his video feed detected a group of insurgents massing a few blocks over. At first, there were just a few. But within minutes, they had almost twenty armed fighters.

Was their sniper overwatching them? *Just like we were doing for our guys?* If that was the case, the enemy knew where the SEALs were and might soon try to maneuver on their building.

Adam peered over the parapet, but the street was still deserted. He ducked back down and told Mark. Fizbo was nearby, watching the F/A-18's video feed from an electronic device called a Rover, basically a small computer with a flat-screen monitor.

"They're moving," Fizbo reported. There were around thirty of them now, almost a platoon-sized element.

The enemy force bounded toward the SEALs, then slipped into a building near the intersection. The Americans waited to see what their next move would be, but none of the insurgents emerged from the building.

What were they doing?

"Hey, Boss, let's use rockets on 'em," one of the other operators said.

Getting permission to drop bombs in Ramadi was extremely difficult, but the Gold Team had sortied from COP Iron with two 84mm Swedish-made Carl Gustav rocket launchers and ten reloads for them. First produced in the 1940s, the Carl Gustav had been used by most NATO countries as an antiarmor weapon for half a century. Its accuracy and hitting power, combined with its portability, made it a favorite weapon inside Naval Special Warfare even though it had been phased out of service throughout the West.

The Carl Gustavs gave the Gold element some serious fire-power slung across their backs. The insurgents outnumbered the SEALs and the squad of soldiers holding the three-story building. If ever there was a time to use that firepower, it was now.

Adam had one of the launchers. Fizbo coached him onto the structure the enemy had taken over. Adam loaded the Carl Gustav.

Dave, one of the other Gold element operators, had the other Carl Gustav. He loaded his, stole a quick look at the target building, and ducked back below the parapet. Then he turned to Adam and said, in a German accent, "I see them!" It was a line from the original *Die Hard* movie when the evil blonde terrorist was preparing to fire a rocket at a police armored vehicle.

Adam started cracking up. Even with all the tension, or perhaps because of it, he couldn't help it. Dave's performance was spot on, and juxtaposed against the backdrop of Ramadi, it was almost surreal.

Then the moment passed. Dave shouldered his launcher and stood up at the far end of the roof. With a fiery whoosh, he let fly with the rocket. A split second later, they heard a muffled blast as it exploded downrange.

Now it was Adam's turn.

Better bring my A game to this rocket business.

The insurgent sniper was still out there. Would he be waiting for Adam's head this time? His windage corrected after that first shot? Maybe he'd trained his reticle just a shade higher this time.

Adam paid little attention to that thought. If they didn't kill these guys, the team would have its hands full if the insurgents got much closer. This was the same neighborhood where Mike Monsoor had died; the enemy in this sector had a habit of exploiting blind spots and tossing grenades.

Keep these fuckers at arm's length or they'll get in around us.

The enemy sniper forgotten, Adam felt a sudden sense of relish. He'd deliver some payback for Mike, but this time instead of a single bullet, he'd send a seven-pound warhead their way at two hundred fifty yards a second. His rocket was set with a slight delay, which would allow it to penetrate the building's walls and explode inside.

In one fluid motion, Adam stood up, took aim, and pulled the trigger.

CHAPTER EIGHT
The Gauntlet

Half a mile from Adam's streaking rocket, a lone insurgent inched toward the SEAL sniper teams of Lieutenant "Jack Higgins's" element. Jack's men, wary of grenade attacks like the one that had killed Mike Monsoor, had set up their hides inside rooms on the top floor of the building they'd occupied. The eyes of al-Qaida noticed this, and came up with a counter to this new tactic. The lone insurgent was the messenger of that latest battlefield evolution.

This interplay between tactic and countertactic made the battlefield in Iraq an ever-changing environment. For both sides, the key to this dynamic was observation. Get eyes on the enemy, understand what he's doing, and figure out ways to stop him. For the Coalition, snipers, aircraft, and drones provided those eyes. For al-Qaida, it was their snipers, plus unarmed men and children wandering the streets to conduct preassault surveillance.

In Ramadi, everyone watched everyone else. Those few who evaded the technology and the many eyeballs would often do telling damage to their enemies.

Staying in the SEAL element's blind spots, the al-Qaida fighter worked his way into the house next door to the one the Americans had taken over. He went upstairs and out onto the roof, still unseen by the snipers. The two buildings were separated by only a few feet, but that did not deter this insurgent. Like something out of an action film, the man jumped across the space and ended up on the roof above the Americans.

Right then, the midday call to prayer began to blare through a local mosque's loudspeakers. The SEALs, long used to this Islamic ritual, noticed it sounded different. As they listened, one of the Iraqi NCOs with them rushed to Lieutenant Higgins and warned him the mosque was broadcasting a message to the insurgents.

Thanks to a group of kids who had spotted the SEALs earlier in the morning, the Jihadist on the roof knew exactly where the snipers had established their hide site. He crawled across the roof to a point directly above one of the firing ports they'd cut in the wall. Before the call to prayer had ended, he swung over the parapet and hurled a grenade into the room below. The Americans had little chance to react as the weapon rolled through the room. Petty Officer "Bill Barnum," the element's corpsman, shouted a warning, but it was too late. The grenade exploded a few seconds later, spraying Bill with shrapnel.

As his brothers rushed to Bill's side, al-Qaida launched a simultaneous assault on all three of the Camp Corregidor SEAL hide sites. Moments before the streets had been empty. Now they swarmed with Jihadists, rushing and bounding and firing from the hips. The snipers opened up. So did the platoon's machine gunners. The enemy poured into nearby buildings and scrambled up the stairs into the higher floors to established support by fire positions. Soon they were hammering the SEALs with machine guns and rifles.

Lieutenant Higgins had been on the bottom floor when the grenade attack took place. As the firefight swelled, he ran upstairs to find Bill seriously wounded. One look at his leg, and the young officer knew they would have to get him out immediately.

This presented a problem. The neighborhood was alive with gunfire and running bad guys. Calling in a helo to extract Bill was out of the question—no way would anyone want to risk a bird to such intense ground fire. CASEVAC (casualty evacuation) by helicopter in such a dense urban environment was fraught with peril anyway, and it was unusual to get a wounded man out that way. In this case, it just couldn't happen, the threat level was too high.

The platoon had inserted into the hide sites on foot. Their vehicles were back at Camp Corregidor, which made evacuating Bill by themselves impossible—unless they carried him through the inferno outside, which didn't make any sense. Such a move would simply get more operators hurt. The only thing they could do was call for help.

Back at COP Eagle's Nest, a mechanized infantry platoon from the 1st Armored Division was standing by for just such an emergency. Before the SEALs had departed on their mission, the company commander had promised to come out should they need armor.

They needed armor. The SEALs radioed COP Eagle's Nest, and the Army launched four M2 Bradley Infantry Fighting Vehicles their way. In the meantime, the operators hunkered down in the hide sites and waited for the Brads to come get their wounded brother. Bullets laced their buildings. The insurgents ducked and maneuvered, always supported by machine gunners and rifle fire. The SEALs didn't have the firepower to overwhelm this many insurgents. All they could do was hold on until the Brads arrived.

Minutes passed, the operators drained their mags and slapped home fresh ones. Then, in the distance, Lieutenant Higgins's men heard the low rumble of Bradley engines approaching. It was time to get out of Dodge.

The lieutenant prepped for the extract. Bill would be carried to the first track by another SEAL, "John Francis," along with four Jundis. The rest of the element would jump into the other three tracks lined up in a column behind the lead Brad.

The snipers gathered their gear and dashed downstairs. Lieutenant Higgins and the others moved to the first floor, ready to dash for their assigned tracks. As they did, the firing died away. One minute, bullets filled the air, spattered the walls of their building, and cracked overhead. The next, the neighborhood fell so silent it seemed like one of those foreshadowing moments in a bad horror film.

Where had the enemy gone? Was this a hit-and-run attack? No doubt they'd heard the Bradleys coming to the rescue. Perhaps their commanders had ordered a withdrawal. Better that than stand up to the cannon carried by the American vehicles.

As the tracks got closer, the Jundis, Bill, and John Francis broke cover and went through the doorway into the midday sun. The other men followed and fanned out to set security.

That's when an explosion blew everyone off their feet. A mushroom cloud of smoke and dirt obscured the horrific scene as it boiled through the street and over the shattered neighborhood.

A Jundi near the point of the explosion was nearly ripped in half by shrapnel. Beyond help, he died a few minutes later. Bill Barnum and John Francis sprawled nearby, their clothes afire, bleeding from numerous shrapnel wounds. The blast broke both of their legs, and as their senses returned, neither man could walk. Two of the other Jundis with them were also down, bleeding and concussed. Almost everyone else had suffered slight shrapnel wounds.

Somehow, once the Muj had figured out where the SEALs had established their position, they had dispatched a couple of men to emplace an IED near the house's front door. Despite the fact that the operators had three-sixty security established, there were always going to be blind spots. It is the nature of an urban environment, a battlefield reality that the most cunning warriors can exploit.

The Muj in Ramadi knew every nook and cranny of this neighborhood. They were able to set the IED in place only a few yards from the front door, before backing off and waiting for the SEALs to pull out after the grenade attack. Whoever detonated the IED had been a veteran of such operations. Instead of blowing it at the first sign of the Jundis and Americans, he was patient. He triggered it only after most of the element had left the house and entered the bomb's kill zone.

Americans back home never really recognized the skill and tactical abilities of the enemy. Much of the U.S. military underestimated their capabilities as well, at least at first. The truth was, in Iraq we faced some of the best-trained and motivated guerrilla fighters ever encountered by a Western army. Some of the ones encountered in Ramadi had been fighting in the city for three years. They were veterans, and they blended their experience with a phenomenal ability to adapt and evolve in the face of American technology, grit, and firepower.

Now, with their bomb detonated, they ambushed the SEALs and

Jundis from concealed positions up and down the street. Bullets scythed through the smoke and dirt, impacting on the road all around the dazed and disoriented men.

Lieutenant Higgins opened his eyes. The explosion had flattened him, knocked him senseless, but somehow its shrapnel had missed him. He lay on the ground, confused and concussed. As his brain reset and got a handle on the situation, he realized what had happened. Looking over, he could see his men down a few yards away. That was enough to kick-start him into action. Higgins got to his feet, staggered to John Francis and dragged him back inside the house.

As he did, the element's communicator (radioman) spotted Bill Barnum and ran across open ground through the enemy crossfire to his aid. The smoke and dust was thinning by now, and the Muj could make out the wraithlike images of the Americans and Iraqi troops as they reacted to the attack. They poured lead into the scene with everything they had.

The communicator pulled Bill back through the doorway and into the house. Bullets laced across the walls and windows, shattering things inside and prompting the SEALs to rush to the aid of the civilians inside with them. The family who lived there was frozen in terror, but several of the SEALs wrapped them up and shielded their bodies with their own. Keeping civilians safe at all costs was the new paradigm in Ramadi, and in this desperate moment, these courageous, but shocked and battered, Americans exemplified the selflessness it required.

The others still outside returned fire and retreated back to the house. They had no other choice. The street was a kill zone, and the Brads were nowhere in sight yet.

For the moment, they were trapped.

A few blocks away, "Phil Glade's" sniper element from Camp Corregidor heard the explosion and learned from the radio chatter that Higgins's men had suffered heavy casualties. Phil made the call to go to their aid. The problem was, he and his men were in the middle of a firefight of their own. Trying to disengage and move several hundred yards through these streets would be an extraordinary challenge.

His men pulled out of the upper floors and took quick stock of things as they reached the ground floor. They slapped fresh magazines home, checked gear, then bolted through the doorway—and into a maelstrom.

Bullets chewed the streets and walls around them. They kept their weapons at the ready, scanning for targets as they bounded through the street. One fire team would move while the other laid covering fire. They shot at the windows above them, and the rooftops seemed to be crawling with al-Qaida. Muj dashed from alleys to spray and pray with their AKs. The SEALs kept going, their extraordinary marksmanship giving them an edge over the enemy's superior numbers.

A few blocks into their gauntlet, they split into two groups and turned down a pair of parallel alleys, still firing as they ran. Around them, the enemy would pop up in a window, or over a rooftop parapet, spray a burst at them with their AKs, then duck down a second later. Bullets pinged and whined, and occasionally a quick-eyed SEAL would drop one of the Muj as he exposed himself. For five minutes, it was like a deadly whack-a-mole game with guns and humans.

The gauntlet lasted perhaps five minutes, but to the SEALs it must have seemed like a lifetime. Finally, they reached the street in front of Higgins's house. Here they ran into a hornet's nest worse than what they'd just gone through to get there. Shooting for second- and third-floor rooms from multiple directions, the Muj had the street dialed in cold. Anyone who moved in it took fire.

Phil Glade and his men hunkered down behind whatever cover they could grab—doorways, walls, building corners—and tried to take some of the pressure off of Higgins. Their M4s, SPRs, and Mark 48s barked and belched flame, forcing some of the Muj to duck and seek cover of their own.

Inside the house, Bill Barnum issued a steady stream of orders to his brothers. He was the element's corpsman, and now as he lay immobile on the floor, he directed his fellow SEALs through treating John Francis and the wounded Jundis. The Bradleys were closer now; their engines' roar could be heard over the cacophony of the gunfight. They just needed to hang on a little bit longer.

With Phil Glade's element outside suppressing the Muj, Higgins's men focused on getting the wounded the care they needed. Bill was in intense pain, and both he and John were bleeding badly. The other SEALs applied tourniquets to their legs and pressure dressing to their wounds. These measures didn't stop the bleeding, but it did slow the loss enough to give both men pain meds.

In the meantime, Higgins was still very dazed from the concussion he'd suffered during the blast. His communicator took over handling all the myriad of command-level responsibilities. He kept in contact with the Bradley platoon, explained the situation, and directed how the CASEVAC would go down once the tracks arrived. Each Bradley could hold six men. Now, with Phil Glade's element, they had more SEALs than space inside the vehicles. They'd have to shoehorn everyone in, plus send the Brads back for a return trip into the fight just to get everyone back to COP Eagle's Nest.

Outside in the street, the Muj seemed to recover from the surprise arrival of Phil Glade's element. The volume of fire they'd been able to deliver had diminished at first. Now, the al-Qaida adherents displaced to new positions in their buildings and opened fire with full fury once again. The gun battle raged with ruthless intensity, both sides seeking to gain the upper hand. He who has fire superiority can dictate what happens on the battlefield. Both sides knew it, and the lead flew as they sought to dominate.

Numbers began to tell against Glade's men. One by one, the incoming fire pinned them down. Soon things were almost as desperate in the street as they had been inside the house a few minutes before.

Down the street, the first Brad turned a corner and came into view, its tracks churning through the dust and debris riddling the roadbed. In the past, the sight of an M2 with its 25mm Bushmaster cannon was often enough to prompt the insurgents to break contact and end a fight. Not this time. Though they had no antiarmor weapons like an RPG, the enemy refused to be intimidated. If anything, the amount of incoming intensified.

The lead Bradley lurched to a stop in front of Higgins's doorway. The SEALs told the crew to work the second and third floors of the houses up the block. The gunner went to work, the big cannon belching shells that blew through walls to explode inside with deadly effect. The gunner raked the enemy positions, blowing insurgents apart.

The Brad crew dropped their ramp, and the first group of SEALs rushed into the street. They piled the wounded inside as others stood in the entrance, firing their M4s over the ramp as it closed. Behind the lead track, the remaining SEALs dove into the safety of the other Bradleys' armored hides.

The Army crews pulled out and raced through the shattered streets to get the SEALs and Jundis back to COP Eagle's Nest. The SEALs dismounted and carried their wounded men and the fallen Jundi to the aid station, where they would be stabilized for evacuation to better facilities, and ultimately back to the States for Bill and John Francis. Though their mission was over, for the Brad crews it had really just started. They'd have to brave the streets one more time to pull everyone out of the third overwatch position the Camp Corregidor platoon had established. Given the speed at which the insurgents placed the IED by the doorway to Higgins's house, the Brad crews expected to run into bombs, rockets, and anything else the insurgents could throw at them. Given their refusal to retreat, the mech infantry guys knew they were in for another hard fight.

They never flinched. The tracks lined up at the front gate and headed out back into the storm.

CHAPTER NINE
Payback

Adam's rocket streaked into the target building, punched through the outer wall, and exploded with a dull thud deep within. Fizbo watched his Rover to see how the insurgents would react to this onslaught. At first, there was no movement around the building, but as the minutes passed, a figure emerged from a doorway on the backside of the dwelling. The SEALs could not see him from their position, but he could not escape the F/A-18's eye in the sky. Fizbo called out to Adam and the others on the rooftop as perhaps twenty others followed the first insurgent out into the street.

At least there were fewer of them.

Instead of withdrawing back toward the Saddam Canal, the gaggle assembled into a semblance of a fighting formation and dashed through the streets and alleys toward the SEALs. Fizbo related their movements and tracked them as they ran into another building.

Adam and Dave took turns popping over the parapet to identify their new location. They could see the building, but they couldn't see any of the enemy within its walls. In the meantime, a smattering of gunfire broke out around the Americans. AK rounds pinged off the parapet and tore more chips from the concrete. It wasn't the sustained firepower onslaught the Corregidor SEALs were facing, but the harassing fire reminded them that there were other insurgents out there—including their own sniper.

The equation could change in a heartbeat if the twenty insurgents got their guns into the fight. Armed with AKs and light machine guns, they could pin down the SEALs and make the roof untenable. Then—who knows? Perhaps they'd try to assault the position, or close to grenade-throwing range.

As Dave and Adam lay prone on the roof, their Carl Gustavs on their shoulders, two other operators crawled to them with extra rockets. They pushed the reloads into the rear of the launchers and locked them home. A slap on their helmets told Adam and Dave that they were good to go. Dave stood up, and brought his Carl Gustav on target. "Fire Gustav!" he shouted to warn the rest of the team. A second later, the rocket left the tube with a hollow-sounding *kathunk*.

The 84mm projectile roared toward the target building like receding thunder. A second later, the rocket exploded into the first floor. This time, instead of a muffled detonation, the neighborhood shook violently as the warhead's shock wave rolled through it.

The enemy was getting close.

Adam's turn. He rose to his feet, the nineteen-pound launcher resting on his right shoulder. Right hand on the handle, his index finger on the trigger guard, he brought his left hand to the foregrip. This is opposite of the Russian RPG, which is fired with the left hand. Exposed now, the seconds ticked as he studied the neighborhood until he locked his eyes on the target house. Smoke was boiling from the first rocket's impact point.

Adam settled his right eye behind the weapon's telescopic sight. A small, upward-facing arrow served as the point of aim. Below the arrow were a series of pluses and minuses that denoted the compensation needed for every hundred yards of range. On either side of those stretched the windage indicators—long horizontal lines that looked like whiskers sprouting from the elevation ticks. At the bottom of the sight, the weapon's integrated range finder provided a digital readout of the distance to the target house.

Adam made a quick series of mental calculations. He was shooting down from the top of a three-story building, which complicated the shot. He wanted to hit the first floor, just as Dave had, so he had to adjust and aim low. There weren't any cross or tick marks to compensate for firing from an elevated position, so Adam made his best guess.

He took a breath, released half of it, and pulled the trigger. *Kathunk*. The rocket shot out of the Carl Gustav's barrel and lanced straight into the building. The ground shook, and a cloud of smoke and debris spewed from the impact point.

There was something almost euphoric about hammering the enemy with such awe-inspiring firepower. There is nothing low key about a Carl Gustav launch; it is loud, dramatic, and powerful. The SEALs on the roof relished the punishment they were dishing out with every rocket.

Six rockets left. Were the insurgents done? The operators reloaded and waited to hear what Fizbo could see on his Rover.

Sure enough, a minute or two later, the Muj bolted from the building. This time, it looked like some of them were wounded. Fizbo reported that the force was down to little more than a squad-sized element—perhaps fifteen men.

To the American's surprise, they refused to disengage. They had the chance. There were plenty of avenues of escape back to the canal the SEALs on the rooftop could not see. But these Jihadists were determined. They stayed in the street and maneuvered forward, toward the Americans.

One of the operators on the roof with Adam carried an M203 grenade launcher under the barrel of his M4. He began to use it as a poor man's indirect-fire weapon—a rifle-mounted light mortar. He lobbed the grenades in a high arc, hoping to drop one down over the buildings that masked their view of the advancing force and hit the Muj while they were out in the open.

The insurgents found another multistory building and poured into it. The SEALs retaliated with another rocket volley. The building shuddered from the impacts, and this time only a few emerged from its shattered interior.

But they still weren't done. About a half dozen ducked and

bounded to within fifty yards of the SEALs, until they took cover behind a wall. The Americans rained 40mm grenades down on them. The explosions wounded several Muj, and that broke their morale. They dragged their wounded back out of the line of fire and vanished into the labyrinth to the south.

The fighting died down after the SEALs repulsed the assault. By now, the Americans had been up for thirty-six hours straight. They were low on ammunition and exhausted. When the Army pulled its patrols in from the Al Iskan and Al Andols Districts, the Camp Lee SEALs knew it was time to depart.

As Adam and the others began to collect their gear, another group of Muj seized a building about three hundred yards away. Concealed inside, they opened up with rifles and light machine guns, stitching the parapet and southern wall of the house with 7.62mm fire.

The last rocket volley had consumed final reloads for the Carl Gustavs. With the amount of incoming they were taking now, the SEALs couldn't pull out without a significant risk of taking casualties when they got into the street.

Fizbo had the answer. The F/A-18 overhead carried bombs as well as AGM-65 Maverick missiles. The AGM-65 carried a three-hundred-pound shaped-charge in its warhead and could be laser guided onto its target. Originally built in the 1970s as an electro-optically guided weapon, it had evolved with the technological times. By 2006 hundreds of them had already been used in Iraq and were well known for their accuracy and remarkable ability to localize damage. With a warhead smaller than a five-hundred-pound JDAM (or joint direct attack munition) satellite-guided bomb, the Maverick could tear the guts out of a building without doing significant damage to the neighborhood.

The Army and Marine patrols had been engaged all day by the enemy. The Camp Corregidor SEALs were still under attack a half mile away, and both Camp Lee positions were taking small-arms fire. As a result, when Fizbo requested an air strike, the chain of command gave the green light. Kindler, gentler, worked only up to a point.

Fizbo coached the F/A-18 pilot onto the target, gave him the nine-line information brief needed to direct his attack, and the Marine aviator made his run. Fizbo warned everyone on the roof to get down—the target house stood only three hundred yards from their position. Even with the directed blast of a Maverick, that was still dangerously close.

Adam and the other operators on the roof hunkered down as the missile left the F/A-18's hard point and flew toward the enemy at seven hundred miles per hour. It dropped out of the sky, punched into the building's outer wall, penetrated deep inside and exploded. The force of the blast was nothing like a JDAM bomb, and the structure didn't even collapse. Still, the havoc it wrought on the insurgents inside was deadly. The firing from within it stopped, and another lull fell across the embattled neighborhood.

The respite from the incoming small-arms fire gave the Americans the opportunity to break contact and get back to COP Iron. They made hasty plans to depart. The Army squad holding security on the first floor would go first. As they headed into the street, Adam, Dave, and the other SEAL sniper team would cover them. If they evoked no reaction from the Muj, the SEALs would leave next, and the two groups would leapfrog back to COP Iron, covering each other as they went.

The squad from the 1st Armored left the house and rushed into the street. The SEALs stayed on their guns, waiting to see what the enemy would do. A block over, in the other overwatch position, the SEALs there began to exfil as well. It didn't take long for the Muj to notice. These al-Qaida Jihadists had been around long enough to know that the Americans were at their most vulnerable during infils and exfils. They realized they had a final, narrow window of opportunity to hit the Americans one more time.

Like the SEALs, they had been fighting all day in the merciless heat, and had to have been exhausted. They'd taken heavy casualties trying to assault the Camp Lee SEALs, which had to have affected their morale. Nevertheless, the Muj leader rounded up enough men for a final assault.

They began to maneuver forward, hoping to cut off the Americans in the street before they could get back to COP Iron. This time, Fizbo didn't need to give the rest of the team a running commentary on their movements. Assuming all the Americans had pulled out, they flowed into the fields of fire established by the SEAL sniper teams. The Americans opened up on them and caught them completely by surprise. One Muj went down, shot dead in the street a few hundred yards from the hide site.

That broke the enemy's morale. The rest of the assault force scattered and retreated. They'd finally had enough for the day. The SEALs grabbed their gear, slapped home new magazines—they were perilously low on ammo by now—and pulled out. Fizbo kept in touch with the F/A-18, whose pilot scanned the way home with his electronic eyes. No sign of any other Muj elements.

Despite their fatigue, the SEALs were in good spirits. Nothing is better for morale than repeatedly hammering the enemy and stopping their every gambit. A month into their deployment now and this was the first time they'd experienced an insurgent assault. The enemy's tenacity, willingness to take casualties, and determination to close on the overwatch sites impressed the Americans, and reminded them that they faced a far tougher foe than their countrymen back home in the States truly realized. That made kicking their teeth in that much sweeter.

Adam reached the street, the Carl Gustav strapped over his back and his M4 at the ready. Right then, the ground shook violently, and a mushroom cloud of smoke and flame rose above the rooftops to the east.

The Camp Corregidor SEALs had just been hit by the IED placed at the entrance to their overwatch position. The radio filled with reports of casualties and the need for immediate evacuation. The Bradleys reported they were on their way.

In a heartbeat, the light mood the day's victory had inspired was wiped away by a sense of complete helplessness. Two of their own had gone down, and the Camp Lee SEALs were in no position to come to the aid of their stricken brothers. Nearly out of ammo, without vehicles or heavy weapons, all they could do was continue their exfil.

Adam felt sick. He and Dave had been cracking jokes all afternoon, feeling that they'd had the situation well in hand. Their Carl Gustavs had done considerable damage to the enemy, and most of the insurgents who had escaped those weapons had succumbed to 40mm grenades and precision gunfire. Now, as he heard the news about the Jundis, John Francis, and Bill Barnum, a wave of guilt struck him. How could he be so glib with his comrades taking such a hit? Those feelings would linger long after the last rifle report echoed through Ramadi's battle-scarred streets.

The Bradleys from COP Eagle's Nest returned to the fight to extract the last of the Camp Corregidor SEALs. Fortunately, they encountered no roadside bombs and the exfil on that flank of the operation went off without further incident.

Adam's element bounded back for COP Iron and made it halfway until they were met by a platoon of Bradleys. Thirsty, hungry, covered with smoke, dirt, and grime, the SEALs and Joes piled aboard for the short ride back to the outpost. They made the last leg of the trip in near total silence, everyone's thoughts on John and Bill.

In the aftermath of the day, the SEALs took stock of everything that had happened. They studied how the insurgents had attacked them and discussed ways to counter their new tactics. These after-action discussions sparked a new battlefield evolution. Hopefully, the next time they went out into the city, they'd be able to catch the enemy by surprise with their fresh ideas.

In the meantime, the thought of that single sniper shot stuck with Adam. He replayed the sound of the 7.62 round smacking off the concrete a few inches from his head. The guy on the other side of that scope had been good. He'd given him only a brief opportunity to take the shot, and he'd very nearly put a bullet in the Illinois native's head.

What had happened to him? In the after-action discussions, it became clear that the enemy sniper had not fired again. Had he been killed? Probably not. The bulk of the SEALs firepower had been focused on stopping the Muj assault element. Nobody even knew from where the insurgent sniper had fired. His hide had been somewhere off to Adam's right, that's as specific as the Americans could get.

He had not taken another shot. The discipline that displayed was remarkable. Had he pulled out after nearly killing Adam? Or had he just gone to ground and provided eyes for the assault element?

There was no way to be sure. But one thing was almost certain: he was still out there, hunting Americans.

CHAPTER TEN
Under Watchful Eyes

RAMADI

In the wake of the November 19, 2006, engagement, SEAL Team Five's two platoons continued operating at a frenetic pace. Between covering Marine and Army patrols, the frogmen went after more IED makers in direct-action raids. With more Iraqi cops on the street, the flow of information from the citizens of Ramadi increased. This gave the Special Forces teams plenty of targets to go after, and very few resisted when the SEALs came knocking at their door.

There were the occasional exceptions. Adam had long since grown accustomed to switching roles depending on the mission demands. One night, he'd go out with his SR-25 and cover American patrols. Another, he'd be blowing doors for an entry team assigned to a kill or capture mission. Even after the hard fight on November 19, Adam continued to volunteer with both the Blue and Gold Camp Lee elements.

One night, during a kill or capture mission against a particularly ruthless IED maker, Adam set a strip charge on the man's front door, stepped clear, and blew it. At the same time, the IED maker had heard the entry team reach his house and had pushed a couch in front of his door in hopes of slowing them down. As he stood in front of the door, the charge went off. Normally, these are such small explosions that only the door suffers damage. This time, in what had to be a moment of supreme karma, the bomb maker happened to be standing in the most optimal place and distance to the blast to suffer from it.

The SEALs pushed through the door, finding the splintered couch in their way and their target lying toward the back of the room. As part of the team cleared the house, Adam, functioning now as the element's corpsman, crouched next to the wounded insurgent and assessed his condition. The strip charge had blown off three of his fingers and studded his face with wooden splinters from the door (and probably the couch). His legs were torn open and bleeding as well.

Whatever fight he had in him was gone now. The SEALs secured the house and kept the rest of the family safe while Adam worked on the wounded Muj. One of the chiefs with the team that night then had a moment of inspiration. Part of the SEALs role in Ramadi was to help prepare the Iraqi Army and Iraqi Police to function independently. They were a long way off from that, but they had made significant progress since the previous spring. To the chief, this seemed like the perfect moment to help mentor the Iraqi medic who had accompanied the Jundi scouts that night.

The Iraqis knelt beside the Muj and as Adam talked them through each treatment step. They applied direct pressure to his worst injuries, then placed a battle dressing on his legs and hand. The Iraqis carried him to a waiting Humvee and evacuated him to the combat support hospital outside the city.

When the team reached the hospital, the Muj was carried inside after being identified to the staff as an enemy combatant. As he was taken into an operating room, an officer assigned to the hospital approached Adam and asked, "Why didn't you just kill him?"

Thoughts of courts-martial, shooter statements, and moments of uncertainty on the battlefield floated through Adam's mind as he struggled to answer that.

Blow me! You think I want to go to prison, asshole?

The words started to form, but Adam managed to hold them in check. His outspokenness within the platoon had already caused some to label him a problem child, and picking a fight with a REMF—a rear echelon motherfucker—would only make things harder on him.

He toned his response down a notch, "Well, I didn't really want to be court-martialed."

The officer thought this over, then asked, "How'd it happen?"

"He got hit on a breach."

The officer nodded. "Okay, is the breacher here?"

"Also me" was Adam's curt reply.

The officer grew agitated. "And you didn't clean up your own mess?"

Adam's temper flared. The son of a bitch was getting on his case for not killing an unarmed man because it meant more work for him. From a rear-echelon type, this was insufferable.

"Look, we didn't use anything unusual. Just a strip of C-two. He was trying to barricade the door. We had no idea he was on the other side when I clacked off the charge."

The officer scowled, then vanished into the hospital's interior. The Muj lived, but he damn sure never made a bomb again.

Such moments were a reminder that as chaotic as combat could be, the politics and consequences of every decision and action would be scrutinized by a lot of Monday-morning quarterbacks. That scrutiny made each decision in the field harder to make. At times, the Muj capitalized on those moments.

Not long after the November 19 firefight, Blue Element from Camp Lee sortied into the city again to conduct another overwatch operation. They returned to the neighborhood of grenade-pitchers, where the Corregidor SEALs had been hit in November and Mike Monsoor had been killed the previous summer. This place was guaranteed action—nobody had any illusions otherwise.

They went in as stealthy as possible. Departing from COP Eagle's Nest, they patrolled toward their target building in the darkness, using no white light at all. They kept noise to a minimum and relied on their night vision to see the way ahead.

When they reached the house they wanted, the front gate was

locked. This neighborhood was like a fortress. Reinforced, nine-foot walls surrounded every compound, including this one. The gate off the street was wide enough to allow entry to a car or small pickup truck. One of the Blue Element SEALs carried a lock pick set, and he stepped forward to use it. A moment later, the gate swung open.

Silently, the team flowed into the compound past laundry hung and fluttering in the soft night breeze. A small stand-alone garage stood nearby, a sedan parked inside. The Americans reached the front door. In Ramadi, the SEALs never knew who would be on the other side of the door. Taking a soft approach and knocking could be an invite to a hail of bullets from some die-hard zealot hiding inside. Conversely, blowing the door risked hurting the very people the Americans were here to protect.

It was a devil's choice.

The SEALs knocked. A moment later, a sleepy-eyed middle-aged man opened the door and greeted the men coldly. The team's commander and interpreter explained the situation. The SEALs needed their house for a few hours. The family would be free to go about their day inside, but they would not be able to leave until the SEALs exfilled. If any part of their property was damaged, the U.S. government would compensate them.

The head of the Iraqi family reluctantly allowed the SEALs to enter his house. The women and children stayed close to him, but their fear and uncertainty was palpable. The fact was, no matter where their loyalties lay, the arrival of the Americans now made their home a target for al-Qaida.

And in Ramadi, there were eyes everywhere, watching.

The SEALs had tried to get into the house as quietly as possible. They'd encountered no opposition, seen no enemy during the infil. Whatever little noise they had generated during their patrol in was most likely masked by the sound of gunfire and explosions in nearby neighborhoods.

Yet on every mission they'd always been compromised. Kids working for al-Qaida kept watch from alleys. Jihadist snipers lay in urban hides observing critical areas. Ordinary citizens revealed what they'd seen in hopes of sparing their families and themselves from al-Qaida's wrath.

As Adam recalled later, "No matter how low our signature, they always knew where we were."

This time the SEALs were determined to surprise the enemy. So far, so good. The team secured the house and set up shop. Some of the operators stayed downstairs to pull security and keep an eye on the family. Meanwhile, the Blue Element snipers climbed onto the roof to establish hide sites along with two machine gunners. The gunners set up to the north, keeping the rear of the compound under surveillance so the enemy could not sneak up on the SEALs from that direction. Adam and his spotter went to the southeast corner of the roof. The other sniper and his spotter took station on the southwest corner. Altogether, six of the thirteen-man element occupied the rooftop.

After all he'd seen in Ramadi, Adam was determined to build a hide site that could not be seen. He wanted to catch the enemy unawares. No more fuck-fuck games of unarmed insurgents celebrating in the street and mocking the Americans. He wanted to catch them, armed and up to no good, then close them out. Surprise would negate al-Qaida's manipulation of the ROEs.

Like most houses in Ramadi, this one had a three-foot-tall parapet running along the roof's perimeter. After what happened in November, popping up over the parapet seemed like a bad idea. As a result, the spotters had brought periscopes along, and the snipers planned to create loopholes in the wall.

When I was in Somalia in 1993, we encountered the same situation. To stay out of sight and be unobtrusive, we would create loopholes in the parapets, then conceal ourselves behind them. We quickly found that knocking holes in concrete, even the substandard stuff used in the Third World, is no easy task. It took sledgehammers and chisels, or explosives to make the holes large enough to be usable. The problem was, either option tended to blow our low signature. Plus sledgehammers are very heavy, and carrying them around in a combat environment is not something any of us liked doing.

We discovered a work around—long, hand-cranked drills. We used them to bore out a hole, then we'd enlarge it with other tools. The noise they made was minimal, and we could do it while remaining under the parapet and unexposed to the rest of the city—something we couldn't do with the sledges.

Camp Lee didn't have any hand-crank drills, so the only options available to Adam and the other snipers were sledgehammers and C2 charges. Using sledges took a lot of time, plus they made a unique sound that would have certainly alerted any insurgents or observers to the presence of the SEAL element. But in Ramadi, explosions shook the city constantly, even at night. The operators settled on using small C2 packets, known as Ghostbuster Charges. They figured the blasts would blend into the background cacophony. Plus, there would only be two used almost simultaneously, which would minimize the enemy's ability to zero in on their location, should they want to investigate the source of the explosions.

Adam set his C2 charge at the same time the other sniper team emplaced theirs on the far side of the roof. A moment later, they detonated them both. Adam's charge created a perfect loophole, but the other charge must have been placed on a structurally weak spot of the parapet. It blew the entire corner off, which created great visibility, but Uncle Sam's taxpayers would have to pick up the repair bill.

The snipers settled into their spots and went to work improving their hides. Dawn was still a few hours away, so they had plenty of time before the insurgents liked to come out and play. Few risked moving around at night, knowing that the technology the Americans carried gave them a huge advantage in the darkness.

Adam positioned his SR-25 on its bipod, its suppressor set back from the eight-by-eight loophole. Using 550 Cord, he strung a tan screen in front of the SR-25's barrel and then built overhead concealment with his poncho liner. That way, when the sun came up, he would not be backlit to anyone looking at his loophole from ground level.

To counter any insurgent attempt to get on the roof, as they had on November 19, the SEALs set up Claymore mines hung against the outside parapet. Any Jihadist who thought he was Spiderman would climb up the wall and trigger a hailstorm of seven hundred polished ball bearings, each precisely an eighth of an inch in diameter. Setting one of those off was guaranteed to turn a human being into a fine red mist.

A few hours before dawn, Adam and his spotter, Bud, were in position and had already prepped their field of view. Using their PVS-22 night scope, they had eyes on an intersection two hundred twenty-one yards to the south. On the northwest corner of the intersection stood an abandoned school. Across the street to the south was a store of some kind that seemed to still be functioning. The rest of the neighborhood was composed largely of walled compounds, one abutting the other. Most shared at least one common wall. Alleys and side streets delineated each block.

Adam's loophole gave him a good, if narrow, view of the intersection. Around 0400, he detected movement at the intersection. At first, only one military-aged male appeared. He was unarmed, but he was looking around furtively. That made Adam instantly suspicious. He focused in on the man and watched him like a hawk. He didn't seem to have any clue there were eyes on him. A few minutes later a truck pulled up and stopped half in and half out of Adam's field of view. Three more military-aged males climbed out. They all stood together for a few minutes, chatting and looking around, then they went toward the back of the truck and out of Adam's view. A couple of them reappeared as they walked into the store on the southwest corner of the intersection.

Who makes deliveries in Ramadi at 0400?

Nobody.

This smelled wrong. Bud and Adam talked it over. Neither man had a good view of the truck, and they could only see the males in the street from about the rib cage up. And most of the time they couldn't see their arms either. They were able to confirm they carried no weapons, but still this seemed very wrong.

The men came back out of the shop, climbed into the truck, and drove off. Adam swapped out with Bud in order to catch a quick nap. The day would be a long one, and both men would take turns ensuring they had something of a sleep cycle.

At 0500, Adam woke up and spelled Bud on the SR-25. The sun was starting to come up by then, so he pulled the PVS-22 off the SR-25's rail mount and stuck his eye in the scope. Yellow-orange light was just starting to stream across the street and intersection below, casting sharp shadows created by the buildings to the east.

From out of the shadows came one of the military-aged males again. He was scowling with that tough-guy, I'm-in-charge sort of look that he'd seen on insurgents' faces before. He stopped in the street, glanced around, as if he were conspiring to do something. The truck returned, and the others piled out again. They disappeared behind the truck, then reappeared briefly. Bud and Adam could only see them from the ribs up again, but it looked as if each man was carrying something heavy with both arms. They went into the store.

The snipers talked this over. It looked like these guys were re-supplying a forward cache, something al-Qaida did all the time. In the heat of a fight, the insurgents knew exactly which building, shop, or house to run to if they needed ammo, water, explosives, or medical supplies. The SEALs had seen it many times, those buildings became focal points of activity during sustained firefights.

Two hundred twenty-one yards. An easy range, but a difficult shot since the men were moving around and Adam could only see them from mid–rib cage to the top of their heads. The elevation would not be an issue this time as the snipers were only two stories up. Wind was light to negligible.

Adam and Bud decided it was doable. If any of the four revealed a weapon or military supplies, the insurgents would fall within the ROEs and they could take the shot. As it stood, they knew something was wrong with the unfolding scene down the street, but both knew if they opened fire, their shooter's statement would be closely scrutinized.

The military-aged men reemerged to gather in the street again. They stood together, talking and taking sidelong glances around the intersection for several more minutes. Adam watched through his scope reticle set on one of them.

Just give me a reason.

No weapons. No military supplies. What if they were bringing in wares for a legitimate business?

As if there were any left in this place.

Adam made the decision. He knew, sensed, and felt these guys were bad. Ordinary citizens didn't act this way in Ramadi. Their scowls, the way they glanced around, the way they postured in that too-cool-for-school sort of way that he'd seen other insurgents mimic, plus their age—it all added up to al-Qaida.

The neighborhood was another indicator. This place was bad karma, one of the P-Sectors that had always been contested whenever the SEALs had gone into it. They'd been given a little more latitude to engage in this area, simply because of the level of resistance typical there.

Adam resolved to engage these guys and close them out. He told Bud, who agreed. The shooter statement remained in the backs of their minds, but this was the right call.

Before they had a chance to open fire, the men by the truck scattered. The truck drove away without at least three of the men.

Minutes passed. The street remained empty, the shop dark and seemingly abandoned.

What were these guys up to?

They hadn't had any visible weapons. Adam started second-guessing himself. Should he have opened fire earlier? Where had they gone? His narrow field of view through the loophole left him frustrated. Bud swept the neighborhood with his periscope, but saw no sign of them either.

Adam checked his watch. Fifteen minutes had passed since they'd last been in the street. Could the truck be going back for another delivery run?

Something black sailed over the west side of the parapet. It hit Bud's leg and rolled onto the roof.

"Mother fuck! Grenade!" Bud shouted.

Adam leaped to his feet to see the device right beside his spotter. Bud kicked it as hard as he could, and it skipped across the roof toward the north wall even as both SEALs flung themselves toward the second-floor doorway.

Adam and the rest of the men on the roof piled into the second-floor main room, but Bud was still trying to get in when the grenade exploded. Shrapnel tore into his leg. He reached the doorway and leapt inside the comparative safety of the main room on the second floor.

Another grenade arched overhead. It landed with uncanny precision in the other sniper team's hide on the southeast corner of the roof, where it exploded.

Adam untangled himself from the pile of pissed-off operators. As he stood up, Bud calmly asked, "Hey, dude, can you look at this?"

Adam went over to his friend and examined his wounds. He'd taken shrapnel in his heel, and his leg had a nasty gash. It looked painful, but not too serious.

"Yeah," Adam said nonchalantly. "You're okay."

He set to work bandaging his brother's wounds.

With their cover blown, their OIC made the decision to extract and get Bud medical help. The SEALs called back to the nearest Army outpost and asked for Bradleys that had been standing by again as a quick reaction force.

As they waited for the Army's tracks to come pull them out, the SEALs crept back out onto the roof to collect their gear and disarm and recover the Claymores. All the while, they kept half-expecting another grenade to come sailing over the parapet.

Once again, the Muj's knowledge of the neighborhood played to their advantage. There was simply no way the SEALs could get eyes on every possible avenue of approach. And these guys knew exactly where the blind spots were. They had reached the street the Americans had entered the compound from and used the outside wall to conceal their attack. How they were so accurate with their throws is anyone's guess. They must have had plenty of practice. Or a career in Major League ball in their pasts.

The Brads arrived, and the team prepared to exfil. They gathered downstairs, promised the family they'd be compensated for the damage to their roof, then made hasty plans for their departure. Every other man leaving the front door would take an alternate approach through the compound to the outside gate. One right, next man left, third man right.

Out the door they went. Left, right, left. The men flowed through the courtyard, then reunited by the main gate in the outer wall. They'd pull security around the Brads in the same manner. Left, right, left, set up and cover Bud's exfil into the nearest track. Once he was in, everyone else would climb aboard.

They began to move. Adam went through the gate at a dead run with the EOD (explosive ordnance disposal) specialist. Three feet away from them lay an IED. Both men froze for a split second as they realized what had happened. It was a repeat of the tactic used on November 19. Except this time, the IED was close enough to kill or maim most of the team.

They called it out and sprinted for the tracks. Everyone else did the same. The Bradleys and their armored hulls were the only thing that could protect them at this point.

The bomb failed to detonate. The Americans got aboard the Brads and the Army drivers threw them in gear and lurched back for COP Eagle's Nest.

Heart still pounding, Adam looked over at Bud. His friend offered a wry smile and said, "Hey, brother, no worries. We'll get 'em another day."

CHAPTER ELEVEN
The Kill or Capture Christmas

DECEMBER 24, 2006

Another fucking day.

Adam sat in the rubble of the abandoned building and took a drag on his cigarette. Two days into this op, and so far it was a bust. They'd been covering Army patrols again in one of the P-sectors, fully expecting a fight to develop, only to be confronted with hours of boredom. December in Ramadi was cold as hell, and the men spent most of the time shivering in their filthy uniforms. To make matters worse, when they patrolled into this empty dwelling, they had to wade through ankle-deep sewage that soaked their socks and feet.

After a few days, these overwatch positions always developed a unique funk. Think football locker room meets Porta-John, foul breath with the occasional spritz of cordite and gunpowder.

Adam finished his smoke, flicked the butt into the debris around him, then regarded his boots. His feet had ached with cold for two days. A few hours ago, they'd started to go numb. Bad sign. He unlaced one boot and shucked it off. The stench that poured forth was so foul that he gasped.

When you can stand the smell of your own feet, you know it's bad.

Trying not to breathe, he peeled off the sweat- and sewage-soaked sock. The flesh beneath was blotchy, red, and reeked of decay. His toes were turning blue. The skin was pruned, as if he'd spent hours in a bathtub.

Trenchfoot. Most of the rest of the team had early signs of it, too.

Adam pulled off his other boot and laid both socks out to dry. As he rummaged around for another pair in his pack, Vic, his spotter on this mission, entered the room. He took one sniff and froze. Nose scrunched, he stared down at Adam, momentarily speechless.

"What?" Adam asked.

"You gotta fucking be kidding me!"

Adam shrugged and returned to digging in his assault pack.

Vic took a step back, "Nope. Nope."

"What is your fucking problem?" Adam asked.

Vic shook his head, "I can't be around you right now."

He vanished through the door, chortling as he went.

Adam found his spare socks and returned his attention to his feet. What a mess. He dried them as best he could, then gave them a coat of powder before covering them with his fresh pair of socks. They'd have at least one more day here, and these would have to last.

Christmas Eve in Ramadi. Back home families were trimming trees and hanging stockings. Closest thing to a stocking here were his shit-coated, standard-issue wool socks.

Adam stretched out under a poncho liner and drifted off to sleep. He needed a few hours of downtime, then he'd be back upstairs on the rifle again.

When he awoke, Vic was waiting for him. "Hey man, how about I get the first watch on the gun?"

"Sure," Adam said.

He grabbed his gear, laced his boots up, and headed with Vic up to the roof to stand the next watch. Then he remembered something and turned back for his pack. Adam's mom had sent the team a few trappings of holiday cheer. Christmas Eve afternoon seemed like a good time to break his out.

"Here," he said to Vic, handing him a Santa hat.

"Fucking awesome!" Vic put it on with a wide grin.

Adam did the same. Most of the other guys had brought theirs along as well, and the men off watch wore them, basking in the sense of irony. Christmas in Ramadi was like Yom Kippur in Tehran.

They climbed the stairs to the roof and low crawled to their hide. The building they occupied was oriented north-south. Adam and Vic took the north end of the roof, their hide situated to cover a street and an intersection to the west. Their view from the roof was a narrow one, offering eyes on part of the street below and only a few compounds on the far block. The nearest intersection was about a hundred ten yards away.

Vic settled down behind the rifle and stuck his eye in the scope. Adam lay next to him, both men still wearing their Santa hats. Vic glassed the street, studied the compounds, and saw nothing out of the ordinary. The two men settled into a long wait. December had been a lot quieter than the first two months of the deployment. The tide had definitely turned against al-Qaida, but that had made the die-hards even more desperate. Still, the hangers-on, the ones in it for the paycheck, and the uncommitted had started to abandon the cause. More and more Iraqi cops were being trained and deployed around the city, and order was gradually emerging from the chaos. Hard fighting still lay ahead. Everyone knew that. But at least they were seeing progress after months of bloody stalemate and attrition.

"Got something," Vic called out.

Through their loophole, the two SEALs could see a solitary figure, slinking around the corner of one of the compounds across the street.

"Hundred ten yards," Adam called.

The insurgent thought he was being sneaky. Not so much. He'd edged to the corner to peer out at the SEALs' position, but he apparently was at lunch when his terrorist training camp covered barrel discipline. Now, here he was in a combat environment oblivious to the fact that his AK-47's barrel was sticking out beyond the corner as he held it at low port.

"Dude has an AK," Vic said.

"I see it. That's what you want," Adam replied.

"Yep."

This was as clear-cut as they came in Ramadi. The shooter's statement didn't even enter into either American's head. Vic waited. The insurgent kept looking up the street toward their hide, still using the corner for concealment. Only the barrel of his AK, a sliver of his shoulder, and head were visible.

Vic held his fire and waited patiently for the Muj to give him a better target. The patience paid off a minute later when the insurgent concluded the coast was clear. He swung around the corner and hugged the wall as he moved up the street straight toward the snipers.

The move gave Vic a full frontal shot, and he capitalized immediately. He pulled the SR-25's trigger and drilled him center mass. The insurgent recoiled and fell backwards. He landed on the ground, with just his AK and feet visible to Vic and Adam. He wasn't moving.

Vic pulled his eye out of the scope and looked over at Adam. "Dude, thanks for letting me take first shift behind the gun. Best Christmas present ever."

The other sniper team on the roof suddenly stirred. Another insurgent carrying an IED wandered into their field of vision. Either they were facing the second string, or they'd finally emplaced without being detected and the insurgents had no idea the SEALs were in their neighborhood.

The other team took the shot and dropped the IED carrier. He tumbled into the street and lay motionless.

If they didn't know the SEALs were in the area before, the enemy knew now. It could have been they were reconning by true believer with these first two guys. The Muj had done that in the past. If they suspected American troops were close by but didn't know exactly where, they would send martyrs into the street to draw fire. Others would watch and look for the muzzle flashes in order to pinpoint the American positions. Then the Muj would launch an assault.

An eerie calm settled over the neighborhood. The snipers stayed extra vigilant, searching for any movement around them. Something was going to happen. Exactly what it was kept their senses on a razor's edge.

Adam was glassing the intersection when movement by Vic's target caught his attention. He focused his spotter scope on the man. He was still lying there, his feet and AK visible and nothing else. It didn't look like he had moved. But what had?

Just then, the tip of a pole came into Adam's field of view.

"What the fuck?"

Adam reported it to Vic. He quickly got eyes on it, too.

Whoever was on the other side of the pole stood inside the courtyard of the nearest compound. He was out of sight, staying low as he fed the pole through the courtyard gate and out toward the corpse.

They watched as the pole poked the dead man's feet. It seemed surreal.

"Did that just happen?"

"Yeah. Yeah it did."

The pole poked the corpse again.

Man that is morbid.

The two Americans watched as the pole-wielder tried to hook the corpse and drag it toward the courtyard gate. He didn't have the leverage to move it far. Finally, the pole withdrew, and the corpse was left alone.

Nothing happened for several long minutes. Then the courtyard gate swung open and six armed men burst through it at a dead run. Each one carried an assault rifle and extra magazines. They hooked left as they hit the street and charged the SEALs' position. One dropped to his knee and brought his AK to his shoulder as he covered his comrades' movement. Another dashed across the street and did the same thing.

The other four kept running in pairs for a few dozen yards before skidding to a stop and dropping to one knee as well. Rifles up, they scanned the way ahead and searched for any sign of the American snipers.

The two Muj behind the main group stood up and rushed forward.

They streamed past their fellow Jihadists, sprinting as fast as they could.

They were bounding by buddy teams. These guys had military training. Good military training. It was the same tactic every single American infantryman learns before ever joining his unit.

In a few seconds, they had advanced almost forty yards. Adam and Vic had waited to engage, but now it seemed like the moment had come to ambush them in the street. As the team prepared to open fire, one of the other SEALs on the roof crawled over to the parapet near them. He pulled a grenade off his chest rig, tore the tape off and shouted, *"FRAG OUT!"*

With a single fluid motion, the SEAL stood up and hurled the grenade with all his strength. Adam watched in complete surprise. He'd flung the hell out of that thing.

It was a world-class throw, just as good as the ones the SEALs had endured in this hood so many times before. Now they at last got a chance to dish it out. The grenade struck the street right in front of the main force of insurgents, now perhaps fifty yards away. Before they could scatter, the weapon detonated in a whirl of smoke and steel splinters.

Two of the insurgents went down with shrapnel and blast wounds. As the smoke boiled through the street, the other four ran to their assistance and dragged them out of the fight. By the time Vic and Adam had an unobstructed view of the street, it was empty.

As usual, the SEALs had an F/A-18 on station overhead. The pilot reported that the insurgent force had withdrawn to get their wounded to medical help—so much for their assault. Yet, Adam couldn't help feeling they'd missed an opportunity. If they'd opened fire on them a few seconds later, none of them would have escaped such a point-blank fusillade. Still, there was something deeply satisfying about paying the Muj back with their own weapon of choice.

The element remained in their overwatch through the night and into Christmas Day. The stench grew insufferable inside the building, and exhaustion overtook the men despite their best efforts to stay warm and maintain a sleep cycle. Finally, on the evening of the twenty-fifth, the team exfiltrated back to a Marine outpost.

As they smoked and waited for transport back to Camp Lee, the outpost began to bustle with activity. The men didn't care; they just wanted hot chow, a shower, and some real sleep in the bunks. The trucks arrived, and the men climbed into the rigs. As they did, a Marine colonel walked over to the platoon's OIC and started talking to him.

Adam and the others watched them converse and felt a sinking feeling. They'd been out for days, their feet were disasters. They were fatigued and cold.

But there would be no break. The team's OIC told the SEALs to dismount and huddle up. They did so in silence, gathering around their leader and the Marine.

"We've got time sensitive, actionable intelligence," the colonel explained. "We have four targets, and we have to hit them tonight. We need your help."

At first, some of the SEALs thought this was a joke. Four kill or capture missions in one night? Then it sunk in. This was real, and they would be going back out in a matter of minutes. The men they were going after were bomb makers. Each one they grabbed would save American and Iraqi lives. They understood the importance, but that didn't stop them from grumbling about it.

Vic looked over at Adam, and said, "Onward Christian Soldiers."

Together, they walked back to their truck and began to gear up for an assault role. The SR-25 would remain behind. Both men would carry M4 carbines. Adam gathered his medical gear. He would be the assault element's breacher, so he grabbed his C2 charges as well.

Then, in the dead of Christmas night, they slipped beyond the outpost's walls and into the shattered streets. The temperature had dropped to below forty-five degrees, so cold the men could see their breath as they moved.

As they approached their first target house, the operator on point and the team's EOD tech spotted an IED. Everyone stopped as the bomb expert inched forward to examine what they'd encountered.

It didn't take long for the EOD tech to discover a second IED. Both had two Russian-made 155mm heavy artillery shells daisy-chained together. One of these shells would have been more than enough to inflict catastrophic casualties.

The team still had a JTAC and an aircraft on station overhead. Through the plan's thermal imaging system, the pilot detected the command wire. It ran from one of the bombs directly to the target house.

The bomb maker had booby-trapped his own neighborhood.

The team worked its way around the bombs to stack up on the target house's front gate. The decision was made not to use an explosive charge to gain entry, but the gate was not one that could be picked. The only other option was a small battering ram their Jordanian interpreter carried.

Adam moved forward to the gate, adrenaline coursing through him. The place could be rigged to blow, and surprise would be the only thing that could protect them. Get inside, collar the bomb maker, and get him flex-cuffed before he could hook that command wire up to a battery and blow the IEDs. Or blow something he'd planted in his house.

A stab of fear struck Adam. He'd gone through this entire deployment in total control of fear. Now, as he thought through this situation, dread swept over him. What if the bomb maker had a trip wire across the gate? Or an infrared trigger?

How many Americans had died in such traps already?

Adam motioned for the 'terp to come up with the ram. The Jordanian was huge, muscled, and fiercely loyal to the SEALs with whom he had worked for years. He hefted the ram and slammed it into the door as hard as he could.

It didn't break.

The sound of the impact echoed through the neighborhood. Certainly, those inside the house had been awakened by it. The team would have only a few more seconds before the inhabitants were up and moving to defend themselves.

The Jordanian backed up, then swung the ram again. It crashed into the gate, but it still did not give way.

They were so exposed in the street. No cover, no protection. What if there were more IEDs nearby that the team had not detected? The longer they remained in place, the greater the risk.

Inside the house, people stirred. The bomb maker and his cohorts would not be surprised now. With that element lost, their only hope was to get in before they could put up an effective defense.

The Jordanian 'terp took another swing. This time, the gate gave way, revealing a small courtyard and the house beyond.

The team poured through the door, Adam third in line. They sprinted across the courtyard and into the house, weapons at their shoulders as the inhabitants shouted and screamed.

The Americans cleared the entry room then fanned out—to find one of the bomb maker's confederates using a baby as a human shield. A SEAL rushed over and pulled the child from his hands as another tackled the coward and got flex cuffs on him. The SEAL held the child only long enough to give him to his mother, who had been silently watching the scene from across the room.

Adam moved with practiced fluidity. *Slow is smooth. Smooth is fast.* His M4 at his shoulder, he worked to clear his section of the house. As he came to a stairwell, the bomb maker suddenly bolted from the darkness and came straight at him, yelling something wildly, arms outstretched as if trying to grab him.

Adam lowered his rifle and push-kicked the bomb maker. The blow stopped the man cold, and before he could recover, Adam kneed him hard in the midsection. The insurgent flailed, and Adam rained blows on him until he finally quit resisting.

In minutes, the SEALs had separated the men from the women and children, then positively identified the bomb maker and one other insurgent. A search of the house revealed an H-rack chest rig, good for carrying extra AK-47 magazines, but nothing else. No bombs or explosives, and the men could not find the command wire the aircraft's pilot had reported.

The Jordanian 'terp questioned the males found in the house and reported that they were being evasive. Had the SEALs had more time, they could have conducted a more thorough search. As it was, they had three more targets to hit. The Americans wrapped up the two wanted men and headed off to hit the next target.

Before first light, the team completed their marathon kill or capture tour of the greater Ramadi area. They returned to the Marine outpost as bone weary as they'd ever been. They handed over their detainees, climbed into their trucks, and drove back to Camp Lee, Christmas over, their Santa hats stowed in their assault packs. Hopefully, they wouldn't be wearing them in this city, or anywhere else in Iraq, come this time next year.

CHAPTER TWELVE
The Face of Victory

Another day in Ramadi came to an end. The shadows crept over shattered buildings as smoke uncoiled upward from mortar and rocket impacts to mingle with the haze that made Iraqi sunsets so striking in Anbar Province. Periodic gunfire echoed through the streets as the denizens of this hellish place slowly settled into their nighttime routines.

As darkness fell, the SEALs of Team Five's Blue Element sortied from a forward combat outpost to patrol deep into the city. They passed through entire neighborhoods that were little more than abandoned rubble. A few blocks further, they came across streets and buildings virtually undamaged, scenes of normalcy unfolding around them. People went about errands. Others sat next to shops and quietly smoked. Scooters weaved through the foot traffic as a few cars eased down the avenue.

Another block—more empty ruins. They slipped around overturned cars, burned-out kiosks, and avoided the dead cats and dogs scattered in the street.

The patrol consisted of about twenty men: perhaps a dozen SEALs, an EOD tech, a Navy pilot who served as their JTAC, a couple of interpreters, and a handful of Iraqi Army scouts the Americans called Jundis. They dashed from alleyway to alleyway, bounding down the streets as they kept their weapons at the ready and searched for potential threats in the windows and rooftops above them. A few blocks later, the postapocalyptic ruins gave way to a bustling neighborhood whose buildings had suffered only superficial blast and shrapnel damage. More scooters. More foot traffic. It looked much like any other Arab city in peacetime.

Except for the looks the SEALs received.

The men on the street paused to stare at the patrol. Eyes narrowed, hate radiating from them, the scowls made the SEALs defensive. Sniper Adam Downs, carrying his black SR-25 7.62mm sniper rifle muttered to a buddy, "Mouth-breathing shitheads."

They'd probably take fire the moment they rounded the corner. That was how things worked in Ramadi. Unarmed males could not be shot. The enemy knew it. They'd stand in the street and watch the Americans go through their own morning rituals, then retrieve a weapon and fire a few shots as soon as an opportunity presented itself. It was a whack-a-mole sort of war, one that sucked the marrow from a warrior's soul. Never knowing who the enemy was, most American veterans in this city came to assume everyone was.

The glares continued until the patrol rounded the block and were confronted with another ruined section of the city. When first in the city, Americans found it odd and even disorienting to see these patches of everyday life juxtaposed amid so much carnage and devastation. It was sort of like seeing the aftermath of a Midwest tornado. In some places nothing was left as the twister cut a swath of devastation through a town. But standing beside that path would be houses and dwellings completely untouched, while their neighbor's home a few yards away was nothing but splinters. The storm of war did the same thing to Ramadi.

Blue Element reached a six-story apartment complex. Aside from shrapnel marks and a few bullet holes on the walls, the place seemed in remarkably good condition. This was an upscale neighborhood, once full of Saddam's cronies and Ba'athists who had gained a piece of the dictator's pie. Now, even the rich here in the city had been reduced to bare survival levels. Though their building was largely unharmed, there was no water in the district. Or power. Or sewer service. Mail service was a distant memory, and every trip out for food and supplies meant risking a family member's life.

The SEALs flowed inside the building and began to clear it. As one of the element's snipers, Adam carried both his SR-25 and an M4 Carbine. Going room to room, making sure there were no bad guys, made no sense with the long-barreled SR. With the suppressor attached to it, the weapon was almost three and a half feet long—far too cumbersome for close-range, room-to-room work. So Adam hefted his M4 when he stacked up on a door with the rest of the team.

Many of the apartments were empty, their residents having had the means and will to flee the chaos for safer areas—like Syria. Then Adam rapped his knuckles on a door up on the sixth floor. An old man opened it and gazed at the American sniper. His eyes fell to his weapon, then back to Adam's face.

For a second, Adam thought he'd be treated to the same sullen expression and menacing glances he'd seen countless times since getting to Ramadi in October 2006 with the rest of SEAL Team Five. Instead, the old man smiled, stepped aside, and gestured for Adam and the others with him to enter.

"Welcome. Please come in, have chai tea with us," the old man said. Adam saw he wasn't that old—perhaps mid-forties or early fifties. But the hard life here, and the place he called home, aged these people well beyond their years.

He led Adam and some of the others from Blue Element into the main room, where he offered his guests a seat. Adam sat down across from a middle-aged woman, her face wrinkled and lined from life in this place. She stared at his black SR-25, which Adam had unslung and now held beside him.

The old man disappeared into the kitchen to brew tea. A young boy appeared, perhaps twelve years old. He came in and sat beside his mother, dark eyes wide as he stared at Adam's sniper rifle.

Adam had seen boys work as the eyes of al-Qaida in the street. He'd heard stories of suicide bombers of all ages. As the boy looked his weapon over, the southern Illinois native stared back, his senses on a hair trigger.

If that kid pulls a pistol, I'll shoot him dead.

A moment later, the boy's brother ambled into the room. Adam judged him to be maybe five or six. He smiled as he took station next to his mother. With a start, the SEAL sniper realized the child was mentally retarded.

Earlier that year, in Samarra, al-Qaida had strapped a suicide vest to a mentally retarded and wheelchair-bound teenager who'd been unofficially adopted by the local Iraqi Police. They wheeled him into the city's main station, where he went to greet the chief of police, as was his routine.

Al-Qaida detonated him and assassinated the police chief.

Adam regarded the child.

What kind of a fucked-up place is this where I have to worry about kids pulling guns and trying to kill me?

When he was the boy's age, he lived in the shadow of a coal mine, the only real industry in Elko, Illinois. Everyone he knew had a parent who worked in the mine, and for decades it had been almost a family tradition for sons to follow in their father's footsteps. Graduate from high school, go to work for the mine, and join the local union. It was a good life, a good wage, and the men would knock off on Friday nights in the fall and disappear into the woods to hunt and fish for the weekends.

What future did these boys have?

For that matter, how did this family even support itself? The head of the house looked too old to work. Besides, with the economy virtually nonfunctional, what work was there?

Aside from laying IEDs and killing Americans, anyway.

Al-Qaida was the economy.

The mother made eye contact with Adam. She said something and pointed at his SR-25.

Adam looked down at it. Before this deployment, he'd gone to sniper school carrying a camouflaged SR-25 through all its rigors. Naval Special Warfare had intended that each sniper would carry the same rifle through training and into combat so that he would know the weapon intimately.

That didn't happen with Adam's class. There was a shortage of weapons, and he had to hand his over to the class behind his. He'd been issued this black one just before they left Virginia Beach for Iraq, and he hadn't had the time to paint it. Or name it for that matter.

The woman said something to him, and Adam shifted his gaze back to her.

"She wants to know if you are a sniper," the element's 'terp explained. He was standing behind Adam.

"Yeah, I am."

The old man returned, carrying a platter of teacups. Adam took one, as did the others in the room. When everyone was served, the old man sat down and offered a cigarette to Adam. He took it, and soon they both were enjoying a smoke together.

The mother said something else. The 'terp translated.

"If I'm walking home from the market and I drop something in the road, will I be shot by a sniper if I pick it up?"

Adam tried to conceal his shock, but the question rocked him on his heels. How the hell was he supposed to answer that?

Do you think we'd shoot an old woman?

Not in normal circumstances, that's for sure. But in Ramadi, where nothing is as it seems, Adam had to concede that the question had merit. He began to think it through.

If he'd been watching through his scope, and the woman dropped something in the street and ran, or left it and moved away, he would consider that suspicious. All American snipers in the city had seen that routine before as al-Qaida's IED planters would use tactics such as that to emplace their deadly weapons and detonation systems.

If she dropped something and ran, she could get shot.

Adam turned to the 'terp and said, "Tell her that if she drops something, pick it up right away and put it back in her bag."

The 'terp translated and the woman nodded. They stared at each other for a moment until Adam added, "Just try to pretend we aren't there. Nobody's going to be mad at you."

They sat in silence and drank chai tea together. For Adam, and most of his fellow SEALs, this was the closest encounter he'd had with Iraqi civilians. Usually, the only interaction he had was through his scope, trying to determine who had hostile intent and who was just trying to survive amid the ruins.

Ruins. Most of the city had no power, but this apartment had electricity. The lights were on, and a nearby television was on with the sound muted. It was set to Channel Two, which played American movies.

Adam's eyes wandered around the room. Typical Iraqi upper-class home. Nicer furniture, nicer cups. Rugs of some value on the floor. It seemed to Adam that Iraq was a classic case of binary economics. The wealthy lived in splendor, but the vast majority of the people eeked out subsistence-level livings in cinderblock and concrete dwellings largely devoid of such luxuries as furniture or electronics. From what he'd seen, there was no middle class. Just haves and have-nots.

His eyes came to rest on a portrait hanging on the wall behind where the old man sat. President George Bush smiled out from the frame. For a second, the recognition of the American president left him astonished. Usually, inside people's homes, the SEALs found photos of Iraqi politicians or clerics. In Shia homes, there was usually a portrait of Moqtada al-Sadr hanging somewhere.

But never President Bush.

The old man saw Adam's fixated gaze and realized at once what had attracted such attention. Solemnly, he said, "George Bush is the only one who cares about us."

After the 'terp translated, Adam nodded. He felt the same way. Back home, most people lived in the myopia of their daily ruts, never looking up beyond their narrow horizons to see that the sons and daughters of the nation were locked in a brutal and pivotal war. The soldiers and SEALs here were the forgotten legions, pushed from the mind's eye by a people seemingly more intent on shopping than service in time of conflict.

But President Bush felt the burden of sending troops into harm's way every day. You could see it with the sincerity of his words at every visit to bases and forts around the country and world. He loved being with the troops. And he tried to set the example for the rest of the nation with his actions and support.

Now here, thousands of miles from the White House, an Iraqi just shared the same sentiments with Adam.

We walk away from this mess now, and a lot more people will die.

The old man knew it. The war had dragged on for three years and the political landscape back home was being redrawn by those opposed to it. The Democrats in the House and Senate had declared the war lost two years before, and had been using it as political leverage against the Republicans ever since.

"George Bush is the only one who cares," the old man said again.

He took a sip of chai tea, then asked, "Why did you let the Democrats take over?"

The 'terp translated and Adam started to laugh, "I'm happy to say I didn't have anything to do with that."

The old man smiled, and the ice broke. More tea was poured, and the rest of the family gradually came in to meet the Americans. The eldest daughter, perhaps twenty-three, sat with her younger brothers. She was a picture of sculpted beauty. Disney princess eyes, long dark flowing hair, skin the color of caramel. Most women avoided Americans, and the SEALs had been told never to interact with them on the street or in houses, as it would offend Arab sensibilities. A teenaged girl appeared as well. She looked to be a year or two older than her brother. Same big, dark eyes as her sister—it was clear she would be a beautiful woman someday, too.

If she lived long enough.

It hadn't been reported much in the media, but the al-Qaida fighters living in Ramadi had taken a page from their Afghan brethren. To cement local alliances with tribal sheiks and leaders, they would marry into the families of the locals—sometimes by force. In some places, al-Qaida had taken over an area simply for the available pool of women. Some they used as little more than prostitutes—slaves to their urges and whims. The women were horribly abused. Those taken or married for political gain were treated perhaps somewhat better, but not much.

Would that be the fate of these two?

The conversation flowed freely, the 'terp serving as the bridge between cultures. What they found was a common humanity that gave them mutual ground from which to build rapport. That, and George Bush.

The clock ticked on into the night, the rest of Blue Element set up overwatch positions on the rooftop. Soon, Adam and those in the apartment would take a shift upstairs while their brothers caught a little sleep in an empty apartment down the hall. In the meantime, the younger kids teased Adam about the green cravat he'd strapped like a sweatband around his head. It was his homage to Tom Berringer's character in *Platoon*, a movie he'd seen dozens of times as a kid. The SEALs kidded him, too. One finally said, "Dude, they're right. You look like Pat Benatar with sideburns."

Then the youngest boy reached for Adam's SR-25.

The mother came unglued. The lightness of the conversation vanished. The child only wanted to touch it. Adam knew he wasn't a threat.

"No! No! No!" the mother shrieked. The boy recoiled, but his eyes never left the SR-25. He looked at it with open wonder and reverence.

For an instant, that look took Adam back to his own childhood. Was this the first weapon the boy had seen up close? He remembered his own reaction when his best friend's father gave him a Ruger 10/22 rifle for Christmas one year. He had held it and looked it over with the same expression. His best friend, Justin, had received one as well. Justin's dad taught them how to use them safely. He taught them how to hunt, and the two boys spent hours hunting squirrels and other small animals with them.

Adam made a gesture, letting everyone know it was okay. The

boy stepped forward and tentatively put a finger out toward the SR-25's barrel. The old man seemed okay with this, but again the mother went crazy.

"No! No! No!"

Was it fear of the weapon that drove this? Or was it fear that her son would grow to love them? There was no way to tell, and Adam wasn't about to ask. The boy retreated and sat back down.

"What will tomorrow bring us?" the old man asked, suddenly serious.

Adam couldn't answer that. How could he? Instead, he asked, "Do you need anything?"

"Diesel fuel. For the generator," the old man replied quickly.

One of Blue Element's chiefs called to Adam, "Don't promise anything, man."

Adam nodded and told the man he'd do his best to help.

The conversation continued until, somewhere long after midnight, it was Adam's turn to take a shift on the roof. He said his good-byes and slipped upstairs, his SR-25 in his hands now. In the morning, the Army and Marines would establish another outpost in the city. This time, it would be an Iraqi police station. The 1st Armored Division had become quite adept at these operations. A leapfrog forward from one COP to another suitable site in a lawless neighborhood, and the ground pounders would seize a building or part of a block that would make a suitable base. As soon as it was secured, a stream of combat engineers would arrive with everything from Texas and Alaska barriers to Porta-John's, sandbags, concrete, and communications gear. As the SEALs looked out for their fellow Americans from these sorts of overwatch positions, the engineers would turn the buildings into a secured compound. From the new base, the Coalition troops stationed there would live with the locals and patrol the neighborhood until al-Qaida's presence receded further into the city like a sanguine tide.

One block at a time, one neighborhood converted and secured. Al-Qaida fought for every inch of the city—they'd declared Ramadi the capital of the Islamic Caliphate of Iraq in October 2006. This would be where they made their stand, and they would stop at nothing to secure victory.

And men like Adam? Every time they pulled the trigger, they had to write a report justifying why.

As he settled down for his first watch that morning, Adam reflected on his encounter with the Iraqi family. He was a two-tour veteran of Iraq. He'd been in firefights large and small. In each, he fought to protect his brother SEALs, or his fellow Americans. For him, that was what the war here was about—keeping Americans alive so they could return to their families.

Now it was something more. Everyone said we could not kill our way to victory in Ramadi. Al-Qaida always found more bodies to throw into the fight, and sooner or later we were going to leave this forsaken place.

The only answer was families like the one downstairs. They needed protection. Their spirit and their belief that this nightmare would end only with America's help had to be preserved until the Iraqis themselves could face al-Qaida on more than even terms.

The Americans went into the Iraqi police station without incident. The engineers came out with all their equipment and gear—their COP in a Can—and set up the force protection. Another neighborhood saved from al-Qaida's clutch. At least for now. The inevitable counterattack had yet to materialize.

Days later, when Blue Element left the apartment and returned to Camp Lee, Adam sat down at his computer. He hated computers. He'd rather be stacking seabags than writing e-mails and had never gotten into games or video consoles. He'd spent his youth out in the woods with his pal Justin, hunting with their Rugers at first, later with bows. That's the life he wanted again.

But what will tomorrow bring?

Adam brought up his e-mail account and pecked out a note to his mother back home in small-town Illinois. He thought of home, the church he'd attended until he left for the Navy and how his mom still attended it regularly. He wrote about the family he'd met and asked her to put the old man, his wife and children into the church prayer list that Sunday.

Their salvation would be our victory.

CHAPTER THIRTEEN
Al-Qaida's Graveyard

The Iraqis worked under the summer sun, seemingly oblivious to the stench. They'd dug out the remains of the soccer field's turf to find the bodies piled, one atop the other. Most had been tortured before being dumped at the stadium. Some had their genitals cut off and shoved into their mouths, others were found beheaded or beaten so badly their arms, legs, and skulls were broken.

Guarded by Iraqi Police and American troops, "Operation Graveyard" disinterred dozens of corpses and laid them to rest elsewhere in the city. This stadium, used as an al-Qaida dumping ground for years, had long since become a place of death and despair, a symbol of Ramadi's fall from one of the urban jewels in Iraq to a modern-day Stalingrad.

This gruesome excavation was a symbolic, pivotal step toward normalization after four bitter years of warfare. In January 2007, attacks on American forces in Ramadi averaged about thirty-five per day. The snipers on both sides continued to play their shadowy roles, and both sides inflicted casualties on each other nearly every day.

Yet after the Christmas Eve firefight, Adam and his fellow SEALs rarely saw the enemy again during overwatch missions and patrols. The population had turned its support to the Coalition so staunchly that if their tips didn't result in immediate action, the people sometimes took matters into their own hands.

In one neighborhood, an al-Qaida sniper opened fire on an

American patrol. The local civilians figured out where he was before the Americans did. They stormed his hide, dragged him into the street, and beat him senseless until the U.S. patrol arrived and detained him.

Those incidents, unheard of a few months ago, became increasingly common through the first months of 2007. In neighborhoods all over Ramadi, the local imams and sheiks banded together in what became known as the Anbar Awakening movement, a grassroots tribal revolt against al-Qaida led by a pro-American sheik. They sent tribesmen to join the police forces, despite the heavy casualties the Iraqi cops incurred from suicide bombers and vehicle-borne IEDs as they manned checkpoints in their districts or on the city's outskirts. The police, once considered little more than a corrupt armed mob, helped turn the tide in the city. Their resolve stiffened even as they suffered terrible blows from al-Qaida attacks.

The SEALs carried out kill or capture missions throughout the next three months, bagging bomb makers and financiers. The locals became so helpful that they sometimes led the SEAL team directly to the door of known bad guys. In one case, an informant knew the exact apartment where an al-Qaida sniper was living. He directed the kill or capture element to the complex, which was less than a quarter of a mile from a Coalition COP. The SEALs gained entry into his home so quickly that the gunman was caught completely by surprise. When the Americans reached his bedroom, they found the sniper having sex. He was so intent on his lady friend that he never heard the SEALs until they dragged him off the bed. Inside the apartment, the entry team found weapons, bomb-making material, and ammunition.

Another enemy sharpshooter removed from the equation.

Success piled on success. After that al-Qaida gunman was pulled from under his sheets, the SEALs never again took fire around COP Eagle's Nest. Since October, the team had played a key role in degrading al-Qaida's midlevel leadership network. Other teams went after the senior leaders with equal effect. Combined with the mood on the street turning against the Jihadists, and the rise of the Iraqi Police force, al-Qaida's resistance in Ramadi crumbled by late spring 2007. By then, Adam and the rest of SEAL Team Five had packed up and headed for home.

At the end of June, a force of some sixty insurgents tried to infiltrate into the city to reignite the fighting. Locals saw them coming and tipped off the Iraqi Police. They in turn warned the Americans in the area, who set up an ambush and wiped the force out. After that engagement, al-Qaida virtually gave up on Ramadi. What had once been named the capital of their murderous caliphate now became the safest city in Iraq. That summer U.S. forces did not sustain a single attack for eighty straight days.

Almost every tribe had joined the Awakening by that summer. The population's decisive turn made all the difference, and despite al-Qaida's attempts to stop the movement by assassinating its leadership, they had lost their grip on the Iraqi people. By the fall of 2007, to be a Jihadist in Ramadi was a death sentence. The locals sought them out, and falling into civilian Iraqi hands was a far worse fate than capture by the Americans. Revenge killings finished off the stragglers.

The caliphate had failed. By making their stand in Ramadi, al-Qaida shot its bolt. Though there remained pockets of fierce resistance throughout Anbar Province and elsewhere in Iraq, the Battle of Ramadi crippled the enemy. Never again would the Jihadists threaten Iraq or the American effort in the country. But like so many other crucial campaigns in military history, it had been a near run thing.

The Marine, Army, and special operation snipers played a key role in ensuring ultimate victory. Month after month, they proved the effectiveness of precision marksmanship in a city battle. Urban warfare is the most intense and casualty-producing form of conventional warfare, and Ramadi illustrated that. Yet the snipers showed that they could affect the battlefield in significant ways. When the Rules of Engagement changed, curtailing the full use of the firepower available to the Coalition, snipers became even more important. Their precision fire saved countless civilian lives, and that was where the real battle in Ramadi was won. Once the civilian population came over to the Coalition's side, al-Qaida's days in the city were numbered.

Snipers also saved the lives of countless American and Iraqi soldiers as well. In the worst days of 2005 and 2006, almost every patrol that sortied into the city took fire. It was often impossible to determine who was shooting at the patrols and from where. In the ruins of the city, there were just too many hiding places, and al-Qaida fighters were masters of camouflage and concealment.

Those losses were mitigated by the presence of friendly overwatching snipers. From their perches atop buildings or in their upper stories, they could scan ahead of the patrols and help keep them safe by taking out threats as they developed. Other times their eyes on the battlefield provided vital intelligence, kept patrols from walking into ambushes, and stopped many an IED-laying team from completing their missions.

The number of lives taken by Coalition snipers during the Ramadi campaign will never be known. Nor will the number of Coalition and civilian lives they saved with their actions. In both cases, though, the snipers decisively affected the flow of the battle. Few battles in modern history were influenced so heavily by so few trigger pullers.

When those men came home, they did so without fanfare. Their share of the credit in the Ramadi victory was largely ignored by the American press, who had long since moved on to other stories. They remain largely anonymous—these Marines, Army, and special operations shooters, despite the fact that they helped turn the tide in Iraq.

Adam returned home with the rest of the team in April 2007. He was ready to call it a career, and dreamed of homesteading someplace. In Ramadi, he'd dreamt of a little farm, some cows and chickens, and mornings in a blind someplace, alone with his bow and his thoughts.

He struggled with the decision right up to the last minute. Ultimately, he reenlisted and served four more years. He spent time in an assault cell and loved every minute of it. While serving with Team Ten, he married and had a son. Right after his son was born, Team Ten deployed to Nigeria to help stand up their new counterterrorism force. While Adam admired the Nigerian troops he helped to train, the separation from his young family proved especially hard on them all. For ninety days, he worked diligently at his assigned task. The poverty in Nigeria was a true eye-opener for him, and by the time the deployment ended, Adam never wanted to leave American soil again.

In April 2011 he separated from the Navy and settled down on a farm. He's at his happiest now in a tree blind, waiting for the perfect buck to come along. His son sits beside him, and as his best friend's dad did when they were kids, now Adam imparts his outdoor skills to his boy.

Ramadi is never far from his heart and thoughts, though. The battle for that city grew in importance until it became a test of wills between the United States and al-Qaida. The resolve of men like Adam and the Americans and Iraqis he served with in the city sustained the fight even in the darkest hours. It was that resolve that finally broke al-Qaida's hold on the city, and eventually to all of Anbar Province.

In September 2007, after a summer free from attacks and violence, the citizen of Ramadi began to dig through the rubble and salvage what they could. The process of rebuilding the devastated city would take years. But one symbol offered them hope. The soccer stadium, once the sight of a grisly mass grave, had been transformed by the Coalition. Once the neighborhood surrounding it had been secured and the bodies removed, engineers descended on it. They rebuilt the stands, laid turf, and striped the field.

Every evening at five o'clock, the citizens would gather in the stands to watch local teams play on the grounds there, made hallowed by the blood of their neighbors. They cheered and reveled in this one aspect of normalcy among the ruins. Youth teams—the children of Ramadi—would play every week as well. Only a few months before, some of them had been the paid eyes and ears of al-Qaida. They had hunted for the Americans, for the SEALs and sniper teams

all the while unwittingly working against the very people determined to secure a future for them. Now at last, they had the opportunity to be kids again.

In 2013, four years after President Barrack Obama ordered a
complete pull out from Iraq, forces opposed to the Baghdad government, some assisted by a wing of al-Qaida once again growing in
strength, retook Ramadi and Fallujah. For the American veterans of
both campaigns, the news came as the worst possible blow. For the
citizens of those battle-scarred city, they once again faced wanton
murder, oppression and violence. Only this time, they had little hope
of salvation. The American troops had all gone home.

PART II

FRONT LINES

CHAPTER FOURTEEN
The Artist

While precision marksmanship has been an enduring part of our military's heritage, snipers have long been treated as the bastard stepchildren of the infantry. It has cost both the Army and the Marine Corps dearly over the years. But in Vietnam, the value of sniping finally sank in with the brass. In the Army, it started when the 9th Infantry Division established an eighteen-day sniper school in Vietnam during the fighting in 1968. By the end of the year, about seventy-five snipers had been trained. They were soon in action, and over the next seven months, the Army credited these men with over one thousand two hundred kills.

In the Reagan era, the Army opened a permanent sniper school in 1987 that has become the foundation of its precision-shooting program ever since.

The Corps developed its own, very stringent sniper program after the Vietnam War as well. The schoolhouse at Pendleton became the nexus of America's most proficient shooters. Over the years, the school has evolved in ways to meet the challenges on the battlefield. Most recently, the Scout Sniper Basic Course was shortened slightly, "Basic" was dropped from its title, and stalking was deemphasized. The current syllabus devotes nine of twelve weeks to precision shooting. This reflects the lessons learned on the battlefields of Iraq and Afghanistan, where stalking targets has proven the exception, not the norm. Instead, combat experience has showed us that a wide variety of different and demanding shooting was taking place in every imaginable environment and terrain. Those dynamics became the core of the new Scout Sniper School in 2010.

The vast majority of the Army and Marine snipers emerging from these schools go straight to line battalions to fill the ranks of the scout platoons. In the Corps, each scout platoon includes roughly twenty snipers and observers, or ten teams. They function as an integral part of each Army and Marine infantry battalion, serving as their commander's eyes and ears. They are true scouts, the best light infantry in the United States military who are capable of sneaking forward to find the enemy and protect the battalion's infantry companies as they advance. They operate in the front lines, and often ahead of the front lines during conventional battles, such as the drive into Iraq in 2003. During the chaos caused by an insurgency, where there are no front lines, the scout platoons have been used to overwatch key areas, interdict enemy rat lines, and ambush IED teams.

Jason Delgado experienced that evolution from conventional warfare to insurgency while serving as a Marine sniper. Dark eyes, a wiry five foot nine, with an easy smile and a wicked sense of humor, Delgado made friends everywhere he went. From behind his scope, he saw it all, from force-on-force in his first combat encounters, to the wild west of the Iraqi-Syrian border where the insurgency mingled with smugglers, drug traffickers and organized crime syndicates. He scored dozens of kills, including one of the most remarkable snap-shots I've ever encountered.

Not bad for a city boy who'd never fired a rifle until he joined the Corps.

When Jason was five years old, he watched a junkie shoot his uncle in the head. Gang wars, drug violence, and pure thuggery defined his world and became his norm long before he'd grown old enough to realize how dysfunctional his Bronx neighborhood was compared to the rest of the country. When he was seven, a turf war broke out on his block, and his house was riddled with bullets.

A sense of hopelessness pervaded the neighborhood, but Jason's dad struggled every day to provide an honest living for his family as a handyman. Part mechanic, part plumber, part carpenter, Jason's dad grabbed hold of any job that came along, but was never able to earn enough to achieve escape velocity from the violence consuming their Bronx neighborhood.

Tyson Bumgardner and a fellow 2-162 scout stand beside a Humvee in northeast Baghad during the running firefight on August 6, 2003.
Via Tyson Bumgardner and Andy Hellman

The Volunteers—2-162's scout/sniper platoon. Most of Kevin Maries's snipers had spent their entire lives around firearms, hunting as kids with their fathers and other family members before joining the National Guard. That experience made them deadly-effective marksmen in the Baghdad firefights of 2004.
Via Tyson Bumgardner and Andy Hellman

A typical sniper overwatch in Baghdad, 2004. Note the Barrett .50 caliber alongside the smaller M24 U.S. Army standard sniper rifle.
Via Nate Gushwa

Nate Gushwa (left) and Darren Buchholz in Baghdad, 2004. Kevin Maries, their sniper section leader, called Nate and Darren the best and most effective team he had during their deployment. *Via Nate Gushwa*

Keith Engle, Kevin Maries's spotter, in the Ministry of Interior hide site where the Volunteers first discovered the Iraqi police torturing detainees in a compound directly below their vantage point. *Via Kevin Maries*

Engle and Maries photographed some of the torture sessions through their scopes. Here, "Yellow Shirt" looks on as his men beat a bound and blindfolded prisoner with metal bars and rubber hoses.   *Via Kevin Maries*

As the interrogation of the teenage boy began, Kevin Maries radioed his commander and threatened to open fire to stop the Iraqi police from harming him if the battalion did nothing to intervene.
Via Kevin Maries

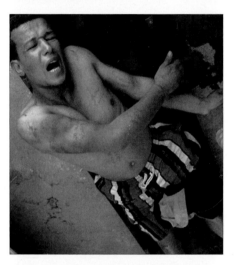

When the Volunteers burst into the Iraqi police compound, they discovered scores of tortured and traumatized prisoners. The Oregonians quickly went to work providing medical aid to them—until they were ordered out of the compound by the U.S. 39th Brigade.
Via Kevin Maries

Lt. Col. Dan Hendrickson (left) and one of his company commanders, Captain Wyatt Welch. Hendrickson seriously considered disobeying the 39th Brigade's order to leave the compound. Ultimately, he did, but he kept Maries and his snipers in the MOI hide site to keep an eye on the Iraqi police. It was a good move, for stranger things were to take place in the hours following their departure.
John Bruning

Randy Mitts in one of the scout/sniper platoon's Humvees. Mitts and Bumgardner came face-to-face with the enemy on August 6, 2004, during a wild melee in northeast Baghdad.
Via Andy Hellman

The 2-162 scout/sniper platoon's overwatch spot on the seventh floor of a partially constructed Baghdad skyscraper. With an exceptional view of northeast Baghdad and Sadr City, the Volunteers were able to ambush the Mahdi Militia mortar teams that had been bombarding their base and the Green Zone.
Via Andy Hellman

Sergeant Andy Hellman. Andy was wounded by an enemy sniper during the firefight atop the skeletalized skyscraper in August 2004.
Via Andy Hellman

Fighting in cities like Baghdad, Najaf, Fallujah, and Ramadi created sniper playgrounds. The ruins and rubble served as perfect hide sites for both friend and foe alike, making these areas treacherous kill zones for those fighting in the streets.   *Via Ron Clement*

Jason Delgado, a Bronx native and one of my snipers from the drive up in 2003. He later served a second tour on the Syrian border, then worked as a contract sniper in Iraq after he left the Marine Corps.
Via Jason Delgado

Jason Delgado with sniper team Sierra 3 in Husaybah, Iraq, in 2005.

Via Jason Delgado

Delgado's position overlooking the Baghdad financial district during the fighting in the spring of 2003. *Via Jason Delgado*

Delgado teaching the craft at Camp Pendleton, California, after his Iraq deployments. *Via Jason Delgado*

As Jason reached his teen years, few options presented themselves. His school was a zoo, the trips between it and his house were almost like running the gauntlet through a war zone. Instead of working at the local fast-food joints between school semesters, the local kids sold crack or served as mules for the drug gangs. These were called "summer jobs" in the 'hood.

Jason took another path. He joined a cadet corps created and run by U.S. Army and Marine Corps veterans. The cadets learned basic infantry skills, absorbed military discipline, and were taught some of the finer points of leadership and scouting. The veterans showed their protégées how to create standard five-paragraph operations orders, and how best to report on enemy forces.

With the city of New York as their backdrop, they went out and executed simulated combat missions.

Jason recalled later, "We were pretty much an urban militia."

The veterans would assign teams, give them missions, and work with other such organizations. They clashed with paintball guns and crept through heavily wooded areas like Van Cortland Park or Orchard Beach to report on "enemy activity" there. Often, the intel given to them by their veteran mentors would be false, which would force the cadets to improvise and adapt on the fly.

Many of those sneak and peak missions took place at night. Jason and his comrades would sleep out in the parks, establishing bivouacs before launching raids on known "enemy" positions. They'd find their tent areas, surround them, and initiate with a barrage of M-80 firecrackers and magnesium blocks thrown into their campfires. The explosions created mass confusion, and as their simulated enemies ran around trying to get organized, Jason's team would storm into the chaos to snatch booty or key pieces of intel.

For Jason, the cadet corps was his escape from a life on the streets that so many of his peers chose. As he said later, "It was either that or sell crack."

Though it may have been an escape at first, the military aspects of the corps, the discipline, and the pure fun of it all gave Jason purpose—and a childhood that he could look back on without regrets. He honed his skills through high school, and dreamed of becoming a Marine infantryman. At home, he began watching war movies. They had a visceral effect on him as he saw Hollywood's version of selflessness in uniform. At times, they reduced him to tears. "It was through those films that I realized I am a Patriot," he later said. He wanted to be a part of that brotherhood.

More truant than student, he graduated largely due to his devotion to Roosevelt High School's swim team. He was an exceptional athlete and spent every moment he could in the water—when not out terrorizing other cadets in city parks.

For all the rough and tumble and competitive aspects of his life, Jason had another dimension to him that he shared with only a few who knew him. Starting in grade school, he discovered a passion for art. He would sketch for hours, drawing cartoons or battle scenes or whatever struck his fancy. It was another outlet for him, a means to express himself in a way not shared by many of those around him.

When he became a sniper, this talent became a key component to his abilities in the field. On surveillance missions, he could draw detailed three-dimensional drawings of target buildings in a matter of minutes, providing accurate and very useful intel to his battalion commander.

After high school, Jason studied art in college before dropping out to join the Marine Corps. He went Marine infantry, puzzled that anyone would enlist in the Corps for any other reason. To him, there was only one purpose for the Corps: to push rifles forward in the face of whatever opposition the enemy could muster. Carrying one of those rifles was every Marine's job.

He served with 3rd Battalion, 4th Marines for eight months before getting a chance to try out for the battalion's scout sniper platoon. The process, known as "Indoc," or Indoctrination, is a brutal weeding-out marathon designed to test the toughness and suitability of prospective Marines. Jason went for it despite his relative newness to the Corps. "Everyone knows Marine snipers are the best trained and most disciplined and well known in the world," he remembered. "I wanted to be a part of the best."

During Indoc, the 3/4 Scout NCOs pushed every button they could think of to draw a reaction from their candidates. It was all part of stress testing them to see if they possessed enough discipline to keep focused in the midst of a rain of crap.

At one point, the candidates were ordered to do pull-ups. Jason hit the bars along with about twenty other Marines, and he knocked out ten in quick succession. An instructor nearby had been counting off, and suddenly he went from ten to three.

Jason let go of the bar and lost it. He started yelling at the instructor in frustration.

"I lost my shit," he admitted. He washed out and was sent back to his line company. It was the first time he had ever failed at something he'd set out to achieve. The failure left him stunned. "It was a rude awakening."

Lesson learned. In the future, Jason swore he'd take the fuck-fuck games and keep focused. After he'd been in combat, he discovered the value of those games. "You cannot control everything; and there are times you cannot help what is going on around you. In those moments, you cannot react emotionally. Those games test your emotional endurance."

He tried out for the 3/4 Scout Platoon again at the next Indoc. The NCOs saw him coming and had already formed a bias. He ignored their extra treatment and worked furiously to prove he belonged. He did well through the entire crucible right up to the very end, when the NCOs interviewed each prospective Marine. After each interview, the NCOs would vote on whether to offer the man a slot in the platoon.

One by one, the NCOs voted "No Go" on Jason. The vote was unanimous, and Jason's heart sank. He'd failed a second time.

I was the platoon sergeant at the time, and I remember watching Jason bust ass to try and make the grade. I remembered his Puerto Rican and Bronx accent, and his dark, intense eyes from his first time through. I also remembered the chip on his shoulder. This time, he'd come back humbled and determined to succeed. Instead of a chip, I saw resolve.

So I stepped in. I said to my guys, "Look, this is the second time this Marine has tried out for the platoon. Okay, he had an attitude the first time, but just coming out and facing all this all over again shows heart enough to work with. I vouch for him."

Jason flourished in our platoon. We worked harder than anyone else in the brigade, and Jason worked harder than almost any of our new guys. Though he'd grown up amid gun violence, he'd never handled a real firearm until the year before in Basic. This actually proved an advantage to him, as he had no bad habits to break. We started teaching him the math behind long-range precision shooting, and all of the NCOs discovered he had a knack for numbers.

"The math and physics made sense to me," he recalled.

He was all heart after he joined us. To hone his skills, Jason spent thousands of dollars out of pocket on ammunition and extra gear—as did most of the platoon. Day after day, we hit the range and I saw him develop into a phenomenal shot.

By the time he went to the Scout Sniper Basic Course, Jason had been so thoroughly trained within the platoon that school seemed easy. He received his class's High Shooter award. To Jason, that didn't seem unusual at the time, as 3/4 Marines had made a habit of sweeping up those sorts of things. He was just glad to be part of the team.

During the March 2003 invasion of Iraq, 3/4 Marines led the charge to Baghdad, and our scout sniper platoon went into combat for the first time. Most of our shooters had never seen action, and they entered the fight amped up, aggressive, and eager to go. I'd seen enough in Somalia to realize that this would be a marathon, not a sprint, but I also knew that I couldn't tell my guys that. They would need to experience it for themselves and settle down as the innate foreignness of battle and death became their daily routines.

This is a process that most noncombat veterans cannot understand. An average American has little association with death, or the threat of it. When somebody dies in a car wreck, or in a street fight, or in some accident, their body is removed almost always within minutes. With death that remote in our daily lives, being confronted with unexpected or violent death is even more deeply shocking and transformative for us. One only needs to remember the sight of our fellow Americans leaping from the Twin Towers on September 11 to know the indelible effect such sights have on us here at home.

In combat, these moments are commonplace. They happen all around us, they claim our friends, civilians, and the enemy. In most of us, there is a switch that such scenes eventually throw within our psyches. It allows us to cope and function. Our first encounters are shocking, no doubt, but then we go numb. Black humor helps, and we make jokes to help normalize the insanity around us. While fighting for the Diyala River bridge, for example, one of the Iraqi soldiers we killed remained in our front for hours. We nicknamed him "Ach-Dead," something that buttoned-down Americans would have probably found offensive. By then, as a platoon, we'd thrown our switches.

It happens in every war, to every soldier, Marine, and sniper who can psychologically withstand warfare. One look at the gruesome Battle of Verdun is all it takes to see the extremes that the human spirit can endure. During that 1916 campaign, German shellfire was so intense that entire companies of French infantry vanished into these barrages. Trenches were ground up, pitted by artillery strikes, then ground up again by subsequent barrages. When French reinforcements were fed into the battle and told to dig in, their spades unearthed shredded pieces of their comrades. They dug anyway, and soon new trenches took shape with corpses embedded in their walls. The fresh troops grew so immune to these horrors that they would sit and eat their rations surrounded by the rotting remains of their brother warriors, knowing that in time, they would probably be entombed in the trench walls, too.

Violent death is shock enough, at least initially. Taking a life is another thing altogether. It never unfolds the way Hollywood portrays. Novelists who have never taken a life, or seen one taken, have created all sorts of heroic final moments, or desperate last stands as their protagonists face the whirlwind with unfettered resolve, killing away without thought or conscience.

Jason Delgado had been no stranger to violence. His world back home in the Bronx had been steeped in it. Yet the scale and nature of what we experienced during the drive up was so much more vast and surreal, it left him hyperalert, edgy, and unsettled. As we fought forward toward the Diyala River bridge, the gateway to southeastern Baghdad, Jason came to grips with the nature of our job as shooters.

It was at the end of March 2003 when 3/4 Marines pushed into a small town we called Buyinah. The Iraqi Army and Fedayeen (Iraqi guerrilla fighters) resisted fiercely, and the fighting devolved into a close-range small-arms and RPG slugfest. Jason, one of our lieutenants, and one other sniper scaled a nearby tower to try and get a better view of the enemy ahead of us. As they did, the enemy fired a rocket-propelled grenade. This one streaked straight at one of our armored vehicles, slammed into its track, but failed to detonate. Jason spotted the smoke plume created by the launch, but couldn't see the enemy soldier who had fired it.

He was carrying an M16A2 at the time, zeroed to six hundred yards. He scanned the area around the smoke plume until movement caught his eye. In an alleyway, a Fedayeen fighter, dressed in black, edged out of a building and moved to a nearby corner. He was armed with an AK; there was no doubt about taking the shot.

Jason leveled his M16, brought his sights onto his target, and pulled the trigger. The shot missed. He took aim again. The Fedayeen had not moved. Jason fired again, and missed again.

He took a breath, let part of it out, and tried to relax amid the din of the battle playing out around him. He focused and pulled the trigger a third time. The Fedayeen dropped his rifle and clutched his stomach. He began to walk with awkward, almost drunken steps. He hadn't gone far when Jason saw him bend over and hunch his shoulders. Then he fell to the ground. As he lay there, Jason looked on as the dying man crossed his legs, then crossed his arms over his chest. He bled out in that position a few seconds later.

Jason stared at the corpse, the shock of his first kill and the peculiar way the man died sinking in. A stay thought ran through his mind. *Hollywood never gets this right.*

The fighting continued. Jason shouldered his rifle and scanned for targets. The hyperness, the overeagerness born from inexperience, drained away. He settled down and felt cold resolve. He was a veteran now.

Not long after his first kill moment, Jason was spotting for a sniper named Jesse Davenport. The battalion had been advancing on the Diyala River bridge, but the going had been tough and bloody. The enemy resisted with surprising intensity, hitting 3/4 Marines with everything they had. No wonder. If the Iraqis lost the bridge, the Marines would have crossed the last obstacle before Baghdad. It was the Remagen Bridge of the Iraq War. If we took it, we'd have a dagger pointed right at the heart of Saddam's capital.

Jason spotted an Iraqi soldier on a rooftop and lased him for Jesse. Eight hundred yards away. Davenport brought his scope on the target, but could only see part of the man's weapon and a portion of his head.

They'd set up a position on a rooftop, so there was little elevation difference to calculate. But a slight breeze was blowing. Jason raised one finger in the air to gauge the wind and said, "One and half right."

"Roger."

Davenport dialed it into his scope. A moment later, he took the shot. The Iraqi suddenly clutched his face and spun out of sight.

"Oh my God! Dude! You hit him!" Jason exclaimed. The veteran in him now marveled at the incredible complexity of the shot. To hit a sliver of a man at eight hundred yards was something only a handful of shooters could ever pull off.

"Jesse, greatest shot ever!"

Davenport pulled his eyeball out of the scope and grinned back. My boys had grown up.

CHAPTER FIFTEEN
Ain't Dyin' Tonight

APRIL 2003

NINE MILES SOUTHEAST OF BAGHDAD

As 3rd Battalion, 4th Marines inched closer to the Diyala River bridge, armor battles raged around the Iraqi's last foothold on the southern bank. Massive, sixty-seven-ton M1A1 Abrams main battle tanks used their 120mm guns to blast a path of pure destruction through every Iraqi strongpoint. Nothing the Soviets produced during the Cold War could stand toe-to-toe with the American tanks, and those Iraqi crews who tried ended up paying an unimaginable price. Here and there, Delgado and his fellow snipers encountered the burned-out remains of T-62 tanks, whose armor proved no defense to American-depleted uranium rounds. In some cases, the 120mm rounds had struck the T-62s in the bow and blown clear through the vehicle to exit the other side. The incredible kinetic energy the round produced created a vacuum in its wake so powerful that it sucked the Iraqi crews through the exit holes that were the size of quarters. Beside the wrecked Soviet tanks there would be a fine spray of human remains drying on the ground in a fan spreading from those exit holes.

Despite being in service since the 1980s, not a single M1A1 had been lost to enemy fire, including during Desert Storm when hundreds of them wiped out the bulk of Iraq's armored forces. It was the closest thing to an invulnerable weapon's system the United States possessed. To the Marines, the Abrams was king of the battlefield. Where those tracks went, the Marine infantry knew they were in the best possible hands.

Until the day after April Fools turned everything upside down.

A civilian truck appeared on the battlefield. Unbeknownst to the Marines, it had been turned into an improvised weapon, packed with explosives including an antitank missile. The driver careened into an M1A1 and triggered his car bomb. The blast destroyed the Abrams and left it a skeletalized hulk that burned for hours.

Jason Delgado and the other snipers of 3/4's scout platoon had never seen such an attack. Mixed in with the Iraqi Army units they were fighting were Fedayeen guerrillas, but this was the first suicide bombing they'd faced. It was a harbinger of things to come as Saddam's die-hards grew increasingly desperate to stop the Marine advance.

On April 3, 2003, the battalion assaulted Al Kut, a small Iraqi town only a few kiloyards from the critical bridge across the river. An artillery barrage paved the way, and Abrams tanks rolled forward with the Marine infantry, but the Iraqis resisted fiercely.

The 3/4's battalion commander, Lieutenant Colonel Bryan McCoy, had gone in with the initial assault force. One of the battalion's scouts, Corporal Mark Evnin, was with him, along with the unit's sergeant major. Just after securing a foothold in the town, the Iraqis counterattacked. Some fifteen fighters and soldiers charged out of buildings and rubble in a human wave, bent on trying to overrun and destroy a nearby Abrams.

The 3/4's sergeant major dashed across a street to help stop the attack. Evnin, a gung-ho kid from Burlington, Vermont, followed. As he ran, an Iraqi bullet struck him in the hip. Three years removed from his graduation ceremony at South Burlington High, Evnin tumbled to the street, critically wounded.

He'd been a new addition to the scout platoon and had not had a chance to go to sniper school before the battalion deployed to the Middle East. Eager to learn, eager to excel, he was a skinny, narrow-faced twenty-one-year-old whom everyone liked because his enthusiasm came from his heart, not from a sense of ambition.

The company medics rushed to his aid even as the Iraqi human wave attack was mowed down. All fifteen soon lay dead near the M1A1.

Mark was loaded into a Humvee and rushed to an aid station about a kilometer behind the lines. Doctors and medics descended on him. Mark was talking, and when asked by one of the docs, he wiggled his toes.

A chaplain rushed over. Mark was Jewish, so he leaned over the wounded Marine and read him the Shema, the first prayer the young Vermont native learned as a child.

"Hear, O Israel: The Lord our God, the Lord is one. . . . And you shall love the Lord your God with all your heart, and with all your soul, and with all your might."

The Chaplain finished and began to read the 23rd Psalm. Mark looked up at him and said, "Chaplain, I'm not going to die."

A MEDEVAC CH-47 Chinook helicopter landed nearby, and the medical staff carried Mark's stretcher to the bird. The helo lifted off and rushed south for a combat support hospital.

But it was too late. During the flight, Mark Evnin went into shock and died. He was 3/4's first combat loss, which was difficult enough on his fellow Marines. But his death hit the scout platoon like a sledgehammer.

For Jason Delgado, learning the news marked the beginning of the most painful and intense period of the invasion. The fighting grew increasingly intense as the battalion clawed the final kiloyards to the bridge. On April 6, 2003, the snipers and infantry of 3/4, supported by armored personnel carriers, or Amtracs, Humvees, and M1 Abrams tanks, finally advanced to the south end of the Diyala River bridge.

They'd reached the last obstacle before Baghdad.

The Iraqis were under no illusions. Should the Marines get across the river, they would be unable to stop the Americans from assaulting into Baghdad. Their capital and the Saddam regime's survival were at stake. Republican Guard units were thrown into the north bank's defense. Fedayeen fighters and artillery were also brought up.

The bridge had suffered heavy damage, which made getting vehicles across it impossible—at least until combat engineers were able to repair it. But the decision was made to assault across in daylight on the morning of April 7. Along with a reinforced platoon from Kilo Company, three sniper teams from the 3/4 Scouts would go across in the initial attack and secure a foothold on the far side. Their precision marksmanship would be relied on to repulse any enemy counterattacks while the battalion fed reinforcements into the bridgehead.

In the morning, both sides launched heavy artillery barrages at each other. Marine 105mm shells pounded the north bank, blowing apart buildings and Republican Guard dug-in defensive positions in preparation to the assault.

The rain of high explosives killed or wounded dozens of the elite Iraqi troops, but their artillery exacted chilling revenge. Just before our attack began, their spotters on the far bank must have seen the Marines gathering to storm the bridge. They called in a fire mission, and three heavy shells landed in quick succession right among the American spearhead. One scored a freakish, one-in-a-million direct hit on an Amtrac parked near the south end of the bridge. The blast wounded several Marines and killed two of the vehicle's crew, Lance Corporal Andrew Aviles and Corporal Jesus Medellin, instantly.

While the Iraqis continued to lob shells at 3rd Battalion, the American barrage lifted. It was time for the assault element to go forward. Jason Delgado and the other scouts charged across the bridge with the Marine infantry. They weaved around shell holes the size of Volkswagens torn in the roadway as two or three Iraqi mortar rounds exploded nearby. Fortunately, none of the assaulting Marines were hit by shrapnel. They pressed on, climbing around debris and ducking whenever bullets pinged off the bridge's steel structure or whined overhead.

When Jason reached the north side of the bridge, he saw the bodies of uniformed Iraqi Republican Guard troops splayed in the dirt, victims of the preassault artillery bombardment. He ran past their ragdoll corpses and into a nearby one-story cinderblock building. He and his spotter climbed onto the roof to cover down on the main road stretching from the bridge northward into Baghdad.

The rest of the snipers found good positions to do the same thing. I came across a short time later with Colonel McCoy. We would need every gun in this fight, for surely the Iraqis would counterattack this position since we were the biggest threat to Baghdad they faced.

Snipers usually operate in pairs, each team covering a particular compass point. This time, the platoon knew where the enemy would be coming from, and we worked together to concentrate our fire on any approaching targets to ensure they would not get close enough to harm the Marine infantry steaming across the bridge to expand our toehold on the north bank.

While behind his M40 bolt-action rifle, Jason heard a warning transmitted over the battalion radio net. The Iraqis were using ambulances loaded with explosives as suicide vehicle bombs. The snipers were told to be on the lookout for anything resembling an ambulance.

"That's pretty fucking low," Jason muttered under his breath.

The snipers had a clear view of the road to Baghdad out to at least nine hundred yards. At the edge of their field of vision was a small rise, then a gentle curve. On either side, pockets of surviving Fedayeen and Republican Guards took potshots at the Marines streaming across the bridge.

A white pickup truck appeared in the road. It rounded the bend, disappeared behind the slight rise, then came into view again, head-on to the snipers. By this time, I had set up shop across the street from Jason. As the rig sped toward the bridge, Jason and I could see the driver wore a green Iraqi Army uniform. He also had on what looked like a long brown leather hat like Russian tank crews wear. A passenger stood in the pickup's bed, wearing a red headdress and hefting an AK-47.

We coordinated our ambush over the radio. At four hundred yards, I gave a short count, and we opened fire simultaneously. Jason's range to target was 395 yards. Mine was 411.

The driver died instantly, struck twice from our 7.62mm M40s. As the truck drifted to a stop, the passenger bailed out. We hit him, too. We later discovered he had a pistol concealed in the small of his back at his waistline. Those shots were Jason's first with his M40 bolt-action rifle.

What were these two guys doing? Certainly they were not the vanguard of a Republican Guard counterattack, but perhaps they were scouting forward to find out the situation at the bridge. Our artillery bombardment probably destroyed communications between their headquarters echelons and the front-line units, leaving the Iraqi leadership in the dark.

The snipers hunkered down and waited to see what would follow. An ambulance loaded with explosives? Another truck bomb? The thought of one of those coming at the bridgehead left the entire scout platoon tense and edgy. Marines have a raw spot for suicide truck bombs. The one Hezbollah drove into the barracks at the Beirut airport in the 1980s killed 241 of our brothers. Though many of the men in 3rd Battalion hadn't been born when that happened, Marines never forget their heritage, history—or old wounds that had yet to be avenged.

That truck bomb in Beirut turned out to be the largest nonnuclear explosion detonated since World War II. Say what you will about the Middle East; the people there know how to build things that go boom.

Whatever happened, Jason and the other snipers were determined to keep the Marines around us safe from such a fate. It was crucial that we stop any vehicle from reaching the bridgehead. But with enemy soldiers and Fedayeen militia still moving around the position, there was no way to establish a traffic control point.

The bolt-action M40s would have to do the job. The snipers resolved to fire into engine blocks at five hundred yards. If the vehicles didn't stop, the drivers would die at three hundred.

What followed was the worst twenty-four hours Jason endured in combat. It was also mine. We remained in our positions without food and without water resupply all day, through the night, and into the next morning as wave after wave of civilian vehicles streamed down the road at us. Some were driven by uniformed Iraqi soldiers.

Some were driven by panicked civilians. They were intermingled, and the Americans at the bridge could not distinguish who was a suicide bomber and who had simply driven into the battle crazed with fear and unable to think.

At five hundred yards, we shot into the engine blocks, but too many times the vehicles kept going. Innocents died, but a lot of enemy fighters did as well. For Jason, the hours became a blur of rage and angst as he was faced again and again with a devil's choice: hold fire as a van or truck crossed the three-hundred-yard threshold even after the warning shots and risk the lives of every Marine on the north bank, or take the shot. Not a man in the scout platoon wanted the deaths of American Marines on his conscience, so we all took the shots. And each time Jason pulled the trigger, his conscience grew burdened with the result. So did mine. We were in an impossible position.

Only later in the insurgency did the Marines learn that the insurgents forced civilians to drive into our checkpoints around Iraq ahead of a suicide bomber. That kept our soldiers and Marines guessing, always wondering if the next vehicle would blow them apart or not. The Jihadists used any means necessary to coerce these innocents into their vehicles. They threatened to kill them, or kill their families. Often, they took families hostage to ensure the civilian would carry out his orders.

And the most insidious part of this tactic was the propaganda value the insurgents made when American troops killed those civilians. They counted on it, and trumpeted America's barbarity on their Jihadi websites. Their willing accomplices in the media followed that lead, and all too many times young soldiers and Marines who were faced with this choice, incomprehensible to their fellow Americans back home, were eviscerated by our own news outlets.

Snipers are not soulless warriors. Snipers are not men without conscience. They are guardians of the infantry first and foremost. And on that bridgehead, the snipers of 3/4 performed that task with all the judgment, skill, and professional resolve they possessed.

But it came at a terrible cost. The Diyala River bridge scarred us all.

In the aftermath, when the platoon was finally relieved, Jason and I drifted back to get hot chow and some sleep. Filthy, stinking, and hollow-eyed, we staggered out of the fight, rage and anguish poisoning our souls.

All of this was made worse by the press, of course. Johnny-come-latelies showed up at the bridge in the wake of the fight to see its aftermath. They didn't report on the armed men in civilian clothes we'd killed. They didn't report on the Fedayeen or the uniformed Iraqis mingled with the civilians who died as they barreled down the highway toward the bridge. They just reported the civilians, and never understood the agony Jason, Jesse, and the rest of us endured as we struggled to make the decisions that kept our Marines safe.

By the time we advanced into Baghdad a few days later, and Saddam's statue fell, Jason Delgado had nothing left to prove to himself, or anyone else. Warriors emerge from the crucible of the fight. Men go into it with expectations of how they will react when touched with fire. The flames sear in different ways. Some break and have not the psychological tools to cope. Others rise to the occasion. And some give up all hope and cast their lot with fate. Men who believe they have nothing left to live for are among the most dangerous—and brave. They don't give a fuck.

When Baghdad fell that April, the snipers of 3/4 no longer gave a fuck. Constant combat and exhaustion had etched away everything but their sense of professionalism and duty. Below both was the rage, nebulous and unfocused.

From atop a skyscraper, Jason and Jesse Davenport watched Baghdad devolve into chaos as its citizens embarked on looting sprees. Random acts of violence broke out in the street below. The two snipers grew jaded to it, and only intervened when somebody below posed a significant threat to innocents still trying to get by with their lives. They were still guardians, but this time, they were protecting Iraqis from other Iraqis.

Atop a fifteen-story building in the government district one day in mid-April, Jesse caught sight of a young Iraqi male as he opened fire randomly with an AK-47. This wasn't celebratory fire—we'd all seen a lot of that since the fall of Saddam's regime. This was a kook with an assault rifle who ran into a street spraying gunfire at the people milling about there.

Jesse took aim with his M40. Jason read off the range: a hundred and eighty yards. The gunman sprinted down the street below, shooting wildly. Fifteen stories in Bagdad usually put us at about a hundred and fifty feet over street level. Jesse had to compensate for the steep angle of elevation. He calculated the shot and placed his scope's reticle low on the target. Snipers call that the "angle of the dangle." When up high shooting down, you aim low. It takes an accomplished marksman to get comfortable with such shots. The Marines and Navy now have a shooting school dedicated to the art of high-angle shooting.

Jesse Davenport was a natural at it. Once again, Jason Delgado witnessed him make an incredible shot only a few could possibly make. The gunman was running erratically, which meant Jesse had to track him. Simultaneously, he factored in the lead necessary to hit him as he moved, the angle of the dangle, wind, and distance.

Jesse pulled the trigger and blew the madman off his feet in a dead sprint. He flopped to the ground, a 7.62mm bullet hole in his forehead. It was one of the most technically challenging shots any of the 3/4 snipers took during Operation Iraqi Freedom.

Not long after, on May 3, 2003, Jesse and Jason were up on a thirty-story building, covering a contingent of Marines ordered to secure millions of dollars from a partially looted bank. Looters still roamed in packs, and the scene below was one of chaos and sudden ignitions of violence. Jesse was spotting for Jason that day, and as they glassed the frenzied scene below, they discovered a group of armed males rushing toward the melee. Several of them carried AKs, and they hefted them about and fired at random.

Not only were they a threat to other Iraqi civilians, they posed a threat to the Marines at the bank. Jesse lased them. Two hundred yards out and thirty stories below. Jason took aim and settled his reticle on one of the males who wore a green and white tracksuit. He carried both an AK and a long, sheathed knife on his belt. He and his pals ran along the street, their backs to the American snipers as they shot up the neighborhood with full auto bursts from their AKs.

These guys needed to be stopped. Jason took the shot. His round missed. The men kept running toward the bank. The New Yorker, perplexed, racked his M40s bolt and drew another bead.

He missed again.

He got up and ran with Jesse to the far side of the roof to see if his zero was off. He aimed at a water tank atop another skyscraper and pulled the trigger. The shot went exactly where he'd wanted it to go.

Why had he missed Green Tracksuit then? As he rushed back to his original position, it dawned on him—he'd been shooting high. Quickly, he calculated the angle of the dangle, set the reticle below Green Tracksuit's waist, and fired.

The bullet hit the man in the kidneys. He spun and dropped as his astonished friends stared at him. They froze, totally captivated by the Shock Factor. Jason chambered another round and waited to see what they would do.

It took several seconds for the spell to be broken, but when it was, the gunmen panicked. Some dropped their weapons, others bolted into a nearby alley, running as if the Devil himself was on their heels. To a man, they left their fallen comrade to die in the street.

That single shot was all it took to break their morale and render them no threat at all to the Marines at the bank. The Shock Factor's power on the human psyche was something Jason would never forget.

CHAPTER SIXTEEN
The 440

HUSAYBAH, IRAQ
SYRIAN BORDER
SPRING 2004

For all its intensity and the toll it took on Jason, the drive to Baghdad was cake compared to his second deployment, this time with 3rd Battalion, 7th Marines.

After a very brief stay at home following the end of Operation Iraqi Freedom I, Jesse Davenport, Jason, and a few others from the 3/4 Scouts were sent to join 3/7 as it worked up for operations in Anbar Province. The battalion arrived on the Iraqi-Syrian border in February 2004, just as the war entered a new and deadly phase.

For the first and only time during the Iraq War, the diverse and fractious insurgent groups attempted to spark a national uprising. Cooperation between the Shia militias and the Al Anbar Sunni rebels took place at a high level, including a secret planning conference later discovered to have been held in London mosques.

The killing of four American Blackwater contractors at a bridge on the outskirts of Fallujah on March 31, 2004, sparked the uprising. Within days, almost every province in Iraq seethed with violence and rebellion. The Coalition was caught completely by surprise, especially in the south where the Shia were considered to be pro-occupation.

All across southern Iraq, Shia militias and insurgent groups struck at the Americans and nascent Iraqi security forces. Entire towns and cities fell into their hands. The militias, including the notorious Mahdi Militia, used their success to terrorize the local populations as they enforced their radical brand of Islam. Shop owners selling Western DVDs were told to shutter their doors. Those who didn't were dragged into the streets of Basra and Najaf to be beaten or murdered. Women who did not cover themselves completely when they went outdoors were shot or beaten—or worse. Couples who dared display affection to each other in public were set upon by the militias, pummeled and left bleeding in the streets as examples.

The British and American forces in the south were spread very thin. Nobody had expected this sudden onslaught, and the majority of the Coalition's fighting power had been deployed in Baghdad or Al Anbar Province. This sudden development threatened the supply lines to Kuwait, and in many places the highways the logistical convoys used were overrun and fortified by the Shia insurgents.

The U.S. had to switch gears. The offensive began just as the first wave of troops were rotating home in what was one of the military's largest relief in place operations ever. Tens of thousands of soldiers and Marines who had been trying to establish order for the past year suddenly found themselves forced to call their families and tell them they would not be home after all. The 1st Armored Division was among the first units to have their deployment extended. Instead of going back to Kuwait, then home, the tankers and mech infantry were thrown into a counteroffensive in the south, supported by the freshly arrived 1st Infantry Division.

As the battle raged from Baghdad to the Kuwait border, the Marines in Al Anbar Province bore the brunt of the Sunni half of the national uprising. The press focused on Fallujah, where the Marines launched an assault into the city to clear the rebels out. Breathless reporters recounted street fights raging throughout Fallujah, but they ignored the broader scope and context of what soon became a transformative moment in the history of the Iraq War.

The battle for Fallujah soon got mired in politics made worse by intervention and micromanaging from Washington. Elsewhere, the Sunni insurgents managed to cut the main supply route from Baghdad through Anbar Province in at least two places. Those bold moves forced the Marines to react; they pulled troops out of other areas and cleared the highway. In Ramadi, the insurgents launched a series of coordinated attacks that rocked the Marines and Army units there. Everywhere, the Americans were reacting to the enemy. The Sunnis held the strategic initiative.

On the western edge of Al Anbar Province stood the city of Husaybah. Long an outlaw stronghold during the Saddam regime, it was sort of Iraq's version of the Mos Eisley Space Port from the first Star Wars movie. When Obi Wan told Luke, "You will never find a more wretched hive of scum and villainy . . ." he could have been referring to this last outpost on the Syrian border. Remote, far from centers of authority, Husaybah was Iraq's lawless Wild West.

The place functioned on greed, corruption, and smuggling. The border crossing was the city's main source of revenue. Everything from oil to booze to weapons came across the frontier there, and the Iraqi security forces manning the checkpoints simply took their cut and looked the other way.

When the insurgency gained traction through the fall of 2003, Husaybah became one of the key resupply routes for the Sunni rebels. Syria was to Al Anbar as Pakistan was to the Taliban in Afghanistan—a safe zone from which to shuttle men, materiel, and weapons into the fight.

Choking off this supply network became the task of 3/7 Marines, starting in February 2004. But the Americans quickly discovered they had been given an impossible task. Every day, thousands of vehicles crossed the border at Husaybah, and checking them all was simply beyond the capabilities of the battalion. They didn't have the men or the resources to do it, and the Iraqi frontier guards could not be trusted. Plus, the smugglers and criminals who had been making these runs for years, and knew how to hide stuff, were now working for the insurgents. Each day, hundreds of semitrucks filled with fruit or other perishables lined up to cross the frontier. Hidden deep within their beds would be weapons, ammunition, and even young foreign volunteers eager to join the Jihad. Short of emptying each truck and searching it from the frame up, there was no way to fully halt the flow.

And it was perilous duty. Husaybah was full of armed criminals, Sunni rebels, and a growing kernel of al-Qaida operatives just securing a foothold in this part of the country. On April 14, 2004, an Iraqi pickup truck was stopped by a fire team of 3/7 Marines. Corporal Jason Dunham approached the driver, who lunged at him when his car door was opened. Dunham

punched and kicked the man, trying to subdue him. As he did, the driver ac-
tivated a grenade. Dunham saw it fall to the ground next to his feet and
knew that it would kill or wound two of his fellow Marines standing nearby.
He let go of the driver, pulled his helmet off and used it to cover the grenade.
Then he fell atop it to further shield his brothers from its blast.

It exploded and mortally wounded Jason Dunham, who died several
days later at a Stateside hospital. His comrades were unharmed by the blast,
and as they recovered from the shock of it, they spotted the driver trying to
run away. They killed him with rifle fire, then discovered his pickup truck
had been full of weapons and ammunition. He'd been one of the mules smug-
gling for the insurgency.

Jason Dunham later received a posthumous Medal of Honor, the first
Marine to be awarded one since the Vietnam War.

But not the last.

The smuggler Dunham's friends had killed turned out to be part of the lo-
gistical support for a new offensive the insurgents planned to unleash in Hu-
saybah. For days, Sunni cells had been infiltrating Husaybah from Ramadi and
Fallujah. More poured over the border by the truckload. Soon, they had at least
three hundred well-armed and well-led fighters deployed around the city. What
followed was one of the most intense, and unheralded, battles of the Iraq War.

APRIL 17, 2004
MORNING

Jason Delgado awoke with that slow burn of anger in his stomach.
From day one on this second deployment, what he was seeing
through his scope flew in the face of the assumptions being made by
his chain of command. While the leadership thought there was only
a scattering of criminals and Saddam loyalists hiding in the rabbit
warren of streets and alleys in Husaybah, Jason sensed something
else entirely was going down.

On their first mission in February, Jason and the other 3/7 snipers
went out to overwatch an Iraqi police station from the local Ba'ath

Party headquarters building. It was the tallest structure in the area, so it afforded a good view. Within minutes of arriving there, though, they took sustained small-arms fire and had to be extracted.

In the weeks that followed, Jason was the only sniper in the battalion taking shots. Whether his experience and training with 3/4 made him quicker to identify threats, or if the others were too concerned about a bad shoot, he didn't know. But they were clean kills against armed men actively threatening Coalition forces. Yet every time he pulled the trigger, his chain of command stuck him in a room and grilled him like he was a criminal. Combat was stressful enough; being hammered like this by his own people for doing his job was almost unbearable.

It didn't help that the sniper section of the scout platoon was undermanned. Instead of ten teams, they were lucky to field three with five men. Casualties over the past year and the demands on the Corps had left every battalion short-handed, so 3/7 was not unique in this regard. Still, the numbers game just added to the burden. They'd only been in country for about six weeks, and already the daily (and nightly) grind was taking its toll.

Jason and the scouts stayed at Al Qaim with the rest of 3/7's headquarters element for only a short time as the battalion settled into its new AO. The town sat about a mile from the Syrian border and the base was only a few minutes' driving time to Husaybah, where a hundred and fifty man company from the battalion had been forward deployed. A week after arriving, Jason and the rest of the snipers packed up and joined them.

That morning, outnumbering the local Marines two to one, the insurgents launched a full-scale assault in Husaybah.

In began with a baited ambush. They detonated an IED on the main road through town, not far from the Ba'ath Party headquarters building. The blast triggered an immediate reaction from Captain Richard Gannon's company. He and a platoon sortied from their outpost—and drove straight into an ambush. Machine guns, mortar fire, and AK-47s raked the platoon. The fighting spread from the street into the nearby buildings.

As it happened, a Marine Recon team had been on the top floor of the Ba'ath building. Now, they discovered the insurgents had taken over the bottom floor and used it as an ambush position against Captain Gannon's reaction force. The Recon guys crept downstairs, burst into the first floor and killed all the insurgents there.

In a nearby building, a squad of Marines ran into a die-hard group of insurgents. Fighting room to room, several Marines were killed. Others were wounded. The casualties piled up. Captain Gannon called for MEDEVAC and reinforcements. More men from his company flowed into the fight, but they were outnumbered and the enemy was well emplaced.

In the chaos of this point-blank urban firefight, Captain Gannon disappeared. For an hour nobody could raise him on the radio or locate him on the battlefield.

Gannon and several of his men had assaulted into a nearby building. It turned out to be full of well-equipped and determined insurgents. They wounded Captain Gannon and killed the other Marines as they fought room to room. As Captain Gannon lay helpless on the floor, the insurgents disarmed him. He was a student of military history, the son of a decorated Vietnam veteran, and a devoted patriot. But now, in this terrible moment, he alone faced a barbaric and merciless enemy, the likes of which Americans had not seen since the Pacific War.

The terrorists executed him with his own 9mm pistol. The same fate would later befall an Army company commander from Task Force 2/2 during the Second Battle of Fallujah later in the year.

At Al Qaim, the remaining scouts and all other available Marines piled into Humvees and raced toward Husaybah to offer their beleaguered brothers assistance. The scouts would sweep into the city from the south while the rest of the battalion struck the enemy from the west. Hopefully, the insurgents would be caught by surprise and trapped between the two elements.

Jason and the rest of the scouts approached a cluster of homes and businesses known as the "440" (there were four hundred forty structures in it). The place was basically a suburb of Husaybah, separated from the main portion of the city by a stretch of open terrain. The Marines dismounted in the desert between the two built-up areas and began to move toward the fighting on foot.

They hadn't gone far when something white fluttered on a rooftop. Jason brought his scope to his eye for a better look. A ten-year-old kid was up there, waving a stick with a white plastic sack attached to it. In previous patrols, Jason had seen other boys doing this as pigeons flew overhead and assumed the kids were just training their birds.

But not this time. There were no birds in the air around him.

Jason watched him for a long moment, considering his next move. His gut told him the kid was signaling the enemy. But what could he do? He couldn't put a bullet in a ten-year-old boy.

The Marines reached a set of railroad tracks. On the other side, a drainage ditch ran parallel with them. It looked like a natural defensive position, except for the heaps of trash strewn throughout its length. The stench boiling up from the ditch was vile, and clouds of flies boiled and buzzed over the mess.

Somebody said, "If the enemy is nearby, I bet they'll be in there."

Jason looked around. The 440 was just to their left, the main part of the city ahead and to the right. From both flanks, an ambush could be executed, and the Marines would have a hard time just trying to figure out from where the shooting originated. They'd walked into a terrible tactical situation, and a feeling of dread welled in Jason.

An officer appeared next to him and said, "Scope that building and see what's going on."

"On it, Sir."

He checked the rooftop. The boy remained in full view, waving his makeshift flag.

That's it.

Calmly, Jason turned to the officer and said, "Maybe we should get into that ditch, Sir."

The officer agreed and gave the order. The Marines began jumping down into the trench. The smell of rot and corruption was nearly overwhelming, and the men were both bitching and laughing about it at the same time.

That's when four machine guns opened fire on the Americans from multiple elevated positions. The fusillade of bullets chewed across the top lip of the drainage ditch as the Marines pressed themselves down as far as they could into the muck. A host of AK-47s unleashed a hail of rounds and added to the cacophony.

In seconds, the insurgent ambush pinned the scouts down. Totally defensive, they couldn't even raise their heads without drawing a crossfire that filled the air around them with cracking 7.62mm bullets.

Jason lay at the bottom of the ditch, listening to the four machine guns rip off burst after burst. The ditch was their salvation, but it also was their death trap. The absurdity of the situation suddenly overwhelmed him. He began to laugh.

Yeah. And the higher ups kept wondering who the hell I've been shooting at for the month. Maybe those geniuses will get the message now.

The guns raked back and forth over the platoon. Several men went down wounded. The situation was getting out of hand. It is in such dire moments that snipers can be the most effective. Usually, the only way to overcome an ambush like this one was to bring in more firepower. Tanks, aircraft, helicopters could dig the scouts out of the jam they were in. Nobody does firepower like the U.S. Marines.

But it would take time to get air support and artillery. The pounding the platoon endured that morning could not be allowed to go on for long. The ditch wasn't that deep, which meant the enemy fighters positioned in the taller dwellings around them would be able to get direct fire on at least some of the Marines as they looked down on them. The insurgents began to find the angles. Another Marine went down wounded as bullets began impacting among the men. As the corpsmen went to work, some of the others burrowed into the trash to conceal themselves from the gunmen out there in buildings overlooking the trench.

Something had to be done, or they'd get picked off one by one. Jason and his spotters, sharp-eyed Joshua Mavica and Brandon Delfiorintino, eased up the ditch wall to try and get eyes on the enemy machine guns. When they reached the top, they used binos and the scope on Jason's M40 to glass the nearest buildings. At a hundred and seventy yards, the trio observed muzzle flashes coming from an apartment complex. Lots of them. Black clad figures moved around inside the rooms as others darted about on the roof.

Find the crew-served weapons.

The air around the sniper team suddenly buzzed with bullets. To Jason, they sounded like pissed-off bees. The enemy had seen their heads exposed above the lip of the trench. Now at least one of the machine gunners had the range on them.

They ducked low and waited out the fusillade. A moment later they crawled back up to the top and continued their sweep. This time they focused on a building about two hundred thirty yards away. On the rooftop, they found one of the machine-gun positions. The gunner wore black man jammies and Adidas running pants. Another man was with him, similarly dressed but carrying an AK-47.

More angry bees. The enemy had seen them expose their heads again, and the two Marines had to go to ground once again.

Half buried in the garbage, the urge to laugh overcame Jason again. Half aloud he said, "Are you fucking kidding me? What the hell have we gotten ourselves into?" The words were swallowed by the din of cracking bullets.

There was no way the scouts would gain fire superiority in this fight. With wounded men, and the top of the trench covered by so many heavy weapons, if they tried to shoot back they would certainly just incur more casualties. Something needed to be done to level the playing field, or they were going to be in for a long and bloody day in the trash.

Carefully, Jason inched back up to the top of the trench, swung his M40A3 over the rim, and stuck his eye in the scope. Technically, a two-hundred-thirty-yard shot at an elevated target was not particularly difficult. Wind was light. Sun was not an issue. Enough of the gunner was exposed above the parapet to make an inviting target. Back on a range in the States, it'd be an easy kill.

But back in the States, nobody was shooting at you. Without any covering fire, Jason was exposed to the full fury of all the guns the enemy had in the fight. He focused on the task, blocking out fear and ignoring the rounds smacking into the dirt on either side of him. The enemy was getting close. He couldn't let himself think of that or the physical reaction to the danger would ruin his aim.

A half breath, and his reticle settled on the machine gunner, just a bit above center mass in order to compensate for the angle. He had the shot lined up. He could see the gunner laying on the trigger, his weapon's barrel spewing flame.

Jason's finger slipped into the trigger guard. More 7.62 rounds streaked over his head. He blocked them out. Nothing mattered but the picture in the scope. He left half his breath out, then pulled his own trigger.

The gunner spun away from his weapon and fell out of view. Jason racked another round into his M40 and drilled the rifleman with his second shot.

The volume of incoming diminished. What next? There were too many bad guys in the apartment complex for his M40 to make much of a difference there. He hadn't been able to find the other heavy weapons yet either. An idea struck him.

Jason took a smoke grenade off his chest rig, pulled the pin, and flipped it over the lip of the trench. The smoke offered a little extra concealment. As it settled over them, Jason called for Joshua Mavica, one of the platoon's radio operators. Mavica came on the run at once, staying as low as possible as he picked his way over the piles of trash at the bottom of the ditch. When he reached Jason, the sniper grabbed his handset and called battalion to request a fire mission using 3/7's 81mm mortar platoon.

The mortarmen brought their A game that day. The first round landed about two hundred yards north of the apartment complex. Jason saw the round explode, lased the distance with his binos, and called back, "Drop two hundred and fire for effect!"

The mortars landed right atop the apartment building and detonated on its roof. They touched off some propane tanks stored up there, sparking a conflagration that roasted the insurgents using the roof for their fighting positions. One of the machine guns and three men were later found to have been up there.

The flames swirled and spread to the top floor. As they did, one of the Marines in the trench stood up and fired an AT-4 rocket into the building. The fire spread until the entire structure was consumed.

Meanwhile, the scout platoon's leadership had been trying to get a MEDEVAC ride for their wounded men. Helos were out of the question—landing anywhere nearby would be a death sentence to the crew given the amount of firepower arrayed against the Marines. A vehicle evacuation was the only possibility, but there weren't any Humvees available. At length, the situation grew so critical that 3/7 HQ sent them an unarmored seven-ton along with a fuel truck. The two vehicles were the last ones at Al Qaim.

They showed up in the middle of the firefight and instantly drew fire. An RPG sizzled over the trench and speared the fuel truck just as it came to a halt a few yards away from the Marines. The rocket punctured the truck's huge tank but failed to explode. That seemed like a moment of inspired divine intervention—if it had blown up, there would have been few survivors in the trench. As it was, the hole it created caused hundreds of gallons of gasoline to spray out into the dirt and flow into the ditch. Soon, most of the Marines taking cover in the trash were soaked with fuel.

The wounded men were carried to the vehicles and extracted as the surviving insurgents fired back with everything they had left. Fortunately, nobody was hit. The apartment building burned on as Marines from one of 3/7's line companies cleared the two remaining machine-gun nests.

Then they moved into the city proper. Jason and the scouts ran into immediate trouble as the streets were laced with roadside bombs. Other Marine elements took sniper fire from well-trained foreign fighters, most of whom were later discovered to be Chechens. They were a cagey and disciplined bunch, and the Americans took more casualties fighting house to house again. At times, the Marine snipers ranged on enemy fighters who were using small children as human shields. The battalion's executive officer, Major George Schreffler, got on the radio and warned the other companies of this new development, telling the Marines not to take any shots that could harm the kids.

As the fighting continued, the IEDs stopped the scouts for almost four hours as EOD teams came out to neutralize them. They advanced a block forward, ran into another makeshift IED minefield, and had to wait again as the specialists rendered them useless. Block by block, they advanced at a crawl, taking sporadic fire as they worked. But the main resistance they'd faced had been broken after the 81mm mortar barrage.

It took fourteen hours of continuous combat to finally break the enemy's back. Late that night, the Marines finally received air support. Cobra gunships made strafing runs on pockets of resistance near the downtown soccer stadium. Those gun runs signaled the end of the offensive.

One hundred fifty insurgents had been killed during the day. The Marines captured twenty more. Captain Gannon and five other Marines were lost. The insurgents wounded twenty-five more. In one day, the battalion lost over five percent of its combat strength.

The end of the First Battle of Husaybah did not end the violence in the city. In the days that followed, the insurgents continued to resist and bring in reinforcements. They learned from their mistakes, switched tactics, and evolved. But they never tried a full-scale offensive again. They didn't need to; what they came up with next was far worse.

CHAPTER SEVENTEEN
The Thousand-Yard Shot

In the weeks that followed the First Battle of Husaybah, 3/7's snipers grew into experts at urban warfare. They learned not to insert into a hide in vehicles. They'd only be spotted by one of the countless kids the insurgents used as their eyes and ears. Early on, they would move into the city in seven-ton trucks, then bail out at their objective. Too obvious. So Jason and the other Marines in the scout sniper platoon switched tactics. They stopped going out with the infantry, stopped using vehicles—convoys of any size were bound to get hit anyway. They also discovered platoon-sized patrols did not work. The insurgents always detected them and countered whatever mission they had laid on for that night. So the Marine snipers took a page from the enemy's book and started infiltrating at night in groups of no more than four. They entered the city on foot, unscrewed streetlights so they could remain in the shadows. Instead of smashing in doors and violently taking over homes so they could establish an overwatch position on the roof, they found a kinder, gentler approach worked much better. To mask as much noise as possible, Jason would tap lightly on a window to get the home owner's attention. Later, he discovered an even more effective trick. Most of the houses had window-mounted air-conditioner units. He could knock on those loud enough to wake the folks inside, but the A/C's motor drowned the sound outside. It made for a very stealthy way to get into a good hide site.

When gaining the high ground didn't work, the 3/7 sniper teams got creative. Like most Iraqi cities at the time, garbage littered the streets. This wasn't just stray packages and wrappers, but heaps of household trash families just dumped in front of their homes because transporting it anywhere was a life-threatening proposition with all the IEDs emplaced in and around the city. The trash heaps made perfect concealment. The snipers made effective use of them and it always surprised the insurgents when they did.

The tactics worked, and the snipers racked up kills. They took out bomb-laying teams, surprised insurgent patrols, and interdicted their supply lines. But at times, it seemed like whatever they did, the enemy always had more willing bodies to throw into the fray.

As the snipers adapted to their environment, the Sunni insurgency they faced underwent a transformation. Many of the local Iraqi leaders had died in the fighting that spring. The Marine and Army's efforts to interdict their supply networks and roll up cells had been extremely effective. The Americans underestimated their successes. Yet those victories came with unintended consequences. As their capabilities diminished, the Sunni turned to the only source of outside help: al-Qaida. They opened the door and let the devil in. Through 2004, al-Qaida's role in Anbar Province grew considerably. In time they would take complete control of the Sunni insurgency and turned it not just against the Coalition but against the Shia as well, hoping to spark a sectarian civil war.

That spring of 2004 was the first iteration in that development. On the battlefield, it meant that 3/7 suddenly faced a host of new threats and sophisticated weapons systems. Al-Qaida brought considerable experience and skill to the IED-making industry around Husaybah. The bombs became far more lethal than ever before. Bigger, utilizing larger explosives and triggered in different ways, they wrought havoc on the Marines and their unarmored trucks and lightly armored Humvees.

On one mission, Jason and the scout sniper platoon rushed to the scene of an IED attack. They found a 998 high-backed Humvee sitting in the kill zone. At first, it looked unharmed. But as Jason drew closer, he saw a fist-sized hole punched in its side. When the scouts dropped the back gate, blood poured out in a wave. Most of the Humvee's crew had been badly torn up.

The Marines had never seen the kind of IED used in that attack. The insurgents had encased it in concrete and left it in the street. It looked just like any other pile of debris in Husaybah. But inside the concrete was a tube with a flechette rocket. When it was detonated remotely, the rocket shot from its tube, broke through the concrete, penetrated the Humvee's sidewall, and maimed the crew.

As the IEDs grew more sophisticated, the enemy brought in a new threat: traveling snipers. These guys never stayed in one town long. They moved from city to city, taking only a few shots and never lingering to see their handiwork. One began showing up every few weeks after the April 17, 2004, fight. Jason studied his attacks and learned his signature—every sniper has one. This shooter was an opportunist. He would stick around for perhaps two to three days at a time, then vanish for a while. He was not a particularly good shot, and he usually missed. He sometimes triggered off more than one round, too, before breaking contact and going to ground.

Then another sniper showed up. This guy was a pro, though Intel was never able to get a handle on who he was or where he had been trained. He was an expert shot, fearless, and disciplined—the kind of sniper who instills paralyzing fear in his targets.

From seven hundred yards, the Pro hit a Marine standing watch in one of the towers at what was later renamed Camp Gannon, the base just outside of Husaybah. The Marine had been scanning the city with binos, minimally exposed, when he was struck in the head with the single shot.

A few days later, the Pro struck again. This time he hit a Marine center mass. His chest plate saved his life. Not long after, he wounded another American in the forearm.

The attacks got into 3/7's head. They made the Marines cautious and reactive, and psychologically it became more difficult to saddle up and head into the city. The 3/7 snipers decided they needed to do something about the Pro. They put together a plan to try and pinpoint him using dismounted infantry to draw him out while the snipers watched from elevated positions. However, by the time they implemented the plan, the Pro had vanished altogether. He never returned to Husaybah.

The 3/7 snipers had an even greater psychological impact on the enemy. During overwatch missions, they protected Marine patrols in the city and killed many insurgents trying to attack the men. The insurgents grew cautious, then skittish. Their fear of the battalion's few sniper teams forced them to cede the initiative to the Americans.

Jason got a glimpse of just how much the enemy feared him and his brothers when a group of elders showed up at their base one day. Most of these Iraqis were either playing both sides or had outright sided with the enemy at that point of the war. They came to the Marines, told them that there would be an anti-Coalition demonstration in Husaybah in a few days. The Marines were happy to see the Iraqis exercising their newfound right of free speech and freedom to protest, so the Americans asked the elders how they could help.

"Would you please keep your snipers away?" was the response.

Of all the things they could have asked for, the snipers had taken center stage.

Between protests and IED attacks, the cat-and-mouse game continued in the city's streets. The insurgents became elusive, hitting and running, increasingly relying on bombs to inflict casualties. The Marines finally decided to search the entire city. The full battalion, along with Iraqi security troops, swept into Husaybah and searched it house by house, building by building. They found a veritable arsenal of AK-47s, machine guns, rifles, rockets, bomb-making equipment, RPGs, and mortar tubes. They detained dozens of suspected insurgents and destroyed all the ordnance and weaponry they uncovered.

The sweep worked—at least for a few weeks. The level of violence diminished, and patrols moved more freely on the streets. Inevitably, the cells got resupplied from Syria, and the attacks escalated again.

Without the ability to control the border crossings, this would be the cycle the Marines would endure for months to come out there in Iraq's Wild West.

One morning in May 2004, two sniper teams sortied beyond the wire on a hunting patrol to the outskirts of the 440 area. Jason led Sierra Three. Sierra Four was the other two-man element. They stayed on foot, moving through the desert carefully, keeping eyes out for any sign they'd been detected. The first two kiloyards of the patrol saw them creep through a series of mines and rock quarries, which served as about the only economic activity in the area besides smuggling.

As they worked their way past the last mine, a burst of automatic gunfire echoed across the desert scape. It hadn't been directed at the snipers, but was close enough to cause the Americans to go investigate. After a few minutes, they saw a shack on the horizon with a single Iraqi border policeman hunkered down behind it holding an AK-47. Beyond the shack, Jason saw five armed men shooting at the Iraqi. Four had assault rifles, but the fifth was armed with an RPK light machine gun.

Sierra Three called to the 3/7 Combat Operations Center and reported the situation. A moment later, COC cleared Jason to engage and assist the besieged Iraqi. The Americans were a long way from the lone cop. So far, most of the shots the snipers had taken in country had been fairly close—usually under five hundred yards. This time, the situation forced a much farther one.

Jason's spotter, Silicon Valley native Brandon Delfiorintino, lased the distance and called out, "One thousand fifteen yards."

Jason settled down behind his M40A3 and searched out the RPK gunner. Snipers are trained to reduce the greatest threat first, and that machine gun was peppering the shack with scores of rounds.

The M40A3 is considered effective out to nine hundred yards, so this would not be an easy shot. Jason had mounted an AN/PVS 10, 8.5power Day/Night scope atop his rifle. He really needed a ten-power scope for this sort of distance, and he wasn't sure he could hit the target with what he had. Perhaps if he missed, he could spook the enemy into retiring.

Brandon was a superb spotter, and Jason loved working with him. The two always seemed to be in sync, always knew what the other needed. Without prompting, he whispered the wind direction and speed—less than ten miles an hour.

Jason set his reticle on the gunner, then raised it above center mass to compensate for the distance. A half breath, release, and he pulled the trigger.

The RPK gunner didn't react.

"Anyone see the splash?" Jason asked.

Sierra Four was spotting for him along with Brandon, but nobody had seen where the round had gone.

Jason racked another round into the chamber and slapped the bolt down. He took aim again. He pulled the trigger and waited.

Nothing. Another miss, and nobody saw where the round impacted.

"What the hell?" Jason said.

He thought it over and decided he needed to do a battle zero on his weapon. He found a berm about the same distance away, told his spotters what he was doing, and took a shot. This time, the round kicked up a big spout of dirt, two and a half mils high and three mils to the right of where he had aimed.

He couldn't dial in any more dope on the scope—his turrets were maxed out. He'd have to compensate manually, but at least he knew where the round was going now. Mentally, he marked the spot on his scope and swung the M40's barrel back on the RPK gunner as quickly as he could.

He pulled the trigger. The RPK gunner flipped over backwards and sprawled on the ground between the other armed men. Stunned, they stared down at him for an instant—another example of the Shock Factor at work—then suddenly bolted wildly. Several ran into a bunker a few yards away, but then one suddenly changed directions. It was a classic case of how the Shock Factor puts a man in autopilot mode after the initial paralysis is broken. A second or two after his brain caught up with his legs, he willed himself to go back for his fallen man.

He rushed back to the RPK gunner. He gave him a quick look, but instead of trying to drag him to the bunker, the insurgent went for the RPK. Jason couldn't believe it. The insurgent had run right back into the area that Jason had already locked down in his scope.

"Oh my God. This guy's a super genius."

Had the insurgent stopped to think things over, let his mind fully catch up to instincts, he would have realized he'd just signed his own death warrant. But the Shock Factor scrambles circuits, and this guy wasn't thinking clearly.

He shuffled to one side slightly until he was standing almost exactly where the first man had been when Jason hit him. He started to bend down, but Jason was waiting for him. The New Yorker dropped the hammer and killed him.

After the second man went down, the snipers reported the situation to the COC. The remaining three fighters had gone to ground in the bunker, so no further targets presented themselves. A few minutes later, the COC ordered the snipers to return to base.

Those two shots Jason took were among the most difficult and longest ones taken by a Marine in Anbar Province. His quick thinking to fire on the berm and get a battle zero ensured his success, as did his knack for physics and math. Only a handful of snipers could have ever made that shot with the rifle and scope Jason carried that day.

Back at the COC, 3/7's leadership was in an uproar. The battalion commander called Jason into a meeting room. As he walked in, Lieutenant Colonel Lopez was sitting there, crossed legged with a finger to his lips. He looked pissed off and intimidating, and Jason's immediate thought was that the officer was affecting the pose deliberately.

"Do you know what you've just done?" he demanded.

Jason looked puzzled. "No, sir."

The sniper gave a brief description of the engagement. When he finished, Lieutenant Colonel Lopez said, "Well, Sergeant, there's only one problem with what just happened."

"Sir?"

"You shot into Syria and killed two Syrian soldiers."

The news left Jason stunned. A full investigation was conducted on the incident—and found that the Iraqi border policeman had been left on his own with a single thirty-round magazine for his AK-47. The Syrians had initiated the fight, and 3/7's snipers had gone to the man's defense. The shoot was deemed totally within the ROEs and justified given the situation. Still, it was another crazy moment in a war that made less and less sense to the Marines fighting it.

The fighting swelled again in the late spring. As 3/7 received replacements to compensate for their combat losses, the new guys found the learning curve in Husaybah to be a steep one. In a matter of days, three new team leaders went down, wounded in action.

The main highway running from Syria east to Baghdad became the focal point of many Marine operations. Keeping it open was a key priority. Denying it to the Marines became the focal point of the insurgent IED-laying effort. To counter that, the snipers spent more and more time overwatching the highway and taking out the bomb layers.

One night, Sierra Three and Four were set up in two different hides, keeping eyes on the road. An Iraqi police station had been built not far from the highway on Market Street, perhaps eight hundred yards from the Marines' positions. The place was a frequent target for the insurgents, who laced it with small-arms fire during hit-and-run raids.

That night, Jason's building trembled violently as an explosion rocked Husaybah. Somebody had detonated a bomb by the Iraqi police station. A minute later, a white Toyota sedan came tearing down the road from the direction of the blast. A curfew had been in effect for months, so civilians knew they were supposed to be off the street at this hour.

Jason watched the car and knew something wasn't right. It passed his hide site, and he decided they needed to stop it. He called to the other sniper team, emplaced a few hundred yards further down the road in another building, and told them to set up a snap checkpoint and stop the vehicle.

The other team rushed down into the street and waited for the car. Meanwhile, Jason and his spotter pulled off the roof of their building and rushed downstairs. They would backup the other team as they searched the vehicle.

As they reached the street, Sierra Four called Jason and told him that the sedan had pulled a U-turn as soon as the driver saw the Marines in the road ahead of it. The car was coming straight back toward Jason's team now.

The transmission had barely reached Jason's ears when he heard the sound of an overreved four-cylinder engine. Up ahead, the Toyota came blasting down the street, doing at least sixty miles an hour.

Jason stood at the side of the road and leveled his M40. The driver saw him, but didn't slow down. He pulled the trigger and put a round in the vehicle's engine block. Toyota makes durable cars. The shot tore into the engine, but had no effect.

The driver didn't stop. Only a few yards away now, Jason heard the driver punch the accelerator to the floor. The engine whined. In a second, he'd be past the Marines. Jason jacked the bolt and slammed home another round, but before he could raise the rifle to his shoulder and take aim, the sedan sped past him.

The New Yorker pivoted a hundred eighty degrees on one foot, eye in the scope and fired a single shot offhand at the fleeing car. His spotter let loose on the car as well with his M4.

The sedan suddenly veered and lost speed. The Marines ran after it. It drifted to a stop, and the driver climbed out about a hundred fifty yards away. Jason and his spotter kept their weapons on him as they ran forward.

The man turned and looked at the onrushing Marines. "Please," he begged, "don't kill me. I have two daughters. I am a good man."

The Iraqi's English was flawless. He had almost no accent. It rocked both Marines, and for a moment they doubted themselves. What had they done? Visions of the Diyala River bridge and the horror there flashed in Jason's mind.

They reached the man. He'd taken a bullet in the back of the right armpit that had grazed his lungs before exiting from his chest. He stood there, repeating that he had children. Girls. He was a good man.

He sat down next to the car as the Marines looked him over. He was in bad shape and needed immediate MEDEVAC. Jason called the COC and requested one, but it was denied.

The man was going to die if he didn't get medical help.

More Marines showed up. Jason took a minute to look the car over. A single 7.62mm bullet hole had punctured the trunk—that was Jason's snap-shot from the hip. The round went through the backseat, through the front seat, and left a hole right at the armpit level. It had been a one-in-a-million fluke bull's-eye. And now, a father would pay the price.

No way would he let the man die. He and his spotter carried him to his sedan. The engine was still running, and an Iraqi hospital was not far away. There in the middle of the night in one of Iraq's most dangerous cities, Jason sped the man through the empty streets unescorted. He reached the hospital and he and his spotter carried him inside.

Not long after, his platoon commander and a bunch of Marines from the CAAT team (Combined Anti-Armor Team) showed up. Fearing another investigation was about to be initiated against him, Jason met with his commander.

"Don't worry, Delgado," his lieutenant told him, "it was a good shoot."

The Marines had searched the sedan and found a collection of cell phones, spools of electrical wire, and all sorts of IED-related tools and gear. Jason started to feel better about that one-in-a-million shot.

It turned out that the man had been arrested by an Army unit a few months before after a weapon's cache had been discovered at his house. Perhaps his "I am a father" schtick had worked on the Army and that was the reason for his release. It had certainly worked on Jason.

But not this time. After the Iraqi doctors stabilized him, a Coalition helicopter arrived and had whisked him away for parts unknown. Jason and the 3/7 Scouts never saw or heard of him again.

A few weeks after that incident, the battalion packed up and headed home. Jason went on to become a sniper instructor for the newly formed Marine Special Operations Command. He stayed in that slot until leaving the Corps in 2009. He returned to the Bronx to pursue his artistic passion by opening Gunmetal Ink, a tattoo shop. He works as a contract sniper and security agent for the State Department occasionally, and spent 2012 in Iraq again. He got to see firsthand how the war played out for the people over there. Gone were the days of bombs and sudden ambushes. Life had returned to normal, and the people of Iraq were busily moving on with their lives.

But in the summer of 2004, that normalcy was a long way off. As 3/7 rotated home, another uprising was brewing in Baghdad. Caught in the middle was a small, close-knit group of citizen-snipers who'd grown up together in the Oregon woods. The moral quandary they faced that summer of 2004 would engulf them in an international incident and trigger almost a decade of media investigations and conspiracy theories.

PART III

OBSERVATIONS AND UPRISINGS

CHAPTER EIGHTEEN
Origins

Daniel Morgan never once backed down from a fight. Six feet tall with broad shoulders and bulging muscles gained from a lifetime of physical labor, Morgan had a knack for finding trouble. Bar brawls, gang fights, and back-alley beat-downs characterized his hard-drinking youth. Ambitious, loyal to his friends, and possessing a sharp mind, he was equally feared and admired by his fellow Virginians.

In 1755 he joined British general Edward Braddock's march against the French at Fort Duquesne, seeing profit and adventure in this first major campaign of the French and Indian War. Serving as a civilian contract teamster, he drove the rule-bound British nuts with his independent spirit and flippant mouth. He also suffered no fools, no matter who they were. When a British officer angered him, he beat him raw and was sentenced to five hundred lashes with a whip for his crime. For most men, this would have been a death sentence. Not Morgan. The British tied him to a post and whipped him until "his back was bathed in blood and his flesh hung down in ribbons." Morgan never lost consciousness, and he even counted each strike of the whip. After that incident, he hated the British Army with singular passion.

Daniel Morgan is the father of the American sniper corps.

After the American Revolution broke out, the Continental Congress voted on June 14, 1775, to raise ten companies of "expert riflemen," including two from Virginia. At the time, Morgan was serving in the Virginia Militia. A patriot committee elected him to be the captain in command of one of these new rifle companies. Morgan leapt at the opportunity. For days, he

rode through the county, using his skills as an orator and leveraging his legendary reputation to recruit the area's best marksmen into his new unit. At
each stop, he would challenge all those interested into joining his unit to a
series of marksmanship tests. Morgan's assistants would set up a board with
the outline of a man's nose painted on it. From a hundred fifty yards away,
each candidate received one chance to hit the target. Only those who did so,
or came close, were allowed entry into Morgan's elite new company. When
he finished recruiting after only a couple of weeks, his company included
some of the best sharpshooters in the colonies.

They were a nonstandard lot. Some things just don't change.

Morgan's men soon made waves with both the enemy and within the
nascent American Army. They never considered themselves average, nor did
they react well to Army chickenshit. They were hard-drinking, hard-fighting
frontiersmen, born and raised in the woods. They thought for themselves,
took pride in their fierce independence, and could live off the land with a
self-sufficiency few could match. They had also learned to shoot from the
moment they were old enough to hold a rifle.

The other militia and Continental units hated Morgan's men. Officers
reviled them and wrote scathing assessments of their unmilitary behavior.
Truth was, they did not fit the army mold. They dressed different, walked
with a swagger, and chafed against routine. They brawled with each other
and others at the drop of a hat, and never once doubted they were better than
everyone else. They developed their own style and rituals. They became a
breed apart, as we still are today.

When they went into battle, they put all doubters to shame. They may
have been a pain in the ass in camp, but in the field they showed their lethality time after time. Light on their feet, masters of concealment and stealthy
movement, Morgan's men inspired terror in the British with their sudden
and deadly accurate attacks.

After serving in the siege of Boston, Morgan's company took part in
the invasion of Canada later that year. In the middle of blinding snow, he
and his men helped storm Quebec, only to be surrounded and forced to surrender. In early 1777, Morgan was exchanged and returned to the American
Army, where George Washington gave him command of an elite, five-

hundred-man battalion of riflemen. *Every man had been handpicked from their Continental regiments based on their precision accuracy with their weapons. Morgan's Riflemen went on to play a key role in the Saratoga Campaign and helped turn the tide against the British. He and his men later helped defeat Lord Cornwallis at Cowpens, and were present at the end of the war.*

Daniel Morgan and his original citizen-snipers set the standard for our community in the years to come. In every subsequent war except Vietnam, militia and National Guard shooters have played valuable roles at the front. Today, that citizen-sniper heritage is embodied in the National Guard infantry units and their scout platoons. These part-time snipers are rarely noticed by the media, and most Americans don't even realize they may have a National Guard shooter working with them in their office or their community's Wal-Mart. Yet since 9/11, these men have served with distinction in both Iraq and Afghanistan, scoring some of America's most notable successes against our enemies.

In the summer of 2003, Oregon's 2nd Battalion, 162nd Infantry was mobilized for service in Iraq. Composed of a mix of college students, mill workers, Hewlett-Packard engineers, cops, and paramedics, 2–162 possessed a backbone of talented noncommissioned officers who had served in their platoons and companies for decades. Some of them had seen combat in Grenada, Panama, and the Gulf. Others had yet to hear the crack of bullets passing overhead, but had trained together for so long that they had become a bonded and well-oiled team. Their bond of friendship and brotherhood ran deep; their families celebrated holidays together, their sons had grown up playing war together, and when they turned eighteen, they joined the battalion. The Volunteers, as they called themselves, were a family—sometimes fractious, sometimes feisty, but loyal to each other to the core.

This small band of seven hundred Oregonians, keepers of the citizen-soldier heritage, would find themselves in the bloodiest and most violent battles of the Iraq War. To that point, no National Guard unit since the end of World War II had seen the level of combat 2–162 would experience in Baghdad, Najaf, and Fallujah. Right there with them, protecting their fellow Oregonians and innocent civilians caught in the violence, were the long riflemen of Staff Sergeant Kevin Maries's sniper section.

CHAPTER NINETEEN
Yellow Shirt

BAGHDAD, IRAQ
JUNE 2004

At five foot five, with John Lennon spectacles and an easygoing smile, Staff Sergeant Kevin Maries does not look like a deadly sniper. If you were to encounter him on the street, his soft-spoken, friendly nature might deceive you into thinking he was an accountant, or perhaps a math teacher. But underneath the benign exterior beats a warrior's heart.

Born in Iowa, his folks moved the family to Oregon in 1976 when he was nine years old. They settled in Albany, a small Willamette Valley rough-and-tumble mill town. As a kid, he developed an interest in firearms—no surprise since his father was a sportsman—and he learned the mechanics of marksmanship long before he was able to drive a car. He has shot competitively most of his life, and has a room full of trophies from those events.

In 1985, after high school, he joined the Oregon National Guard, where he served initially as a TOW missile anti-tank gunner. Later, he became a medic and transferred to an engineer unit. In 1991, he found his true calling in the Guard when he joined 2nd Battalion, 162nd Infantry's scout/sniper platoon. He graduated from the National Guard's scout-sniper school in Little Rock, Arkansas in 1993. At the time, most of the instructors were Marines, and Maries was part of the first class to graduate from it.

The Volunteers considered the scout/sniper platoon to be the battalion's elite element. Only the best soldiers were selected to join it, and only after they underwent an extensive series of tests and interviews. Each prospective candidate had to be a seasoned infantryman whose tactical acumen was challenged with a weekend of field exercises known as the Scout Indoc. One bad decision during those training battles and the candidate would be rejected.

The scout platoon had two components: a reconnaissance, or recce, section designed to serve as the eyes of the battalion, and a sniper section composed of three two-man teams. The thirty men who filled the platoon's ranks represented the best light infantrymen in the entire Oregon Guard.

The surest shots and the most patient, observant soldiers who were admitted into the scout platoon were selected to become snipers. Kevin Maries made it through the selection process thanks to his stone-cold demeanor while under stress and his ability to recall incredibly minute details. He spotted things through his scope that others never saw. He was persistent, cerebral, and impossible to fluster. He made a natural candidate for the sniper section.

When Maries joined the scout platoon, the Vietnam-era M21 rifle was long out of the Guard's inventory. This was the Vietnam-era variant of the M14 made famous by such men as Chuck Mawhinney. In 1988, the Army transitioned to a new sniper weapon system called the M24. Based on the Remington 700 civilian bolt action rifle, the M24 has an effective range of eight hundred and seventy five meters. It holds five 7.62mm rounds, though some units use .300 Winchester Magnums. The Volunteers received their M24s starting in 1992. By the end of the decade, the 2–162s snipers carried a mix of M24s and the deadly .50 caliber M107 Barrett semiautomatic. Maries' loved both weapons, but he had a special affinity for the M14. Later on during his service with 2–162, he acquired several match grade M14s from the Guard's marksmanship unit and pressed them back into service with his snipers.

2–162.

Sergeant Wes Howe, a fellow National Guard sniper, served with Maries for years and was awed by Maries's natural shooting ability. After Kevin won the state's sniper competition in 2001, which made him Oregon's top shot, Howe marveled at Maries's "incredible score with an M24." Kevin had long earned a reputation among his peers as the state's preeminent sniper.

By 2003 Maries had become the sniper section NCO. In that role, he molded the 2–162 shooters into a close-knit, meticulous bunch who prided themselves on their attention to detail. He was also responsible for recruiting and mentoring new candidates for the sniper section. He handpicked each man for the unit and imparted his knowledge to them with the acumen and patience of a schoolteacher.

In the summer of 2003, the battalion received orders to deploy to Iraq. The Volunteers' commanding officer, Lieutenant Colonel Dan Hendrickson, ordered Maries to increase the sniper section to include five two-man teams. To do so, Kevin had to accelerate his normal recruiting process. He pulled in a number of talented privates, including a prior service veteran named Keith Engle. Through the course of that summer, the scouts tested those privates relentlessly. When the process ended, Maries had sent almost two dozen of the prospects back to their line companies. He kept only Engle and Private Nate Gushwa.

That fall, the Volunteers were allotted only one slot at the sniper school in Little Rock, Arkansas. Jim Schmorde was originally slated to go, but he suffered a knee injury in training that delayed his depature. So Maries gave the slot to Nate Gushwa, who left the battalion to attend the school in January 2004. He graduated on Valentine's Day and caught up with the Volunteers at Fort Polk, Louisiana, shortly before the unit headed out the door for Iraq.

Engle grew up in the mountains south of Bakersfield, California. Before age five, his dad had taught him to shoot with a .22 Marlin 18, which he used to hunt rabbits and squirrels. His Marlin had no rear sight, yet he developed a knack for nailing targets on the fly that confounded his older brother, who later joined the Army. When Engle was fifteen, he outshot his brother when he came home on leave from Korea. Keith teased him about that for years afterward.

His brother was the second man in the family to serve in Asia. Engle's dad had done a combat tour as a medic during the Korean War. Though he rarely talked about it, his military service helped to inspire his sons to join the Army. Out of high school, Keith enlisted as a TOW antitank missile gunner.

After his four-year contract ended, Engle got out, came to Oregon, and settled at the coast. He found a job as a commercial fisherman—hard, rugged work that demanded long hours and physical stamina. He was at sea on 9/11 when the Towers fell, but as soon as his feet hit dry land, he reenlisted. He joined the Oregon Guard and was pulled into the scout platoon after a series of drills with the 2–162. Maries saw his potential and picked him for the sniper section.

The two formed an interesting combination. Engle's blood ran hot; Maries's ran cold. Engle tended to be more emotional and excitable, while Maries was analytical and detached. As the two learned to work together, Maries made a concerted effort to show Engle how to control his emotions while out in the field.

Six months after mobilizing for duty overseas, the Volunteers departed the United States. They flew to Kuwait in March of 2004 just as Sunni and Shia insurgent groups forged an alliance intended to create a nationwide uprising against the American-led Coalition. In April, as the battalion drove north across the Kuwait border destined for their new base in eastern Baghdad, the Shia and Sunni groups struck simultaneously throughout the country. In the once-quiet southern provinces, members of the Badr Brigade and Moqtada al-Sadr's ragtag Mahdi Militia attacked Coalition bases, convoys, and patrols. Al-Sadr's men seized control of dozens of southern Iraqi towns, including the holy city of Najaf. Meanwhile, Sunni groups west of Baghdad rose up against the U.S. Marines, leading to ferocious fighting around Fallujah, Ramadi, and other key cities.

With only a minimal load of ammunition, the Volunteers had to fight their way into Baghdad a year after the initial invasion. As they reached the southern suburbs, a sixty-man force of Syrian foreign fighters ambushed their column, wounding three Americans. After blowing through the ambush and evacuating their casualties, the Oregonians finally reached their destination later that night.

The battalion took over a small base built around the former Iraqi Olympic training facility. Known at the time as Forward Operating Base Provider, later renamed Patrol Base Volunteer, Kevin Maries and the other snipers found some interesting things in their new home. Saddam's psychotic son, Uday Hussein, had frequented this place, and the scouts discovered his mangled Ferrari abandoned in one of the base parking lots, towed there after U.S. forces blew him up in late 2003. Inside the Olympic training facility, his snipers discovered a bloodstained room with a drain in the floor that their interpreters later explained was Uday's personal torture chamber. Apparently, he used it to punish the Iraqi national soccer team whenever they lost a match.

The scouts spent their first nights in Baghdad sleeping first in a gravel parking lot, then later in a drained Olympic-sized indoor swimming pool. Rocket strikes echoed through the city. Mortars exploded, gunfire rattled periodically in the distance. This was not at all what the Volunteers had been led to expect while training up for the deployment at Fort Hood, Texas. There, they'd been told resistance in the capital was minimal and the few roadside bombs encountered were small, Coke-can contraptions that had little effect. Instead, they'd driven into the middle of a well-armed national uprising that rocked the entire country. They faced roadside bombs so large they were destroying M1 Abrams tanks, and an enemy both skilled and capable who knew the terrain.

Getting a handle on the situation became Lieutenant Colonel Hendrickson's first priority. He deployed the sniper teams out onto hide sites all over their new area of operations, and Maries's men soon found excellent spots in Baghdad's busy high-rise buildings from which to observe the goings on around their patrol base. In downtown, they actually took over the observation point my sniper section had built on the Sheraton Hotel in 2003 after our Marine battalion helped capture the capital. It provided an excellent vantage point of the area, and Maries's snipers were sent there to help protect the Western press corps still working out of the hotel.

The Ministry of Interior (MOI) building was another one selected by Maries as a prime vantage point. From the fifteenth floor, his sniper teams could watch several key intersections in northeast Baghdad. On the floors below them, American civilians and military personnel worked from shabby offices and cubicles as they propped up the Iraqi bureaucracy that would eventually replace them when the transfer of authority took place later on in the summer. The place hummed with activity at all hours of the day.

The Oregon snipers took over the entire fifteenth floor. Being workout fanatics, they dragged exercise equipment into one of the interior rooms and created a makeshift gym. During scrounging trips to lower floors, they acquired chairs, tables, and even a mini-fridge that made life on their floor a little more comfortable.

During one of those scrounging trips, six-foot-two-inch-tall Sergeant Darren Buchholz discovered there were more than just bureaucrats in the building with them. Buchholz, whom Maries had pulled into the sniper section in 2001, wandered onto a lower floor none of the other snipers had yet visited. To his surprise, he found a Caucasian female secretary sitting at a desk outside a closed office door.

Dressed in nothing but BDU pants and a tan undershirt, Buchholz approached the secretary with an air of brassy authority.

"I wanna talk to your boss."

The secretary smiled warmly and led him through the office door.

Buchholz stopped in his tracks. He had intended to requisition a few chairs from the woman's supervisor. Instead, he found himself in an ornate room full of elegant wood furniture that was totally out of place in a building that looked like it had been decorated by the Salvation Army. It felt like he'd walked into a CEO's office in an otherwise down-at-the-ears strip mall that had been leased out to county services.

The walls were covered with photographs of world leaders and generals posing with the dapper, gray-haired man sitting behind a desk at the other end of the room. He was dressed in an expensive suit. A pistol lay on his desk within easy reach.

Buchholz stared at the man, who quietly asked, "Can I help you?"

The Fortune 500 setting knocked the swagger out of Buchholz. Deferentially, he introduced himself and explained his purpose and mission in the building. The man rose from his chair. For a second, Buchholz thought the man might reach for his pistol, but he simply came around his desk to shake the Oregonian's hand.

Despite the suit, the man possessed a steely, almost sinister sort of aura that unnerved Buchholz. The man was clearly used to this reaction, and took charge of the encounter. He gave Darren his business card that indicated he was one of the senior-level members of a particular "Other Governmental Agency," and asked if he could do anything for the Oregon snipers working upstairs.

Buchholz was surprised by his helpfulness, but he wasn't about to take advantage of it. Politely, he extricated himself as quickly as he could and beat a hasty retreat upstairs, never to return to that floor.

It was the first indication that things were not as they seemed in the Ministry of Interior building.

Maries established a rotation for his five teams that kept them moving between the Sheraton, the MOI, and rolling out with the scouts as they patrolled the city. Usually, two teams would man each observation post for a week to ten days at a time. A fire team from the scout platoon usually provided security. At the MOI, the Oregonians took to sealing themselves onto the fifteenth floor by chaining and locking the stairwell doors.

Every few days, a logistics run would be made and food would be delivered to the men under the guise of normal working traffic into the building. The snipers and their spotters rotated time on their weapons, ensuring that Lieutenant Colonel Hendrickson had eyes on his section of Baghdad 24/7.

During those first weeks in Baghdad, Maries and his men saw a lot of things go down from their observation points. Suicide bombings, car bombs, mortar and rocket attacks took place almost every day. It did not take long for Moqtada al-Sadr's Mahdi Militia, the primary Shia insurgent force in Baghdad, to discover that the Volunteers had moved into their neighborhood. They targeted 2–162's base every day with sudden mortar and rocket strikes. Periodically, a car or van would cruise by the entrance and blast off a few rounds from an AK. Once in a while, they'd even fire RPG's at the base.

On the MOI observation point, the snipers made a concerted effort to pinpoint the mortar and launch sites used to hit their base. This was no easy task, and even when they did see a launch, the Coalition forces in the area usually could not react fast enough to catch the mortar crews before they vanished into the byzantine streets of Sadr City, a massive slum that made up most of eastern Baghdad.

Between long stretches on the OPs, the snipers took turns going out on dismounted and vehicular patrols with the rest of the scout platoon. These missions led to the snipers' first taste of battle.

One night in the late spring of 2004, the scouts had dismounted from their unarmored Humvees in what turned out to be a very hostile neighborhood. Darren Buchholz was with the platoon that night. Usually, he carried a Barrett .50 caliber sniper rifle and a scoped M14 that he loved for its semiauto capabilities, but on this mission he'd brought along his M4 with a PEQ-14 laser designator for use with his night vision goggles. While in the street, the scouts spotted a light flashing intermittently on a rooftop two hundred yards away. Moments later, somebody sprayed the street with automatic weapons fire. The scouts took cover and searched for targets. After a moment, the scene went quiet.

As the scouts continued with the patrol, the light flashed again from the same rooftop. Seconds later, somebody laced them with machine-gun fire again. This happened several more times until the scouts realized what was going on. There was an insurgent standing on the rooftop, signaling his fellow fighters with a flashlight. Each time he used it, the other insurgents would make a hit-and-run attack on the platoon.

Buchholz found a stable firing position in the street and waited for the man on the rooftop to return. Through his night vision goggles, he spotted the insurgent reappear. Buchholz illuminated him with his PEQ-14. Wind was minimal; the night was warm and still. He pulled the trigger and smoke-checked the insurgent with a single shot from his M4.

After the patrol, the platoon learned that the man on the roof was an Iraqi cop, and he'd been signaling the enemy while atop the local police station. It was one of the first indications the battalion picked up that the Iraqi Police, which was predominantly Shia, had been penetrated by Moqtada al-Sadr's Mahdi Militia.

Others evidence accumulated. That spring, the Volunteers received numerous distress calls from the neighboring police stations claiming to be under attack. The Oregonians would send a platoon out to the rescue, only to be ambushed en route. Other times, they would show up and find everything normal at the station. As they drove back to Patrol Base Volunteer, Mahdi Militiamen would spring an ambush. At times, the police even gave the Mahdi fighters free access to their armories. The insurgents took what they wanted, then vanished into the streets where they used those weapons against our troops.

From the observation point I had established the year before on the Sheraton Hotel, the 2–162 snipers witnessed many unsavory acts by the Iraqi Police. More than once, Buchholz saw them beating people during routine traffic stops. Engle observed them doing similar things as well. The Oregonians grew disgusted by the behavior of their erstwhile allies, but could do little about it besides report it up to the battalion operations center.

In 2004, most of the police had been recruited since the invasion from the ranks of the Shia Iraqi population. This was part of our de-Ba'athification program designed to sweep away the last vestiges of the despotic Saddam Hussein regime. Before the 2003 invasion, the police were largely composed of Sunni, who served as the oppressive bulwark for the dictatorship.

During the 2003 drive on Baghdad, my sniper section discovered how brutality was a mainstay of Iraqi police operations. We had been scouting toward the capital, several kiloyards in front of the main body of our battalion, when waves of nausea overtook me. I'd come down with some sort of stomach bug the night before, and I'd languished all morning in our Humvee's right seat, trying not to puke all over our Blue Force Tracker as we searched for the enemy.

We rounded a bend and I ordered our driver to halt. As soon as the Humvee stopped, I bailed out, grabbed an ammo crate, and made a beeline toward the side of the road. In seconds, I was running at both ends, praying that we wouldn't end up in a firefight. All I had was my 9mm pistol, which I kept holstered on my flak jacket for easy access. Between retches, I drew it and held it at my side, wishing I'd brought my rifle with me when I had slid off the truck. Of course, my gunner thought this was hilarious, and he busted out laughing while manning his weapon in the turret of our Humvee.

Meanwhile, the rest of my men dismounted and set up security. Several of them pushed up the road to clear the police station. They came back a moment later and said, "Hey, Boss, you've got to come see this."

When I was finally able to get off the crate, I followed them into the station. At first glance, it looked like a typical small-town, down-at-the-ears constabulary office. That was until the men showed me the torture chamber. The Iraqi cops would take prisoners back there, strap them onto a metal bed, and go to work on them. A car battery sat nearby with jumper cables attached. The other end of the cables dangled from hooks in the nearby wall. During sessions, these would be clipped to the bedsprings to electrocute the prisoner. The sight of such a barbaric thing filled us with grim resolve. This regime had to be destroyed.

We saw that sort of thing in nearly every police station we cleared. In April 2003, as the Iraqi Police returned to work for the first time, our unit went out on joint patrols with the cops to help put an end to the looting going on. Lieutenant Casey Kuhlman, my company executive officer, rolled out on one patrol that encountered a bank robbery in progress. The Iraqi cops caught one of the looters as he tried to escape and began beating hell out of him. On one hand, this was their country and their way of doing business. Stuff like this was going on all over Baghdad. On the other hand, this was not the way we did business, and we were here to bring a new era to the Iraqi people. Clearly, this wasn't the way to start it off. Plus, a news crew had come along for the ride, and Casey worried that this could end up being a very bad media moment. Finally, he walked up to the Iraqi police commander and said, "If you or your boys beat someone else like that today, I'll put a bullet in the back of your head before you can throw the second kick."

The cop nodded in understanding. The prisoner was loaded into a vehicle and taken away to the nearest police station, where I have no doubt a metal bed and a car battery awaited him.

Some things you cannot change overnight. When the Volunteers showed up a year later, they discovered the same behavior, different actors. The Iraqi police uniform still represented repression and fear to the people, and beatings were just part of a day's job on the street. The Shia cops turned out to be just as bad as the Sunni ones. There was a lot of payback to dish out after decades of brutal repression by the Ba'athists.

That spring, as the Oregonians tried to get a handle on the chaos, a small number of American military police injected a dangerous new dynamic into the equation. It started at the end of April when media reports surfaced alleging that American MPs were torturing detainees at Abu Ghraib prison. Photos taken by the abusers found their way into the press, and these shocking images made international news for months afterward. America lost the moral high ground in Iraq and received near universal condemnation for the twisted behavior of a few bad American cops.

The media spent weeks publishing scores of horrific photos from

Abu Ghraib. The story not only didn't go away, the scope and depth of the scrutiny increased. *The Economist* called for Secretary of Defense Donald Rumsfeld's resignation. Editorials blasting the administration, the U.S. Army, and the effort in Iraq filled hundreds of newspapers from the *Denver Post* to France's *Le Monde*.

This happened just as the American occupation of Iraq was about to enter a delicate new phase. Since the end of the initial invasion in the spring of 2003, Iraq had been governed by the Coalition Provisional Authority, a civilian agency headed by Paul Bremer, a career diplomat. This was a temporary arrangement, and Bremer planned to hand power back to an interim Iraqi government on June 30, 2004.

For the men and women patrolling the streets, Abu Ghraib stirred up massive anti-American sentiment. The ranks of the various insurgent groups swelled with indignant and hate-filled volunteers, some of whom came from all over the Muslim world to join the battle.

In the weeks that followed, the violence in Iraq intensified. In retaliation for Abu Ghraib, al-Qaida kidnapped, tortured, and beheaded American civilian contractor Nicholas Berg. His execution was videotaped by his murderers and posted on the Internet.

The Oregon snipers saw an uptick in attacks from their vantage points at the hotel and the MOI. While out on patrols with the scout platoon, they also detected a shift in the mood of the locals. Everyone in an American uniform was paying the price for what had happened at Abu Ghraib.

On June 4, 2004, the battalion lost two enlisted men and a promising platoon leader during a firefight on the edge of Sadr City. The Oregonians had rushed to the rescue of a New Jersey MP unit that had been hit by rockets, roadside bombs, and machine-gun fire. A secondary bomb detonated, killing five Americans altogether. The ambush was carried out by a cell of Mahdi Militiamen and was witnessed by several Iraqi reporters who were working for Western news agencies, including the Associated Press. Within minutes of the attack, film and photos of the dead and dying Americans were published on the Internet. Various news outlets picked them up and used them for months after. One of the reporters embedded with the enemy that day, Karim Kadim, later received an American Pulitzer Prize for photojournalism for his work during the uprising.

Aside from the firefight downtown, the snipers had yet to do anything they felt to be substantive. Maries and the rest of his section seethed at what was going on. A week after the June 4 attack, the scout platoon captured several members of the Mahdi Militia cell that carried out that operation, but the snipers were minimally involved in that coup. It seemed that everyone else in the battalion was contributing while they were sitting on their hands in the two observation points. Their frustration level grew daily.

On June 17, the snipers rotated assignments again. Kevin Maries and Keith Engle took the MOI observation point along with Darren Buchholz and one other team. Darren had lost his spotter a few weeks before and had not picked up a new one yet, so he had been working with Maries and Engle. This time, the snipers brought with them two "Fisters"—forward artillery observer—whom they hoped would help them take out the mortar and rocket teams operating out of eastern Baghdad. They would be up there for almost two weeks this time, and the snipers settled in as best they could. They shucked off their heavy body armor, left their helmets and BDU tops with the rest of their gear to stay as comfortable as possible, then took turns glassing the neighborhood. Each team had an M24, a semiautomatic Barrett .50 cal, several M4s, and Buchholz's venerable scoped M14.

One night, while Buchholz was on watch, two gunshots rang out. They seemed to have come from the nearby Iraqi Police Academy. Buchholz began glassing it. A few moments passed. Suddenly, a door to one of the academy buildings flew open and a hunched-over Iraqi cop appeared. He dragged a limp body across a courtyard and into another building. A second cop pulling another limp figure followed not long afterward.

Buchholz called Maries and Engle. The snipers conferred. This smelled like an execution. Maries radioed the battalion operations center and reported the incident. The Volunteers were later told that prisoners at the academy had rioted, leading to a crackdown by the Iraqi Police that resulted in several injuries, but no deaths. The Oregon snipers didn't buy it, but they hadn't seen enough to prove the story was a cover for something more sinister. They couldn't even be sure that the bodies dragged from the building were dead or just unconscious. Maries told his men to keep a close eye on the academy and watch for anything further that was suspicious.

A few days later, the Iraqi Police conducted a raid in Al Betawain, a Sunni Baghdad neighborhood that included a small population of African immigrants. They rounded up dozens of men, about half of whom were Sudanese. Some of them lacked passports and work papers. The police arrested them on the spot. Others displayed their documentation, which the Iraqi cops confiscated and demanded a bribe for their return. The police detained anyone who couldn't pay the bribe. They also arrested a few who did shell out the money. The detainees, which included elderly men and young boys, were bound and blindfolded and packed into waiting buses.

That afternoon, Keith Engle was on watch. He had his own .50 caliber Barrett beside him, Maries's M24 bolt-action rifle, their spotting scope, and a pair of M22 binoculars. Instead of using his scopes, he happened to have the binos in hand when a bus drove up alongside the Police Academy's main wall and lurched to a halt. A bunch of police officers appeared, some of whom were armed with sticks and rubber hoses. They began pulling men off the bus and lining them up single file.

Keith observed this with great interest. He had heard nothing of the Al Betawain raid, and this was the first time any of the Oregon snipers had seen prisoners delivered to the academy.

The Iraqi police shoved and kicked their detainees until they were lined up to their satisfaction. Engle counted thirty of them. Toward the front of the line, two cops grabbed a prisoner, who tried to resist. Bad move. The cops dragged him out of the line and threw him into the dirt. Another Iraqi policeman rushed over to help. Together, the three began whipping the detainee with rubber hoses.

Engle's jaw dropped. He'd seen police beatings before, but the sheer viciousness of this one left him spellbound in horror. He pulled his eyes from the binos and called to one of the forward observers, "Go get Sergeant Maries. He needs to see this."

Maries, who had been on his sleep cycle, appeared next to Engle a few minutes later and asked, "What've you got, Keith?"

He pointed down to the bus. Maries got behind his spotter scope and watched the tail end of the beating. It had lasted five minutes. The detainee had been flayed from head to foot by the rubber hoses and was flopping around in the dirt, wracked with pain. At length, the police pulled him to his feet and pushed him back into the line.

After that, nobody else offered any resistance.

About a dozen police now patrolled the line of detainees. After a few minutes, the entire group was led into a walled compound next to the Iraqi Police Academy, where they disappeared into a rectangular-shaped building.

More buses arrived. Each one parked in the dead space between the compound and the academy. The drill was always the same: the police would herd the detainees off the bus, line them up, and lead them into the rectangular building. By the end of the day, Engle counted ninety-three detainees offloaded from three buses.

This compound, which had been virtually unused prior to this development, began to bustle with activity. More cops showed up until eighteen stood guard around the rectangular building. Others periodically went inside, retrieved a prisoner, then took him to a smaller building on the other side of the compound.

The next morning, Maries, Engle, and Buchholz watched as a group of cops congregated on a small concrete pad in front of the rectangular building. A wooden overhang shielded them from the summer sun as they stood around, talking animatedly to each other. Some of them held rubber hoses and aluminum bars that the snipers recognized as spreaders for U.S. Army–issue cots.

They smoked and joked for a while, then two cops tied handkerchiefs behind their necks, covered their mouth and noses with them, and approached the main entrance to the building, hefting a rubber hose and a bar. They flung the door open and plunged inside. Some of their brethren gravitated toward the windows, which the snipers could not see through.

Minutes passed. The two cops emerged, smiling and laughing. The others clustered around them as they began talking. Through their scopes, the Oregonians saw the two cops use their hoses and the cot spreader to pantomime beating somebody. They hammered at their invisible subject, then pretended to be their victims. They cringed and cowered. The other Iraqi cops burst out laughing. Two more of them put on handkerchiefs and went into the building. They came back with fresh tales to tell the others.

Maries reported this to the battalion operation center, but since the Volunteers had already become jaded about the behavior of the local police, the battalion took no action. To those who weren't witness to the beating beside the bus, this seemed like normal Baghdad cop behavior—thuggish and wrong, but not the U.S. Army's problem.

The refusal to do anything rankled Maries. He had seen enough of how the cops operated to know that what was going on in this little compound beside the academy represented a level of violence not seen on the street. Though he had no conclusive proof, it appeared that the police were systematically torturing their detainees.

And it continued throughout the day. Pairs of cops would enter the building with blunt weapons, emerge and be replaced by two more. Each time they came out, they would recount to the other officers waiting outside what just happened.

While the snipers kept watch over the compound, forces far above their pay grade clicked into motion. Paul Bremer disbanded the Coalition Provisional Authority two days ahead of schedule and turned over control to the interim Iraqi government. After a year of occupation, Iraq was once again a sovereign nation, which meant that the U.S. military had to defer to the new government in the course of its operations.

Bremer boarded a flight home on the morning of June 28, 2004, just as Keith Engle took a shift behind his Barrett. For the past few days, the activity in the compound had settled down to a grim routine. The eighteen guards on hand took turns going inside the building carrying blunt objects or hoses. They never took food or water inside, and the snipers hadn't seen the prisoners since the first day they'd been brought in. As a result, they had no way to determine their condition, or whether they were actually being harmed.

The police broke the routine later that morning when two of them dragged a prisoner out of the building and dumped him in the middle of the compound's courtyard. A gaggle of cops piled on him, hoses and spreader bars flailing. They kicked, punched, and beat him as he rolled in the dirt, hands tied behind his back and his eyes blindfolded. Finally, the police lifted him off the ground and flung him, headfirst, against the side of a white pickup truck. The detainee collapsed in a heap, knocked cold from the impact.

Maries joined Engle in time to watch the beating. Keith fumed with anger and wanted to start shooting cops to put an end to the mistreatment. Kevin Maries calmed him down, "Look, we're going to sit tight, observe, and report." Besides smoke-checking guys who need it, this is the primary mission snipers have. Engle, who had not yet been with the section for a full year—and had not gone to sniper school yet either—forced himself to be more patient. He stowed his emotions, though inside he still seethed. Later he recalled, "I was indignant. It was like watching your neighbor abuse his dog and being unable to do anything about it." He felt sick.

As the cops hauled the unconscious man back inside the building, Maries reported the incident over the radio to the battalion operations center. This time, the level of violence the snipers witnessed, combined with the other reports, alarmed Lieutenant Colonel Hendrickson. Had the incident happened the day before, he would have gone to investigate. But that morning, Bremer was somewhere in the air en route home and that left the Iraqis in charge. Hendrickson no longer had the authority to burst into an Iraqi Police facility and demand to know what was going on. It was their sovereign business now, no matter how ugly.

The next morning, June 29, 2004, Maries was on watch behind the scope when a group of guards gathered at the concrete pad. All at once, they poured into the rectangular building, armed with 2x4 wooden boards, more hoses, and cot spreaders. A few cops remained outside and took station at the window to watch whatever was going on inside. About a half hour passed with no further activity, then a group of Iraqi civilians approached the compound from a driveway that led to the Ministry of Interior's main entrance. The snipers concluded that these new arrivals had come from the very building they were observing from.

The guards rushed to open a gate, and the civilians walked into the compound with an air of authority. Leading the group was a paunchy and balding middle-aged Iraqi who sported a Saddam Hussein mustache and spectacles. He wore a pale yellow button-down shirt, green slacks, and carried a holstered pistol on his right hip. He held a sheaf of papers in one hand.

Maries called the rest of his team. Buchholz and Engle showed up and got behind their scopes. Maries had the M24. Buchholz and Engle manned the Barretts. All three fixed their eyes to their optics, dreading what they might see next.

Right away, they noticed how the Iraqi cops deferred to the man in the yellow shirt. Some took it to the extreme and acted obsequious. Upon Yellow Shirt's command, several of the uniformed officers scurried off to the rectangular building to fetch a table and some chairs. They carried them outside and placed them in the shade of a tree in the courtyard. Another cop placed a ream of blank paper on the right side of the desk. The man in the yellow shirt passed his paperwork to a minion, who sorted it and created two haphazard stacks on the desk. Somebody else put a black ballpoint pen beside one stack.

Maries, Engle, and Buchholz realized something very bad was brewing. They grabbed their digital cameras so they could document whatever would go down next. By now, there was a mix of uniformed cops and men dressed in civilian clothes hanging around Yellow

Shirt. Who the plainclothed guys were kept the snipers guessing, but the uniforms seemed almost afraid of them.

Yellow Shirt gave another order. The uniforms armed themselves and went into the rectangular building. A few minutes later, they whipped, beat, and pushed about thirty prisoners out into the courtyard. Maries noted the detainees seemed weak and unsteady on their feet. They stumbled across the courtyard until the police shoved them to the ground near a Toyota pickup truck. Without shade, the mid-morning sun beat down on them. Already the temperature was over a hundred degrees. This new development had cowed the prisoners, who crossed their legs and kept their heads bowed. Some trembled with fear.

The cops went back in and pulled another twenty more men out. Arrayed in four loose rows, some of the detainees couldn't even stay upright. They slumped to the dirt, bound and blindfolded.

The man in the yellow shirt stood by the desk and waited. A few other Iraqi Police, dressed in dark gray slacks and sky blue uniform shirts, hovered nearby. Several other men, all in civilian clothes, wandered around near the table, talking amongst themselves.

Then some cops strutted over to the rows of detainees, selected one man seemingly at random, and dragged him over to the table, where the man in the yellow shirt tried to get him to sign some kind of document. To Maries, it looked like they were trying to coerce him into signing a confession.

The man refused. An Iraqi policeman and a civilian Iraqi, both holding rubber hoses, threw him to the ground. He landed on his bound hands and lay on his back, still blindfolded. A cop carrying an AK-47 in his right hand stood nearby, watching casually with his left hand stuffed in a pants pocket.

An order was given. The two men wielding hoses slammed their weapons down on the prisoner. They tore his shirt open so the rubber would do more damage to his skin. Another Iraqi police officer appeared with a cot spreader. He began to beat his legs. The man in the yellow shirt peered down at the prisoner, then stepped forward until he was by his side. He spoke to him, but apparently did not get the answer he wanted. The beating continued. Another hose-carrying policeman stepped up to take his turn. Looking down at the prisoner, he rolled his sleeves above his elbows and laid into the man, who was still lying on back. Moments later, yet another policeman boot-stomped the prisoner's head. The man in the yellow shirt reached for his pistol. His fingers touched its butt, but he didn't draw it from the holster. The police continued the beating.

Engle had seen enough. Behind his Barrett, he begged Maries to let him engage. Buchholz was at the same point. All three snipers had their crosshairs trained on Yellow Shirt and two of the most violent police officers. One word, and their fingers would have slipped into their trigger guards, and three men would die.

The man in the yellow shirt did nothing for a few moments, choosing to regard the action while still next to the writhing man. Then he thrust his hands out, as if to halt it. He began making hand gestures that appeared to indicate he was coaching them on their technique. The cops paid close attention to the lesson. Meanwhile, another detainee, this one in dark pants and a dark shirt, was culled from the ranks and taken over to the table. They forced him to sit and listen, blindfolded, as the police continued working over the first man.

It dawned on Buchholz right then what was going on. He said later, "We were watching a torture-training exercise. With live victims."

Engle could barely contain his rage. He had Yellow Shirt in his scope. Three hundred yards, an easy shot. "Do you want me to take him out?" he asked Maries.

"No."

"Come on, Kevin."

"No."

The beating finally ended, and the police pulled the prisoner over to the desk. The man in the yellow shirt stood next to him, as did several police officers and a civilian-dressed Iraqi. Not long after, he was pushed back to the main group of detainees.

Then it was the dark-clothed prisoner's turn.

This went on for about half an hour. Maries radioed reports to the battalion operations center, giving a running commentary at times of the beatings.

A few prisoners signed the paperwork, and they were not beaten. Most did not, and the police unleashed an escalating level of violence. They struck one detainee in the head repeatedly with a spreader bar. Engle captured one of the blows with his camera. The cop was in mid-swing and the bar glowed silver with the reflection of the morning sun.

The police seemed to grow frustrated. When the next prisoner was dragged to the table, the beating commenced before Maries even saw the man's mouth move. He never had a chance to sign the confession. The police simply lit into him. The man in the yellow shirt reached for his pistol again as two cops knocked the detainee down and slid a spreader bar under his legs in order to raise his feet off the ground. A third police officer began whipping the soles of the man's feet with a black hose.

That was enough for Maries. Though outwardly calm, he'd watched the situation grow ever more violent with growing disgust and moral outrage. The battalion staff had taken his reports, but had offered no guidance or response. Now, as the man in the yellow shirt played his fingers across the butt of his pistol again, Maries decided it was time to end this.

He keyed his radio, "Okay, you've been taking my reports all morning. Nothing's been done. If they continue to escalate, I'm going to shoot somebody."

The NCO on the horn at the ops center replied, "That is not within the Rules of Engagement."

Maries bristled at that. "I know what the ROEs are," he barked, "and if they escalate, I will engage with deadly force."

Lieutenant Colonel Dan Hendrickson, who was at one of the downtown hotels, heard this. He cut into the conversation, "Negative. You will not engage. I'm on my way."

It was a direct order from his commanding officer. Maries seethed, but acknowledged it.

Maries checked the time. It was about 1130. The beatings had been going on since 0900. He knew it would take Hendrickson up to an hour to get to the compound from the hotels. In the meantime, all he could do was watch and wait.

Right about then, the police officers returned to the cluster of detainees. They reached down and yanked a teenaged boy to his feet. Blindfolded and bound like the rest of the prisoners, the boy quailed in his captor's grip. He looked perhaps fourteen years old.

Eye in his scope, Maries saw this and recoiled. He was a father of two young children, and the thought of what lay in store for the boy made his stomach churn. For just a moment, he lost his legendary composure.

"Oh Jesus Christ . . . what are they going to do to that kid?"

The cops led the teenager over to the table, where the man in the yellow shirt was waiting.

Maries fingered his trigger and whispered, "Not the kid. Not the kid."

Things were about to get really ugly.

CHAPTER TWENTY
Where Shades of Gray Are Found

Every sniper has faced a moral choice while looking through his scope. When your career involves watching people who don't know they are being watched, you're bound to see sordid and questionable things. You'll see the worst of human nature; you may see the best as well. Life behind the scope is not one of moral black and whites, not when so much of the world exists in shades of gray. In those moments, our spiritual constitution is tested. In our profession, we have to make choices, we have to take that leap into the chaos of moral ambiguity. When we do, some of us never recover from the hardest decisions we've had to make.

Head down and stooped like an old man, the boy looked like he had already been worked over and now sensed he was in for more. His narrow, lime green blindfold was wrapped tight against his face, and the Iraqi police had tied his wrists with yellow cord. The cops parked him in front of the table and untied his hands. The boy's shoulders sagged; his arms fell to his side. One of the uniforms pointed to the paperwork as he said something to the boy, which seemed a pointless gesture since the boy obviously could not see anything.

The boy shook his head.

The Iraqi cop pointed to the paperwork again. The boy shook his head one more time. The police were not pleased.

Eye glued to his scope, Maries watched this with a sick sense of helplessness. He had been ordered not to engage and kill our erstwhile allies. The consequences of an American sniper killing a uniformed Iraqi police officer could have severely damaged the United States' relationship with the freshly established interim Iraqi government. Unlike the street fight several weeks before, these cops had not made any overt hostile act against U.S. troops. There would be hell to pay if they started dropping these guys. It would mean inquiries, maybe even a court-martial and jail time. At the very least, their careers would be over.

Kevin understood all of that. But how could he allow these thugs to beat a boy with an aluminum bar? He began to run through his options. There weren't any.

Then, to his surprise, the cops gave him an out. They gave up on the boy without inflicting any punishment on him. They tied his hands again and returned him to the main group of prisoners. The police pushed him down next to an older man whose left hand hung at an odd angle. Maries studied the two and concluded the older man was the boy's father. The father's wrist looked broken.

Right then, a green Humvee rumbled through the compound's main entrance. Maries and Keith Engle breathed a sigh of relief as they watched the rest of their scout platoon reach the scene. Lieutenant Colonel Dan Hendrickson dismounted from the lead truck, his face set with an expression of pure anger as he sized up the situation.

Dan Hendrickson did not see the world in shades of gray. He'd spent his life as a protector and warrior—first as a regular army officer, then later as a lieutenant in the Corvallis, Oregon, Police Department. Now he served as the battalion commander for 2–162. To him, laws were in place for a reason; he adhered to them and upheld them with everything he did as a cop and a Guardsman. He expected his men to do the same. Before leaving for Iraq, he'd repeatedly told his staff to "do the right thing." He was determined to get the battalion through their Iraq deployment by seizing and holding the moral high ground. He had to be the example for the other seven hundred American citizen-soldiers he'd taken into Baghdad with him.

Hendrickson stood next to his Humvee regarding the prisoners.

Bound, bloody, and bruised, they languished in the sun. Some appeared to be unconscious. The Iraqi Police, some of whom were holding AK-47s and other weapons, congregated under the overhang at the front of the rectangular building. Engle and Maries saw anger and surprise on their faces.

Flanked by members of his staff, Hendrickson strode up to the Iraqis and demanded, "Who's in charge here?"

One of the Iraqi police officers countered, "What's the matter? Why are you here?"

To their left, some of the prisoners were moaning. A few screamed in agony. Through the battalion interpreter, Hendrickson repeatedly asked who was in charge. The Iraqis evaded the question. An argument broke out. The uniformed Iraqi Police grew still and docile. The civilian-clothed ones became belligerent.

Maries and Engle watched this unfold from their scopes. The man in the yellow shirt remained at a distance. Then a small group of scouts, led by the platoon leader, Lieutenant Ross Boyce, moved around to the back of the rectangular building. The snipers kept a close eye on the police just in case the tension broke into outright violence.

At the back of the building, Lieutenant Boyce and his men discovered a bamboo enclosure. Upon entering, the Americans found bloodstains on the building's rear wall. Then the stench hit them: the pungent, heavy reek of rotting corpses. The air was thick with it, and the men would smell it in their uniforms for days after.

There was a door in the rear wall. Sergeant Tyson Bumgardner, a keenly intelligent NCO of about twenty-two, moved to it and made ready to gain entrance. "Bum," as he was known within the platoon, had joined the Guard at age seventeen while still attending Churchill High School in Eugene, Oregon. Now, half a world away from the sleepy college town he called home, he opened the door to a charnel house beyond his worst nightmares.

From his sniper hide three hundred yards away, Maries saw them disappear inside and swung his scope over to his battalion commander. Lieutenant Colonel Hendrickson remained locked in an argument with the civilian-attired Iraqis. They continued to stonewall, and his pissed-off meter was clearly about to be pegged. Hendrickson was known around the battalion as a blunt, no-nonsense officer who did not tolerate red tape or bullshit. The Iraqis were throwing shovelfuls of the latter at him.

Finally, the man in the yellow shirt stepped forward and announced he was a major with the Iraqi Police. Hendrickson directed his attention on him and demanded to know what was going on. The Iraqi major ignored his question and wanted to know why Hendrickson had burst into his compound. The situation escalated further, and both leaders were soon shouting at each other through the battalion interpreter.

Just inside the back door, Bumgardner and Boyce stopped in their tracks as the acidic reek of urine assailed their nostrils. Beneath it lingered another odor, one of corruption and filth. Recalled Boyce, "It smelled like a Third World morgue."

The men were in a narrow hallway with two doors set in intervals on the left wall. Bumgardner stepped to the first one and flung it open. Three surprised Iraqi police officers swiveled their heads to him and froze. The Oregon sergeant had caught them in the middle of torturing a bound and blindfolded prisoner.

Blind fury spurred Bumgardner into the room. He pushed the prisoner out of the way as the Iraqis began yelling in broken English, "No! No! No! This is not what you think! Is okay!"

Bumgardner grabbed the nearest police officer by the neck and pushed him into a wall. Tyson, who stood well over six feet and was built like an NFL tight end, dwarfed the cop. He pinned him in place and held the cop's neck in a vise grip.

"What the hell are you doing?" he shouted at the terrified policeman.

"Hey Tyson, why don't you come on out now?" said a calm voice from the doorway. Bumgardner tore his eyes from the cops' and saw Master Sergeant Jeff McDowell, his old platoon sergeant, waving for him to step back into the hallway.

That broke the spell. He released his hold on the man and went into the hallway to compose himself. Meanwhile, Boyce and McDowell cut the prisoner loose and gave him some water.

Captain Jarrell Southall, a middle school history teacher in his civilian life, stood beside Tyson and trembled with rage. He was the battalion's personnel officer, but he also spoke Arabic and was a practicing Sunni Muslim. For those reasons, Hendrickson had brought him along. Southall had his nine millimeter pistol unholstered and held low.

McDowell and Boyce finished tending to the prisoner—to the utter bafflement of the Iraqi cops, then walked back into the hallway. The Oregon Guardsmen exchanged glances and wondered what lay behind door number two.

In the courtyard, the scout platoon's medic and combat lifesavers went to work assessing the prisoners. Kyle Trimble was one of the latter. He'd gone to high school with Tyson Bumgardner and had made the decision to join the Guard together with him. Tyson had become a squad leader in the scouts while Kyle had been waiting to go to sniper school when the deployment came up.

The wounds the prisoners had sustained affected Trimble deeply. The men showed signs of being burned. Their faces, backs, and arms were covered with lacerations and purple-red bruises. One had a suppurating gunshot wound to the knee. The bullet's entry wound was a ragged, infected hole ringed with blue-black rotting flesh.

As the Oregonians began triaging the prisoners, Trimble noticed several of the Iraqi policemen staring at him. They seemed puzzled. He got the sense that the Iraqis did not know they were doing anything wrong, as if flaying flesh off captives with rubber hoses was just a normal day at work.

Recalled Trimble, "The vibe they were giving us was very, very strange."

Under the unsettling gaze of the Iraqi cops, Trimble opened his combat lifesaver bag and busied himself with tending to some of the lesser injured men. Mike Giordano, the platoon's medic, focused his efforts on the most severely affected, some of whom lapsed into unconsciousness as the Americans moved them into the shade.

Back inside the building, Lieutenant Boyce nodded to Bumgardner and told him to open door number two. The young sergeant turned the knob and pushed through it into a room about the size of half a basketball court.

It was jam-packed with moaning, suffering men. Some lay semiconscious in their own urine and feces, bleeding from open wounds. Some seemed delirious. Others had fallen into stupors. The prisoners who still had the strength sat cross-legged, chins draped on their chests. The smell was so overpowering that Bumgardner nearly vomited.

To Jarrell Southall, the room looked like photos he'd seen of Dachau and Buchenwald—the Nazi concentration camps the U.S. Army liberated at the end of World War II. The room felt like a furnace. Without open windows or air-conditioning, it was easily over a hundred degrees inside. There was no water in sight. Even if there was water available, the prisoners would not have been able to drink. Every one of them had their hands tied behind their back with the same yellow rope Maries had seen on the teenaged boy.

The Iraqi Police had been nothing if not thorough.

Southall tried to talk to a couple of the prisoners, telling them in Arabic that he was a Sunni Muslim. At first, nobody responded to him. Then Southall recited the Shahada, the Muslim profession of Faith.

"I bear witness that there is no deity (none truly to be worshipped) but Allah, and I bear witness that Muhammad is the messenger of Allah."

That broke the silence. Several of the Sudanese captives began to tell their story. Southall listened as they recounted their sudden arrest, how their passports and work visas had been confiscated by the police. A few told him that even after they paid bribes for the return of the documentation, they were detained anyway. Others didn't have the money for a bribe. They were among the first arrested.

Southall reported all this to Lieutenant Boyce, who had seen enough. He went back outside and found Lieutenant Colonel Hendrickson in mid-argument with the man in the yellow shirt.

"Sir," Boyce interrupted, "I think you need to come see this."

Hendrickson followed his young lieutenant into the building

and saw for himself the condition of the other detainees. Captain Southall, Bumgardner, and Master Sergeant McDowell reported to their commander that they had found torture implements and photographs taken while the police officers tortured the fourteen-year-old boy Maries and Engle had seen dragged to the table.

Southall had learned that the cops had been pouring some sort of chemical agent into the eyes of their prisoners during these torture sessions. Others told him they had been burned, or had been electrocuted with a lamp whose bulb had been broken. The scouts searched the area and found the chemicals and the lamp, as well as more hoses, sticks, and aluminum bars.

Already furious at being stonewalled by the Iraqi police, the sights and smells roused him to immediate action. He ordered Sergeant Major Brunk Conley to get all the prisoners outside so they could be assessed and treated. As Conley set to that task, Hendrickson stormed back outside and told his men to disarm the Iraqi cops.

The move stunned the police. They gave up their weapons grudgingly, but made no move to resist. Soon, a stack of AK-47s rose in the courtyard. The torture implements were laid out nearby. Some of the scouts began taking photos to document this evidence.

From their observation point, Maries and Engle watched all this unfold with a sense of tremendous satisfaction. Engle saw Lieutenant Colonel Hendrickson spin one police officer around and pin his hands behind his head. Hendrickson had been a cop himself for too long not to take part in the disarming and detention of these thugs.

When Conley began getting the rest of the prisoners outside, Engle spotted the man who'd been knocked unconscious when he had been slammed into a car a few days before. He got on the radio and told Lieutenant Boyce what had happened to the man so Giordano could check him for head trauma. Within minutes, the platoon's medic had put him on a stretcher with a neck brace and began giving him intravenous fluids.

As the other scouts rounded up the Iraqi Police and put them in one spot so they could be watched, Hendrickson turned his attention back to the Iraqi major. The major flatly told Hendrickson, "We have done nothing wrong here."

Behind them, the scouts carried a writhing, screaming man out of the building and set him under the overhang. Kyle Trimble and Doc Giordano rushed to his side.

"How can you say that?" Hendrickson demanded.

"These are hardened criminals!" the major declared.

Hendrickson thought of the fourteen-year-old boy and guffawed. The major demanded that his men receive their weapons back. The Oregon commander refused. The shouting match continued for a few more minutes until, seeing nothing was going to be accomplished, Hendrickson turned and walked away. He radioed the battalion operations center and talked directly to his executive officer, Major Edward Tanguy. Tanguy reported the situation to 2–162's higher headquarters, the Arkansas National Guard's 39th Enhanced Brigade. He reported the situation and the conditions at the compound to the brigade executive officer, who told Tanguy to stand by while he talked with the 39th's commander, Brigadier General Ronald Chastain.

While Tanguy and Hendrickson waited for guidance from General Chastain, the scouts continued to work on the prisoners. The Americans went from man to man, removing their blindfolds and cutting the yellow cords that bound their arms so painfully. Kyle Trimble and Giordano focused on the writhing man who had been carried out of the building a few minutes before. His filthy blindfold had been tied so tightly to his face, and had remained on for so long, that it had damaged his eyes. Trimble had to cut it off, then peel it from his face. The man's eyes were shrunken back, a sure sign of extreme dehydration. He wailed in agony as the two Americans spoke gently to him and tried to start an IV.

Trimble attempted it first, but he couldn't get the tiny flash of blood in the cotton stuffed in the backside of the needle that indicated he had found a vein. He tried again. The man began to sob. Unable to open his eyes, his hands scrabbled weakly in search of whoever was assisting him. His fingers found Trimble's boot, and he grabbed hold for a moment.

"Thank you, thank you," he said in English through broken teeth.

The man was wearing a sweat suit soaked with perspiration. Trimble knew he had to get fluids into the man or he would most likely die. Fluids would only be a start—he needed hospitalization fast.

He punctured the man's skin again with the needle, gently moving the tip into what he thought was a vein. This time, he saw a tiny dot of blood bloom on the cotton. Then the vein collapsed. He started over. Same result.

Giordi tried next. As he worked to get the IV started, Trimble cut the man's sweatpants off him and began pouring bottles of water over his legs to cool him off.

"Thankyouthankyouthankyou," the man cried to his unseen saviors.

Trimble cut his sweatshirt open to get more cool water on his body. His chest and stomach were a latticework of bruises, gashes, and lacerations.

"Kyle, he's too dehydrated to get a needle in him," Giordi said. Kyle nodded, knowing that the only solution was to go in rectally.

"I got this, keep working," the medic told him.

Kyle stood up and went to find another patient. As he moved through the rows of prisoners, the Sudanese called out, thanking him over and over. The Iraqi detainees were quiet, sullen, and looked tense.

Against the wall of the rectangular building, Trimble noticed an Iraqi prisoner with a brown-black bandage wrapped around one arm. He went to his side and the stench of rotted flesh hit him before he could even kneel down. The man regarded him with utter hate in his eyes. Trimble later said, "He gave me the look of death."

Trimble helped him to his feet. The man offered no resistance. After moving him away from the main group of prisoners, the Oregonian eased him to the ground and unwrapped his bandage.

A suppurating, prurient wound ran along the length of his arm. He'd been gashed by some sort of ragged weapon, and without antibiotics or immediate medical care, it had become infected. The infection had turned gangrenous. It seemed almost pointless to treat it. Kyle knew it would almost surely have to be amputated at this point to save the man's life.

He began to clean it anyway. Carefully, he covered the wound in iodine to disinfect it, then he poured antibiotic ointment on it. The stench appalled him, but Trimble forced himself to make no sign of the revulsion he felt. As he started to wrap the wound with fresh gauze, he chanced a look in the prisoner's eyes. They were softer now, the hate replaced by gratitude.

Lieutenant Boyce was standing near Lieutenant Colonel Hendrickson when Ed Tanguy came back over the radio.

"Sir, the Thirty-Ninth Brigade says to stand down."

Dan Hendrickson was a man of supreme self-possession who concealed a deeply caring and emotional nature with a gruff and stoic demeanor. The scenes around the compound had already caused his indignation to crack that wall. Now Ed's words left him dumbfounded, unable to hide their effect.

Ross Boyce stiffened. He thought he hadn't heard the order right. "What? What?!" he sputtered.

In the MOI, Kevin Maries had tuned a radio to the battalion frequency. He, Keith Engle, and Darren Buchholz heard the order and stared at each other in complete astonishment.

"What are they talking about?" Engle managed. "We're doing the right thing here."

Maries, ever the picture of calm, could only utter a curse. Buchholz, who had been watching his friend Kyle Trimble treat the prisoners, felt a swell of pure outrage. To him, the entire operation looked like a "torture training" exercise. How could this be acceptable in anyone's rulebook?

Especially coming less than two months after Abu Ghraib.

The order left the snipers in momentary disarray while Hendrickson stood next to his Humvee and battled to regain his composure. At length, he keyed his radio and told his exec, "You need to tell the Thirty-Ninth Brigade this is not something we can walk away from."

"Roger."

Ed called the 39th Brigade and relayed the message. In the meantime, the rest of the scouts learned of the order. Once they recovered from their shock, they worked even faster. Hendrickson had given them a few extra precious minutes to do what they could for the worst affected prisoners.

The seconds ticked off too fast. Tanguy's voice came over the radio, "The order stands."

Hendrickson was not having it. "We cannot turn this over to the Iraqi Police."

The Oregonians had no legal authority to be there. Thanks to the early changeover of power, they were infringing on the activities of a sovereign nation's police force. Had this all happened three days before, the scouts could have arrested the entire Iraqi Police detachment and released the prisoners themselves. Not now.

No legal authority, perhaps. But the moral authority was clear to every American in the compound. Kyle Trimble recalled, "No matter who these prisoners were, you have to provide medical aid to those in need. That is common humanity."

Nobody was under any illusions here. If Hendrickson pulled out, the police would win. It would vindicate their sense that they had done nothing wrong. The beatings and torture would continue. Several of the prisoners were already urgent medical evacuation casualties. If the Americans left, these men faced agonizing deaths.

"Volunteer Six," Tanguy called to Hendrickson, "The Thirty-Ninth Brigade says you need to leave. Now. There is no discussion here."

The cop from Corvallis refused to give up, "Have you talked to First Cav?" The 1st Cavalry Division was the 39th Brigade's higher command. Hendrickson was trying to go above Brigadier General Chastain's head, a very risky move.

Major Tanguy had heard enough from the 39th Brigade to sense that the Volunteers were skating on thin ice. If Hendrickson pushed this, Tanguy feared he would be relieved on the spot.

"Six, Thirty-Ninth Brigade says you need to leave now," Tanguy reiterated.

Hendrickson frowned in abject disgust and looked at Boyce. *Options?*

An idea came to Boyce, "Sir, Brigadier General Jones's office is in the MOI main building. We can walk over there and we can grab somebody from his office to come see this. Or, if he's there, we can get him to come see this for himself." Jones was the 1st Cav's assistant division commander.

"Okay, let's do it."

Boyce, Hendrickson, and a couple of the scouts began walking toward the compound's main gate. They had three hundred yards to cover. They walked in silence.

They had only taken a few steps when Major Tanguy radioed, "Six, we need confirmation that you are leaving."

Hendrickson tried to buy time, "I'm having trouble hearing you."

Tanguy wasn't buying it. The 39th Brigade was breathing down his neck. It felt to him like they were not going to wait much longer to fire his battalion commander. He needed to impart the sense of urgency he was feeling.

"Six, we need confirmation you are leaving," he repeated.

"You're breaking up," Hendrickson said again.

Ross Boyce could hear the tension rising over the radio. The escalation made him fear his commander was about to be relieved, too.

Hendrickson stopped walking. He'd grown up the son of a U.S. Air Force F-86 Sabre Jet pilot who had fought in the Korean War. He'd played football in high school and at Cabrillo Junior College in Santa Cruz, California. His life had been founded and built around discipline, attention to detail, and following orders. He had never disobeyed a direct order.

He wanted to disobey this one. Badly. If he did, and he was fired, Major Tanguy would take over the battalion and the Volunteers would be withdrawn anyway. What purpose would it serve to push the 39th into firing him?

He turned to Ross Boyce and spoke over the radio, "Okay, 2–162, we're leaving. Now."

Sheer disgust greeted the order among the scouts. Captain South-all initially refused to leave. So did some of the scouts. Kyle Trimble tried to get the prisoners in need of urgent medical care evacuated with the platoon, but that request was denied. "At least let us finish what we're doing here," he pleaded.

No luck. Trimble was able to finish wrapping the gangrenous arm in a new bandage, grab his combat lifesaver gag, and get to the Humvees as the rest of the platoon mounted up. Mike Giordano was forced to stop working on the desperately dehydrated man and join the rest of the platoon as well.

The Iraqi Police looked triumphant. Several started for their AKs and torture implements. Fearing reprisal and a possible shoot-out, the scouts lowered their weapons and warned the Iraqi cops away from their guns.

When the last Humvee passed through the main entrance, the Iraqi cops knew they were in the clear. Captain Southall watched them pick up their weapons and head for the prisoners. With hope of salvation gone, the Oregon snipers saw terror bloom in the eyes of these helpless men.

Maries pulled his eye from his spotter scope and spoke to his snipers. Back in Oregon, he had handpicked each one of them. He was their leader, their mentor. Most had learned more about the snip-er's craft from Maries than they had at the schoolhouse in Little Rock.

What had just happened left them reeling. The high ground was gone, stolen from them by their own chain of command. The ugly, real world grayness had swallowed them whole.

Yet, this thing wasn't over. The snipers were Hendrickson's trump, and Maries knew it. The 39th Brigade hadn't said anything about pulling out of the MOI position. For now, he and his men weren't going anywhere.

CHAPTER TWENTY-ONE
The Lifesavers

All afternoon, the snipers studied every move the Iraqi cops made. A small American military police unit showed up. They talked with their Iraqi counterparts for a short time, then left. As soon as the last American cleared the compound, the cops went right back to beating and torturing the detainees.

Keith Engle seethed at the sight. He wanted to engage. So did Darren Buchholz, who lay beside Maries with his Barrett .50 cal. Maries controlled his own helpless rage by going stone cold. They documented everything and continued to report each development to the battalion operations center.

The American MP unit returned that afternoon. With their return, the beatings ceased. Not long after, a motorcade of black armored SUVs rolled into the compound and parked near the overhang. They were armored and had smoke-black tinted windows. Maries, Engle, and Buchholz all began taking photographs as men dismounted. Engle snapped his photos through a pair of binoculars. Maries worked with his spotting scope. So did Buchholz.

The Oregon snipers recoiled when they saw who they'd just caught on camera. The men who dismounted were all Caucasian Westerners. They had black bulletproof vests and carried folding stock variants of the AK-47. All of them were dressed in civilian clothes. They moved swiftly and with professional acumen to set up security around their rigs. A moment later, another white male, this one dressed in a slate gray business suit, appeared from one of the SUVs.

"Who the hell is that fucking guy?" Engle asked in shock.

He had medium-length gray hair that almost looked like a pompadour from three hundred yards away. He walked with a stiffness that seemed to Maries to indicate he was not an American.

Maries studied these new arrivals as they headed to meet with Yellow Shirt. The guys with the AK-47s were clearly the gray-haired man's personal security detail. Since reaching Baghdad in April, the snipers had seen all sorts of contract security types, especially down at the hotels. All of the American companies issued their people M4 rifles and .45 caliber pistols. The only mercenaries he'd encountered carrying Soviet bloc weaponry worked for a British company called Parson Limited.

Because of this and the more formal way he walked, Maries began to think of Gray Hair as a Brit.

Whoever he was, the Iraqis treated him with deference. He met them at the overhang in front of the rectangular building. The cops clustered around him. In the far back of the circle stood a tall Caucasian-looking male in a black shirt. Nobody had any idea who he was.

The MP's moved to the gray-haired man's right and listened to him as he addressed the Iraqi Police. Heads nodded. A few of the Iraqis spoke. The meeting lasted a half hour, then the gray-haired man walked out of the compound and headed for the Ministry of Interior's main building. Maries leapt to his feet and told his men to stay put and keep their eyes on the compound. He set off to find the gray-haired man.

He dashed downstairs as quickly as he could, but by the time he got to the lobby, the man was nowhere in sight. He searched several floors and then gave up.

Maries returned to the hide site just in time to see a gaggle of civilian Iraqi officials show up at the compound. The man in the yellow shirt talked with them for several minutes, then turned and gave some orders to his minions. A few minutes later, the cops began lining all the detainees up in the courtyard again. The snipers counted ninety-three altogether.

The Iraqi cops brought the prisoners cigarettes, food, and water. Those who could ate. Others were too far gone to do so. They smoked in silence as the snipers covertly examined them through their scopes. Thirty-five of the ninety-three were Sudanese. They also noticed a Caucasian detainee in the mix.

The Iraqi officials left just before 1800. The MPs were long gone by that point, and the snipers figured their departure would herald a new round of beatings.

Not this time. The cops appeared to be in enforced merciful mode after the arrival of so much brass. Soon, they let the prisoners bathe in the courtyard. Just before sunset, they selected a dozen men, escorted them to the main gate and let them go. The prisoners hobbled out into the street in front of the Ministry of Interior and disappeared into Baghdad traffic.

The next day, the police released another batch of prisoners. With great satisfaction, the snipers saw the fourteen-year-old boy and his broken-wristed father in the mix. They were lucky to escape. Eventually, Maries and his men saw the police release about sixty of their prisoners. What happened to the last thirty-three remains a mystery.

While the snipers kept watch over the torture compound, Lieutenant Colonel Hendrickson tried to find out who gave the order to withdraw from the compound. He could not get a straight answer. Instead, the 39th Brigade ordered the Volunteers to remain silent about the incident. It was not to be discussed anywhere.

Kept in the dark and told to stay quiet about what they had seen did not sit well with the Oregonians. There'd already been friction between the Arkansans and the Volunteers, and this caused even more. Here, in the wake of Abu Ghraib, was a story of a group of citizen-soldiers who had done the right thing. They had displayed compassion, humanity, and mercy at a time when the world's media was flaying the United States for the abuses caught on camera at Abu Ghraib.

After 2–162 pulled out, the torture at the compound was eventually stopped. Between the arrival of the MPs, Gray Hair, and the Iraqi officials, two-thirds of the prisoners survived their treatment. Had Maries's sniper section not escalated the situation and forced Hendrickson to go check it out, many of those ninety-three men surely would have vanished. This would have been the perfect counter to Abu Ghraib had the chain of command seized the public relations opportunity and released the news through U.S. Army channels. The gag order ensured that wouldn't happen.

Throughout history, America's citizen-soldiers have proved to be independent souls and often resistant to Army regulations and discipline. In this case, the moral outrage the Volunteers felt trumped the 39th Brigade's gag order. They wanted answers, and they wanted the story of what had happened to those prisoners known.

Several of the Volunteers, including Lieutenant Colonel Hendrickson, detailed the events of June 29, 2004, to *Oregonian* reporter Mike Francis. Mike embedded with the Volunteers several times during the deployment and proved to be a stalwart friend of the Oregon soldiers. They trusted him. The photographs the snipers shot found their way into his hands, and he gathered numerous eyewitness accounts through the summer of 2004.

The men believed they were violating an unjust order, but were also well aware that by doing so, they put their own careers at risk. That didn't matter. Hendrickson's mantra—do the right thing—had permeated down to the youngest privates. The hard right is never easy, but they were prepared to suffer the consequences. To them, the country needed to know what had happened.

The story broke with a front-page feature in the *Oregonian*. Media outlets all over the world picked up on it. Instead of focusing on the selfless actions of the Volunteers, the majority of the ink spilled over the incident lambasted the order to withdraw from the compound. Numerous attempts were made to find out exactly who that order came from. While there was suspicion that it came from above division level, nothing was ever confirmed.

After Francis ran his story, an Air Force major general held a press conference in the Pentagon, where he announced that none of the Oregonians would be punished for violating the gag order. The truth was, any JAG officer would have known that it was an illegal order in the first place. Hendrickson and his men had every right to disobey it.

During the research for the story, Mike Francis discovered that the interim Iraqi government felt enough outrage over the Volunteers' arrival in the compound that one of its first official acts was to lodge a protest with the U.S. ambassador. The diplomats were walking on eggshells in hopes of building a solid relationship with the new Iraqi government. Instead, the incident had created sharp tension between the new Iraqi government and the U.S. authorities, which was probably one of the reasons the gag order was issued. Nobody wanted to make a bad situation worse.

On July 4, 2004, the *Boston Globe* ran a story about the incident based on an interview with a Coalition Provisional Authority official named Steve Casteel. Until June 28, Casteel had been in charge of the Ministry of Interior. When the changeover took place, he became a senior American adviser to the MOI and was primarily responsible for building and structuring Iraq's law enforcement capabilities. He helped organize a number of Iraqi police units, including the special commando battalions that were later accused by international organizations of many heinous crimes.

In the article, Casteel described the incident on the twenty-ninth as a turf war between some American MPs and the Iraqis at the MOI, a battle that went all the way to the prime minister's office. His version of events categorically denied the Iraqi Police were abusing prisoners. Instead, he claimed the MPs overreacted after seeing the Iraqi cops drag some detainees outside into the sun.

Casteel's version of events did not match the reality documented by 2–162's scout platoon. When Mike Francis's story ran, complete with photographs of the Iraqi Police in the middle of beating the prisoners,

Casteel's account and the *Boston Globe* article were completely discredited.

Upon returning home, 2–162's snipers identified Casteel as the gray-haired man who entered the compound late in the afternoon on the twenty-ninth. Though he declined to be interviewed for this book, it is probable that whatever he said to the Iraqi Police that day helped secure the release of the prisoners.

Exactly who the prisoners were and why they were arrested also remains unclear. The Sudanese swept up in the Al Betawain raid claimed they were innocent of any wrongdoing, and quite possibly that was true. However, many of the Sudanese males we encountered in 2003 had come to Iraq to fight as volunteers for the Saddam Hussein regime. Some were tied to al-Qaida, which had used Sudan as a base of operations for years prior to 9/11. During one fight in the spring of 2003, I smoke-checked three Sudanese who were fighting alongside a Fedayeen group that had launched a counterattack against our regiment.

In 2004 and 2005, the United Nations Refugee Agency (UNHRA) documented repeated instances of forcible eviction, assaults, murders, and blackmail against the Sudanese immigrants living in Iraq. This campaign of terror was carried out by Shia militia groups—the same ones that had penetrated the Iraqi police force. Between December 2004 and February 2005, seventeen Sudanese immigrants were killed in these militia attacks.

Why were the Sudanese targeted by the Shia militia groups? The easiest explanation is that many of them had come to fight for Saddam in 2003 and the fall of the regime trapped them in the country. They had been volunteers of a Sunni regime that had oppressed the Iraqi Shia population for decades. The militias went after them as payback.

Another answer is that at least some of the Sudanese were a link in the al-Qaida Iraq network that was just taking shape in 2004. By targeting them, the Shia militias and the police had hopes of unraveling, then destroying, as many al-Qaida nodes as possible.

Whatever the case, many of these Sudanese tried to flee Iraq, only to end up confined in camp K-70 in Al Anbar Province only a few kiloyards from the Jordanian border. They languished there for years in harsh conditions until the Romanian government opened up a special refugee facility for them in Timisoara. By early 2009, 138 Sudanese had reached Romania safely, including 40 children.

Whether innocent or not, the fact was the Shia militia had made terrorizing the Sudanese in Baghdad a priority. The Al Betawain raid could have been part of that campaign.

As for the other prisoners, Lieutenant Colonel Hendrickson and the other men on the ground that day believed that some of them may have been criminals or insurgents. This was the main reason why Hendrickson did not immediately order the prisoners untied when the Volunteers first entered the compound. Only after seeing the torture facility inside the rectangular building did he give that order. Whatever the case, one thing was abundantly clear to the Volunteers: guilty or innocent, no human being should ever have to endure what those prisoners had. Though many aspects of what happened that day are clouded in shades of gray, that part will always be black and white for the Oregonians.

For 2–162's scout sniper platoon, the day represents a lost opportunity. Ninety-three prisoners were in that compound on June 29. Had they been left to do the right thing, all ninety-three would have made it out alive. Despite the order to withdraw, they saved sixty men. Their actions that day were noble and just. They could take pride in what they were able to accomplish given the minefield of politics, ethnic warfare, and international diplomacy they encountered.

Yet it is the fate of the lost thirty-three that continues to weigh on the Oregonians. They had entered a chamber of horrors, one that scarred them as Buchenwald scarred the GIs who stumbled upon it in 1945. Even eight years later, the memories of that day are raw and spiked with pain. Recalled Kyle Trimble, "We were denied closure. We never got it. And now, we live with that every day."

CHAPTER TWENTY-TWO
Off the Chain

Maries's snipers spent July in the triangular rotation established earlier in that spring. The routine soon devolved into tedium. Day after day, they sat atop the MOI and the Sheraton watching and waiting. The Shia Uprising ended in late June, crushed by additional American forces. A tenuous calm marked the mid-summer days as the Mahdi Militia melted away to lairs throughout the city to recruit, re-equip, and rebuild.

To a man, 2-162's snipers felt they could have been doing much more than watch and report activity around northeast Baghdad. They drafted creative plans designed to maximize their value on the battlefield. Some of the men wanted to use the scout platoon to insert them into key locations around the city where they could set ambushes or take out local Mahdi leaders that the battalion's Intel shop identified for them.

Lieutenant Boyce, the scout platoon commander, wanted to employ his snipers more dynamically as well. He listened to his shooters and looked for ways to exploit them if and when the lull in the fighting ended. Until that day arrived, the rotation continued, and the snipers grew increasingly frustrated.

For the time being, the rotation stayed the same. Truth was, the battalion was still searching for the best way to approach its mission. Finding the balance between helping rebuild the neighborhood and killing the bad guys living in it took a delicate hand, and Lieutenant

Colonel Dan Hendrickson understood all too well that every civilian casualty simply increased the level of resistance his men would face the next time they patrolled the streets.

In an environment like Baghdad in the summer of 2004, snipers can bring all sorts of force multipliers to the table. They can over-watch specific areas to deny them to the enemy. This is particularly useful when trying to keep major roads open to vehicular traffic. Put a sniper team atop a building near a freeway, and those shooters lock that area down. They could deal out death to any cell of insurgents unlucky enough to enter the kill zone to plant a roadside bomb. The minute their shovel hits the dirt, they will end up well aerated by our shooters.

Snipers can also take out heavy weapons teams. Machine guns, mortars, artillery—they are the best casualty-producing weapons on an asymmetrical battlefield. In 2004 the Mahdi Militia possessed ample quantities of all three weapons. They had even mounted heavy machine guns on flatbed trucks, like the "technicals" seen in the movie *Blackhawk Down*. While the firepower these weapons can pour out at our troops can be deadly, the crews themselves are almost defenseless to a well-emplaced sniper team. When covering a friendly patrol, we make a point of searching for these weapons, and they become our top-priority targets. We remove those threats with our precision fire. Take out the machine-gun crew and that deadly weapon won't rake through our men. Kill the mortar team and no more rounds explode among them. Once again, our capabilities on the battlefield can be used to save American lives.

A smart enemy knows that these crews are vulnerable, and they will support them with whatever forces they have available. I learned this firsthand during a mission in Somalia in the spring of 1993. At the time, the security situation inside Mogadishu, the capital, was spinning out of control. Dime-store warlords carved out mini-fiefdoms in the city's streets, stealing food relief supplies from the UN in order to gain power over the starving populace. He who had the food controlled the people in desperate need. We had been sent in to create order out of the anarchy and help the UN regain control over the distribution of relief supplies. Not surprisingly, the tin-pot warlords did not like this at all, and as our deployment wore on, the level of violence escalated.

One night, we established a hide to overwatch several large warehouses full of heavy weapons, tanks, and armored vehicles that belonged to Mohamed Farrah Aidid, Somalia's most powerful warlord at the time. We had inserted into the area ahead of an American raiding force whose mission it was to seize Aidid's weaponry. Nobody expected a fight, but when we planned the operation I did not want to take any chances. Should Aidid's men decide to give us a scrap, my men would be out on a limb, in need of speedy support or reinforcement. Just in case that happened, I brought a machine-gun team and a forward air controller with us and set up on a rooftop overlooking the warehouse complex. That gave us additional firepower, plus access to air power and all the killing force of our AH-1 Cobra helicopter gunships.

In hopes of dissuading Aidid's men from fighting us, we planned a major show of force just before the raiding element hit the warehouses. In this case, a pair of Cobras were to roar overhead and intimidate the crap out of the street warriors. Believe me, there is nothing more gut-liquifying than the sight of an AH-1's business end pointed your way, bristling with Hydra and Zuni rockets plus a 20mm machine cannon.

The best laid plans . . .

While our hide remained undetected that night, we heard all sorts of unusual sounds coming from the warehouses. Engines rumbled in the darkness. Men shouted orders. Come dawn, we discovered they'd set up two ZSU-23 antiaircraft gun systems around the warehouses. Manned and ready to fire, they posed a deadly threat to our Cobras. I had a direct line to our task force commander, General Jack Klimp, who ordered me to disable the first ZSU without hurting the gunner. Our objective that day was to seize weaponry, not start a firefight and cause casualties among Aidid's men.

I aimed at the ZSU's ammunition feed tray and took the shot with a Barrett .50 cal. The bullet went straight through the feed tray and struck the gunner, blowing him back over his seat and out of sight.

Okay, so that didn't go so well.

What followed wasn't any fun either. The other ZSU opened fire on our building, its quad 23mm cannons raking the front facade. My spotter screamed, "They're tearing the building apart! You gotta stop them!"

I swung my heavy rifle over until the sight settled on the ZSU's gunner. He went down with one trigger pull. At that point, Aidid's men opened fire from all over the warehouse complex. Bullets keened and whined around us. So much for avoiding a fight with a show of force. We'd been compromised.

Two Russian-built tanks had been pulled out of the warehouses during the night. Some of Aidid's men broke cover to try and crew them. We could not afford to face those monsters; their main guns would turn our building to rubble in minutes while their coax machine guns pinned us in place. We ignored everyone else to stop this threat. Not a Somali made it to the tracks, but we had a tiger by the tail. There were too many fighters for us to tackle, and they knew where we were. I could see this ending badly if we didn't have help soon.

Thank God we planned ahead. Our forward air controller spoke into his radio, and a moment later two Cobras thundered directly over our building and waded into the fight. Their twenty-millimeter guns spewed shells, knocking Aidid's men right out of their sandals and leaving the battlefield dotted with dead and dying Somali mercenaries. Soon they were dropping buildings with well-placed rocket shots.

We prevailed that day. Looking back, it could have ended much differently. Without the air support, I'm not sure we would have been able to survive. Fortunately, we had backup. But I often wonder what would have happened had those Cobras not arrived so quickly after we had neutralized the antiaircraft guns.

Being detected and overwhelmed by numbers or firepower is a sniper's worst nightmare. In the unconventional fighting we employ, we are in our element when isolated and working in small teams. Our ability to move with stealth and speed, use concealment to avoid detection, and carry out surprise attacks where the enemy least expects them are key assets that make snipers a force multiplier on the battlefield.

Unfortunately, American infantry leaders are often loath to use us to the best effect. If given a choice, a battalion commander is almost always going to try to overcome resistance with firepower and crushing weight of numbers. The idea of sending a sniper section forward to break the enemy's will, or eliminate key weapons, seems far too risky. Naturally casualty-averse (and rightfully so), the prospect of seeing their snipers detected and overwhelmed before help can arrive causes our chain of command to be reluctant to employ us. We've tried to change that mind-set and show our battalion commanders what we can do by giving them sniper employment classes, but the conventional mind-set remains. When our brethren have been overwhelmed on the battlefield, such as in late 2004 when Iraqi insurgents took out two USMC sniper teams, those commanders who tend to err on the side of caution see their decisions justified. And so, when serving with regular line infantry units, snipers are often underutilized.

But there are always some battalion commanders willing to think outside the box. They're the ones we love. They give us the flexibility we need to maximize our effect on the battlefield. They take risks, and they pay big dividends. I loved working with those officers during my time in the Corps. They exist all over the U.S. military and can rise to the occasion in creative and unusual ways when circumstances demand it.

Fortunately, the Volunteers had just such a commander. Lieutenant Colonel Dan Hendrickson, 2–162's police officer and citizen warrior, never considered "inside the box" a comfortable place to be. He could be a stern disciplinarian and taskmaster, but he also listened to the officers and men in his command. Ideas percolated from the bottom up within the battalion, and Hendrickson was open to new ideas from anyone in his chain of command. That flexibility would serve the Volunteers well in the dog days of summer when all hell broke loose once again in the streets of Baghdad.

After going to ground toward the end of the Shia Uprising in the spring, Moqtada al-Sadr gave a rambling, hate-filled speech on July 23, 2004. In it, he attacked both the United States and the current Shia-dominated Iraqi interim government.

A week later, a joint Iraqi-American operation in Karbala captured al-Sadr's senior commander in that city. The Shia cleric demanded his release to no avail. The situation escalated until August 3 when American troops surrounded al-Sadr's house and tried to kill or capture him. Somehow he managed to escape. Once clear of the American trap, he contacted all his senior leaders and told them to send the Mahdi Militia into the streets. Kill Americans. Resist to the death.

Two days later, the Second Shia Uprising broke out. For the next week, the Oregon snipers found themselves in the fight of their lives.

CHAPTER TWENTY-THREE
Gushwa's Thirty

The best snipers are men who make the most out of whatever circumstance they find themselves in. They are versatile, skilled, and intelligent. The best of us are fleet of foot and fast to react to the chaos of combat. Once in a fight, they dominate the enemy.

Sometime this happens from behind their scopes. Sometimes it happens with whatever weapon is at hand. When a fight comes to them, it is the enemy who suffers. In a fluid environment like Baghdad—or any other urban area—a sniper's got to be ready to fight at a moment's notice in any situation, mounted or dismounted. Countless times during the war in Iraq, our snipers were ambushed while either infilling or exfilling an area. Those sorts of situations become run-and-gun-type firefights that resemble some of the scenes in *Blackhawk Down*.

I had this happen to me while in Somalia in January 1993 after our sniper section wrapped up a patrol to the UN food distribution site in downtown Mogadishu. We climbed into our three Humvees and drove back through the city toward our base of operations at the soccer stadium. That day, I rode in a soft-top Humvee that had no turret or heavy weapon. Our other two rigs carried a Ma Deuce (a Browning .50 caliber M2 machine gun) and a Mark 19 grenade launcher. Those two Humvees were armored, our soft top was not.

We'd been traveling down Route 31 October, the capital's main drag, when we came to an intersection about a kilometer and a half from home. So far, it had been a milk run.

But at the intersection, Aidid's fighters were waiting for us with a "technical"—a Toyota pickup with a machine gun mounted in the back bed. They'd emplaced the rig on a side street that ran parallel to our road and used the intersection that connected the two as their kill zone. When we drove by, they poured fire at all three of our vehicles. The surprise attack riddled our lead truck with bullets. Our trail one got hit, too. Somehow my truck lucked out.

In these sorts of situations, the best thing to do is just blow through the kill zone. Aidid's men had figured that out and had deployed technical at every intersection for five blocks. Every time we crossed a side street, they hammered us. We put the pedals to the floor as our gunners opened fire. The technical crews would blast away at us, then speed down the parallel road to another intersection, leapfrogging the other Toyotas already waiting for us. This way, they rolled the ambush down closer and close to the soccer stadium and gave us no respite.

I had a kid named Lassiter on the Mark 19 that day. He was a great Marine, very reliable, and extremely trustworthy, which is why we took him out on missions with us. At the third or fourth intersection, he was ready for the ambush and sent a 40mm grenade right into the waiting technical. Granted, Toyotas are excellent, reliable vehicles, but they just can't take a grenade strike. This one exploded and burned quite nicely.

We reached the stadium and the surviving technical pulled off and raced into the city's dark heart. After we rolled through the gate, we discovered the enemy had shot out all four tires in our lead rig.

Our gunners and our speed made all the difference that day. It also taught us that part of a sniper's job is to be prepared for any kind of combat, be it a stalk in a ruined cityscape or a road warrior–esque running gun battle. That was a lesson I took to heart, and in the years to come I always tried to train my sniper teams to be as versatile and flexible as possible.

There's no other way to fight an asymmetrical war.

Fortunately for the 2–162 Scouts, Kevin Maries recognized that need for versatility long before the Volunteers deployed to Iraq. He made sure his snipers cross-trained on every weapon available to the scout platoon. His section drilled with machine guns, M4 carbines, M16 rifles, pistols, and even grenade launchers. They learned to clear jams, load, break down, and clear each weapon.

When the battalion moved to Fort Hood for its predeployment workup, the snipers even manned Humvee turrets and practiced hitting targets while on the move. Anytime the snipers could pick up an additional skill set, Lieutenant Boyce and Staff Sergeant Maries were all for it. They pressed ahead and made the most of every training opportunity.

Specialist Nate Gushwa missed that part of the battalion's time when Maries gave him the one available (and coveted) slot to the sniper school at Camp Robinson in Little Rock. Maries had seen in this young soldier something unique. He had a fire, a grit that impressed everyone. He kept himself in superb physical shape as well. Since being pulled into the scout platoon, he earned a reputation as a workout fanatic. His tattooed arms were roped with muscles.

Some men are born shots. They have that instinct coded into their DNA. Some men have a phenomenal knack for math and can do the ballistics and environmental calculations in their head on the fly while in the middle of high-stress situations. Others, like Nate, just seemed to know where to lay the crosshairs. It didn't matter the weapon either. Nate could shoot the hell out of anything from a Crossman pump to an M240 Bravo machine gun.

Born and raised on the Oregon coast, Nate's dad was the pastor for the local Baptist church. His maternal grandfather taught him to shoot when he was old enough to carry a rifle, and he would hunt raccoons at night with his grandfather, armed with Ruger 10–22 rifles. He was twelve when his grandfather gifted him with his first firearm, a Winchester 94 30/30. Later on in high school, he purchased a Remington 700, the civilian version of the M24 bolt-action rifle he later used in Baghdad. No matter the weapon, one elemental lesson from his grandfather stuck with him. Time and again, he told Nate to take a few easy breaths before taking each shot as a way to calm his system and steady his aim, a lesson he took to heart so well it became an ingrained part of his shooting style.

He grew obsessed with precision accuracy. He practiced his marksmanship nearly every day on a mini-range he'd set up for his BB gun in his backyard. As he got better, he made his targets smaller and smaller. Whenever he could, he went off into the woods to shoot targets or hunt black-tailed deer. He grew into a confident sharp-shooter, and before he left high school he could take out a milk jug at six hundred yards with a scoped, customized rifle.

Being a trained shooter, not a natural one, I have nothing but respect for men like Nate Gushwa. Before I joined the Marines, I'd never fired a weapon. I learned everything in the Corps, and while I excelled with an M40 and the Barrett .50 cal, I never developed that touch with our pistols. That's actually not unusual. Most of us shooters are better on one weapon than others.

Nate Gushwa was the exception to that rule. On a lead-filled day in Baghdad, that unusual ability played a key role in the largest battle fought by 2–162 Infantry since the end of World War II.

AUGUST 6, 2004
NORTHEAST BAGHDAD

The frantic call reached 2–162's operations center just after lunchtime. An Iraqi police station north of Sadr City reported it was being blitzed by an all-out Mahdi Militia attack. Without assistance, they were sure to be overrun and killed to the last man. Minutes later, the Iraqi Police called in to say another station was under attack as well. Mahdi Mili-tiamen were boiling out of the Sadr City slums and pouring en masse into the area, which on American maps was labeled Zone 22. They were battling the cops (supposedly), laying roadside bombs, and set-ting up fighting positions and barricades in the streets.

Lieutenant Colonel Dan Hendrickson launched the scout platoon to go investigate. Lieutenant Ross Boyce had five Humvees that day. Four were armored M1114s that could withstand direct hits from most types of RPGs. The fifth, which Boyce put in the middle of his column, was the platoon's "Rat Rig." This was a soft-topped, unarmored Humvee commanded by Sergeant Andy Hellman. Andy was a low-key, unassuming scout of average build and stature whose dark eyes hinted at the cagey intellect he possessed. He'd driven around Baghdad all spring in the Rat Rig, taking pride in the ridiculous level of risk such excursions entailed.

Boyce was running lean that day, as many of his men were home on leave. Maries and several sniper teams were still deployed to the MOI and Sheraton, leaving only fourteen men to crew five rigs. Out of necessity, sniper Nate Gushwa manned the turret-mounted M240 Bravo machine gun in the lead Humvee. Darren Buchholz was supposed to go along, too, but he injured his back shortly before the platoon departed and could hardly move. Nate saw him suddenly crumple to the ground next to his Humvee as he was loading his gear aboard. The men carried him to the battalion aid station, where the medics shot him full of painkillers and corticosteroids. He dragged himself back to his room and passed out, feeling utterly awful that he could not roll with his brothers.

Boyce's platoon reached Zone 22 and checked in at the first police station. This time, the cops looked legitimately terrified. They reported that they'd been under fire all morning, and that the enemy was moving in large numbers throughout the area. Right about then, the platoon heard gunfire, and Lieutenant Boyce mounted up his scouts and headed off in search of the fight.

Moments later, the platoon rolled northward up to a three-way T-intersection. Just as they slowed down to figure out which way to turn, a column of Humvees came barreling through the intersection, running flat out east to west. The last rig screeched to a stop directly in front of the Oregon platoon, and one of the dismounts popped open his door and spun out into the street. The 240 gunner went cyclic on his weapon, spraying bullets down the street. The soldier in the street took a knee and fired his M203 grenade launcher in the same direction.

In the lead Oregon Humvee, Trimble and Gushwa watched this unfold only a few yards from their hood. The dismount in the street blew through his entire chest rack of 40mm grenades in a matter of seconds, then turned to the scouts and shouted in a thick Arkansas accent, "Do not go down there! RPGs. RPGs."

Their truck began rolling. The dismount fired a last M203 round as a parting "fuck you" to the Mahdi army, then pivoted and dove into his Humvee, which sped away with the 240 gunner shouting one final warning, "Do not go down there!"

Sergeant Dustin Paul, Trimble's truck commander, asked, "Hey, Lieutenant, what do you want to do?"

Boyce radioed his rigs, "This is our job, guys. Let's go check it out."

Gushwa heard the order and was startled by it. "What? Right? Isn't that the way they just told us not to go?"

Paul relayed that to Boyce, but the platoon leader insisted, "We're recon, we gotta check this shit out."

Dreading what would happen next, Trimble turned right and gave it some gas. The rest of the platoon followed. They drove into a ramshackle slum full of ugly, low-slung buildings built one atop the other. They passed a broken rocket-propelled grenade lying in the street. UXO—unexploded ordnance—is never a good sign. Heads on swivels, the platoon inched deeper into the neighborhood.

Gushwa scanned the road ahead, swinging his turret left and right in a forty-five-degree arc. The scouts had attached a .50 caliber ammo can to this 240 Bravo and linked four belts together to give Gushwa eight hundred rounds of ready lead. The machine gun sported a Trijicon TA648MGO 6x48 green dot scope—perfect for knocking down targets at long range, but awkward in a close-quarters fight. The street was so narrow that if they did roll into an ambush, the scope would not be an asset. Nate handled the 240 with confidence, though he had not fired a live round through a machine gun since basic training some two years before.

They'd only gone a short distance when Kyle Trimble spotted a crowd of black-clad figures in the street ahead. They wore the green armbands of the Mahdi Militia, but did not appear to be armed. Some of them turned in surprise as the Oregon Humvees approached. Others bolted for nearby alleyways and buildings.

The rain of shit began right there, and it was on like Donkey Kong. Gunfire erupted along the left side of the street sending bullets spanging off the lead Humvee.

Gushwa shifted the turret to the left and saw three men with weapons. A quick six-to-ten round burst dropped all three. He spotted another man shooting from the corner of an alley. He shifted fire and killed him with another controlled burst.

Suddenly, a figure stepped out of an alley to the right of Gushwa's rig. Trimble glimpsed him just as he raised an RPG launcher. He could not have been more than fifteen yards away. A puff of smoke, a flash, and the rocket shot from the launcher's barrel. It skipped across the hood of Trimble's Humvee and detonated beside his left window. The blast rocked their truck just as Gushwa dropped him with a snap-shot from his 240.

The rest of the platoon drove forward into a sea of muzzle flashes. Dozens of Mahdi Militiamen appeared on rooftops, in the street, in alleys, and atop compound walls. They fired from windows and gardens and from the road itself, standing fearlessly and fully exposed. The Oregonians poured lead downrange, cutting them down one after another. Undeterred, more Mahdi rushed to join the fight until it seemed like the platoon was fighting its way upstream. The level of enemy incoming never slackened despite the carnage the scouts inflicted.

Another RPG sizzled past Gushwa and clipped the truck's radio antennae. Bullets laced the armor plating, raking their Humvee from fender to fender. Trimble floored his accelerator, but the Humvee's turbo failed and the heavy, armored rig wallowed along at less than thirty-five miles an hour. It was a slow motion nightmare for the Oregonians. Another RPG flew at them, only to ricochet off the street and explode under their Humvee. The blast lifted the rig into the air and flung them around in their seats. A split second later, a roadside bomb detonated, studding the Humvee with hunks of shrapnel that Trimble later found embedded in their vehicle's armor plating. One fist-sized piece of metal spanged off the back of Gushwa's turret just above his head, then fell behind the rear shield with a dull thud.

"Go! Go! Go! Blow through it!" Boyce ordered. Trimble's rig wasn't up to the crisis. It limped along and was savaged by the incoming. Fourteen men in five Humvees were at the mercy of the Mahdi Militiamen. If they scored a mobility kill, the platoon was sure to be faced with a terrible choice: leave those in the crippled rig behind, or make a last stand and die together.

Gushwa meted out short bursts, playing his machine gun like an instrument. He fired, shifted, fired, shifted again. Trimble was in awe of his skill on that weapon. Though it had been two years since he'd fired a 240, and had never pulled the trigger on one while in a moving Humvee, Nate's natural ability to shoot anything with a stock and barrel made him deadly effective that day. He hunkered down behind the scope, making split target acquisition decisions as he scanned the forty-five-degree arc in front of the platoon. If the person had a weapon, Nate pinned him with the green dot sight and pulled the trigger. He kept his ammo use to a bare minimum as he carefully triggered off less than ten rounds a burst.

Behind him, though, the Mahdi hammered the other trucks. An RPG skipped across Andy Hellman's Rat Rig, singeing its soft top but miraculously doing no damage. Behind the Rat Rig, Tyson Bumgardner saw the desperation of the moment and rolled down his window. He was in the front right passenger seat, serving as a truck commander that morning. Now he stuck his M4 through the window in his door and opened fire. The fight had engulfed them so quickly, he hadn't had time to switch off his iPod, which had been connected to the Humvee's speaker system. They rolled through the fight with Pantera's "Cowboys from Hell" as their soundtrack.

Death metal filling his ears, Tyson drained his magazine, dropped it out, and grabbed another one. Just as he slammed it home, a Mahdi fighter stepped into the street and opened fire with his AK-47 from only a few yards away. Bumgardner swung his barrel and triggered a three-round burst that hit the man in the chest. Seconds later, more Mahdi boiled from an alleyway, armed with a mix of AK-47s and RPGs. The scouts fought back furiously.

Lieutenant Boyce's truck was directly behind Gushwa's. His gunner, John Ash, was a mountain of a man, at least six foot three. His height worked against him in this fight, as he was probably the most exposed American that afternoon. Manning the .50 caliber machine gun, he saw a Mahdi Militiaman dash from the alley and aim an RPG at his truck. The man was less than ten feet away and clearly had no fear for his own safety. Just as he raised the weapon, Ash blew him apart with his Ma Deuce. Boyce watched one of the man's arms cartwheel over his Humvee's hood spraying blood and gore.

The fight continued, block after block. The Mahdi had studied the way the Americans would fight from their Humvees and tailored the ambush to counter those techniques. Instead of picking only one side of the road for a linear ambush, they alternated sides at each block. Just as the American gunners zeroed in on targets, they'd reach an intersection and take fire from the opposite side. The gunners had to spin their turrets one hundred eighty degrees to reengage.

Behind the platoon, a group of militiamen pushed a pair of cars across the road, then set them afire. This effectively blocked the scouts from backing out of the firefight should the lead truck go down. Seconds later, mortar fire rained down on the street. The Mahdi had also preplanned indirect fire for their kill zone, but the platoon had managed to push farther down the road than they had anticipated.

For all their cunning, the ambush had been triggered prematurely. The Mahdi had been preparing roadside bombs when the Volunteers showed up, and now the Humvees passed stacks of mortar rounds and artillery shells arrayed alongside the street to await emplacement as IEDs.

For over a kilometer, the seesaw, slow-motion battle raged. In the trail Humvee, Sergeant Randy Mitts blazed away with his M4, just as Bumgardner was doing. Mitts was a former Marine of imposing stature who came to Oregon after his service to work as a computer software engineer. Deeply religious, he arrived in Baghdad with the spirit of an avenging angel, determined to exact revenge on the Muslim world for 9/11. Now he found himself in the fight of his life, in a race to take out RPG men before they could fire their weapons on his brothers.

A brazen Mahdi fighter sprinted into the road behind Mitts's truck. Before his gunner could take him out, he triggered an RPG that exploded directly under the Humvee's rear axle. The back half of the rig lurched upwards, then slammed down with enough force to jar fillings loose.

Mitts grabbed his radio and reported, "We just took an RPG in the ass!"

It was a Groundhog Day moment. Every block brought more of the same—rockets, machine guns, AKs. The men fought back with ruthless desperation. In their wake, the road looked like a slaughterhouse. Bodies lay bleeding and torn along the length of the kilometerlong kill zone.

Many of those had been killed by sniper Nate Gushwa. His weight lifter's muscles bulged as he worked his machine gun and mowed down targets. Swinging left again, he spotted a heap of clothing on the side of the road. It looked suspicious, so he put a burst into it. The 7.62 rounds tore apart the clothing and revealed a 155mm artillery shell hidden beneath. This was the weapon of choice for roadside bombs as they could disable an armored Humvee.

Seconds after he shot up the pile of clothing, Nate's head whipsawed backward and slammed against the rear of the turret. He remained there, pinned in place for a second before his head jerked forward and hit the turret ring. He disappeared into the Humvee.

Somebody called, "Nate's been hit! He's down!"

Trimble heard him fall out of the turret, unconscious, and knew they were in real trouble. Without anyone to crew their 240, the Mahdi fighters in front of them would pour it on without fear of retribution. It would be open season on their rig. If it went down, the platoon would either have to fight in place and hope help arrived, or back out through the kill zone to the nearest intersection to make an escape. Ugly propositions at best.

The problem was, they didn't have anyone else to get up on the gun. The platoon was running with such a skeleton crew that only Kyle and Sergeant Paul remained in the rig. Paul was on the radio, calling out targets from the front passenger seat. In full battle rattle, getting Gushwa out of the way and climbing into the turret from that spot in the Humvee was difficult at best. In a Humvee being thrown around by repeated explosions, it would have been borderline impossible.

Sergeant Paul shook him. Blood streamed down Gushwa's face. One eye was covered with it.

"Nate! Nate, are you okay?" Paul said repeatedly.

Gushwa slowly regained consciousness. He hadn't been hit by any of the incoming after all. The Mahdi had created a trap, stolen from the pages of the German Army circa 1944 that was tailor made to take out Humvee gunners. They had strung a wire across the road right at gunner level. As Trimble navigated through the kill zone, the wire struck Nate right across the front of his helmet and caught on the mount for his night vision goggles. The sudden impact rammed his helmet into his forehead, opening a gash, then flung his head into the back of the turret. Later, at the Baghdad combat support hospital, he was told that if he hadn't had the neck muscles he'd developed in the gym during countless workouts, the wire would have ripped his head off. Instead, it tore two of the tendons in his neck and left him with lasting nerve damage.

If the wire had hit Nate three inches lower, it would have killed him instantly. Three inches higher, it would have slipped over him without inflicting any injury. Had that happened, the wire would have struck Ash in the turret of the next Humvee. With his taller frame, the scouts figured later that the wire would have hit him square in the neck at thirty-five miles an hour and decapitated him.

Nate would worry about the wounds later. In the moment, he realized how terribly vulnerable the platoon was without a man on the 240 above him. Groaning in pain, his eye stinging and blurred from the blood that had poured into it, he pulled himself into the turret with sheer determination. Once upright again, he grabbed the 240 and rotated right. Two running figures appeared in the scope. One was wearing a white shirt, carrying an RPG launcher. A teenaged male ran along behind him, carrying extra rockets. Before they had a chance to shoot, Nate walked a ten-round burst through both of them that knocked them off their feet. Launcher and reloads skidded along the ground as Trimble sped past them.

Trimble was amazed by his friend's grit. The scouts later estimated that Gushwa killed at least thirty insurgents with his 240 Bravo. He'd been so accurate and sparing with his ammunition that he hadn't even needed to reload. He'd fired about five hundred rounds, all while being pummeled with rockets, bombs, and bullets as Trimble bobbed and weaved through the street. Hitting moving targets from a moving platform is one of the most difficult shooting situations a sniper can face, no matter what the weapon. Nate Gushwa, less than a year removed from sniper school, showed a unique level of marksmanship on a weapon he had not used in two years. The versatility and skill he displayed that day was nothing short of spectacular.

The platoon rolled through the last block of the kill zone, their rigs battered but intact. A UAV, an unmanned aerial vehicle, drone aircraft arrived over the battlefield right after the scouts escaped the kill zone. The UAV's video camera captured over a hundred Mahdi fighters still alive and moving in the street. Scores more lay dead or wounded. The Volunteers had been outnumbered probably ten to one. Trimble credited their survival to Gushwa. He later recalled, "His shooting was key to getting us out of there that day."

As they cleared the area, their adrenaline highs drained away, leaving them exhausted and shaking. As they gained some distance from the enemy, they allowed themselves a collective sigh of relief.

That was until the technicals began chasing them.

CHAPTER TWENTY-FOUR
The Man Who Lost His Shoes

Kyle Trimble steered the scout platoon out of the fight. His crippled Humvee lurched through the final block of the kill zone and came to an earthen dyke that defined the east side of Zone 22. Rather than trying to take one of the side streets, Trimble drove up the slope and slid onto a narrow dirt road that ran along the top of the dyke. The other four trucks followed, and soon they were running southeast, the city to their right and farms to their left.

Behind them, the Mahdi seethed with fighting ire. Instead of melting away into their urban jungle to nurse their wounded and bury their dead, some of the militiamen piled into waiting pickups and bongo trucks. They sped after the scout platoon, armed with machine guns, AKs, and RPGs.

The scouts were trying to figure out how to clear the area. They'd never been on the dyke before, and they didn't know this area of Zone 22 well at all. The maps they had were unreliable at best. As they worked through their next move, the gunners spotted the mounted Mahdi force coming at them. The enemy drivers selected a north-south running side street that ran parallel to the dyke. Between breaks in the maze of buildings, the scouts caught fleeting glimpses of the technicals closing on them.

Trimble's rig still set the pace. With its turbo out, he managed to coax only about thirty-five miles an hour out of the Humvee, which was far too slow to be able to outrun their pursuers. Within minutes, the technical drew even with the American trucks. The two sides runned and gunned through the neighborhood, taking snap-shots at each other whenever there was a clear field of fire.

Gushwa stayed focused on his forward sector of fire. By now, his head throbbed with pain. His neck was so swollen he could barely look left and right. Blood continued to drip into his eye. For him, the chase became a surreal blur of colors, sounds, and shouted commands.

Up ahead, he saw a taxi go right through the dyke from east to west. As it crossed the dyke, all he could see was the vehicle's roof.

"Stop! Stop! Stop!" he shouted to Trimble. Kyle jammed on the brakes and the Humvee slid to a halt in a cloud of dust.

Some Iraqi bulldozer had cut a makeshift road through the dyke so the people of Zone 22 could move back and forth into the farmland on the east side. Nate had seen it just in time. The Humvee's front tires stopped less than a meter from a sheer, ten-foot drop. Had the taxi not driven through it at that exact moment, Nate and Kyle never would have seen the cut until their Humvee fell into it.

Those 1114s were tough, but a plunge like that at thirty-five miles an hour probably would have killed or severely wounded everyone inside.

Behind them, the other drivers skidded to a stop as well. Boyce saw their predicament clearly: unmoving now, sitting atop a dyke without cover or concealment, they were easy targets.

He ordered the platoon to back up, then dive off the left slope of the dyke. Down they went onto a rural road that intersected with the one the taxi had been using. There, they swung around in a U-turn and drove north for a ways before climbing back onto the dyke.

The maneuver threw off their pursuers, and the scouts sped north of Zone 22 into another neighborhood, marked Zone 50 on their maps. There, they drove off the dyke, looped west, and linked up with Dan Hendrickson and another company of Volunteers on the west side of the 'hood.

While Lieutenant Boyce briefed Hendrickson, the platoon's

medic climbed aboard Trimble's Humvee and went to work on Nate's wounds. Mike Giordano was not your typical medic. Gruff and growly, he often told the scouts, "I'll save your life if I have to, but I ain't your personal Jesus."

The tough-guy comments concealed the medic's gentle side—at least until he started working gently on Nate's head. He stopped the bleeding, bandaged him up, and asked him if he was good to go. Gushwa, now that the adrenaline had drained away a second time, felt like crap. His head swam, he was seeing gray dots, and his neck felt like it was on fire.

But there was no one else to man the 240. From the look of things, Lieutenant Colonel Hendrickson was about to order them back into the fight.

"Good to go," Nate told the medic. Giordano slapped him on the shoulder and climbed off the Humvee to go check the other men out.

In the meantime, the rest of the scouts began to check out their rigs for battle damage. All of them had been shot up. Staff Sergeant Paul's Humvee had been hit the worst. Its radio antennae had been torn off by the Mahdi gunfire, and shrapnel studded its metal hide. The men even pulled chunks of concrete off the back hatch.

Lieutenant Boyce came back to the platoon a few minutes later. The news wasn't good. The Mahdi had launched attacks all over Zone 22 and 50. They were in the open, shooting at anything American, attacking Iraqi police stations and Iraqi Army patrols. Hendrickson had brought up reinforcements—everything the battalion had available—and had ordered them to advance to contact down three of the main roads in northeast Baghdad. Hendrickson had tried to get air support. None was available. He tried to get artillery support. That was denied. The 39th Brigade did not want to have to rebuild the neighborhood if the Oregonians chewed it up with 155 and 105mm shellfire.

Failing that, he tried to get tanks. No luck. Everyone had their hands full that day. For heavy support, the battalion could count on a single platoon of Bradley Fighting Vehicles loaned to them from the

2/7 Cavalry. Hendrickson ordered the Brads to patrol down to the ambush site the scouts had just survived. To support them, Boyce's men would push down into a market area the Americans called Route Rogue, a few blocks north of the morning's kill zone. Charlie Company would cover the flank.

Hendrickson mounted up and rolled with the scouts. Trimble led the way again, this time turning onto Route Rogue in the heat of the mid-afternoon sun. Normally, this area bustled with activity. Rogue was the place to go in northeast Baghdad if you needed to buy consumer goods—sort of the Iraqi version of a Best Buy outdoor sale. Open market stalls and run-down storefronts lined the street. Iraqi merchants would stand beside their televisions, refrigerators, DVD players, and movie kiosks to hawk their wares and dicker with customers. Every time the Volunteers had visited the area during the day, the place was humming with activity.

Today, not a soul stood on the street. The shops were shuttered, the merchandise dragged inside to leave the sidewalk kiosks and stalls bare. The scouts stayed mounted and crept forward into the silent neighborhood. As they passed alleys and side streets, Nate could see crowds of people moving around on the blocks both north and south of the road they were on, as if business were usual over there. Obviously, they'd been told to stay clear of this one.

They drove past one alley, and Nate saw a man with an RPG lurking in its depths. He traversed left but couldn't get a shot on him before they drove past the mouth of the alley. He called up the contact, but by the time the second rig reached the alley, the man had melted into the crowd on the other end.

The platoon continued its slow advance down Rogue until it reached a larger intersection. Here, Hendrickson ordered a blocking position established. It was a tough spot to guard. The neighborhood was honeycombed with a maze of little alleys and side streets, none of which were large enough to accommodate Humvees. But they could certainly be used by the Mahdi Militia to attack the platoon. The gunners kept a close eye on them.

The battalion commander dismounted, carrying a Beretta M12 9mm submachine gun he'd grown fond of since the Volunteers had found it during a raid earlier in the year. Hendrickson carried it with him during meetings with local civilian leaders. In case there was trouble, the Beretta seemed like the perfect room-sweeper.

At the platoon's rear, Randy Mitts climbed out of his rig, as did Tyson Bumgardner. Hendrickson went over to talk with them just as Nate noticed a group of civilians coming toward them from an alley a few blocks away. They seemed to be excited, eager, as if they were about to watch a good movie. Tyson and Mitts spotted them too and kept a careful eye out for anyone with a weapon.

Was this a Bull Run moment? In 1861, as the Union and Confederate armies met at Manassas, crowds of civilians gathered with picnic baskets to watch the show. Some of them got trapped in the pell-mell Union retreat at the end of the battle.

To the south, the sound of gunfire swelled in the distance. The distinct rapid-fire *boom-boom-boom-boom* of the 25mm autocannon mounted on our Bradleys echoed across the neighborhood. The 27 guys had driven into the kill zone. Rashes of AK-47 bursts resounded next. Explosions followed. A fierce firefight soon raged only a few blocks away. The sounds echoed and bounced around the buildings, streets, and alleys, which made it impossible to pinpoint the origins of the gunfire.

Nate glanced back that way, saw nothing, then returned his eyes to the crowd. They'd inched even closer. He saw no weapons, but the chances of somebody with one pushing through the mass of people to take a potshot at the Americans seemed likely. He flipped the safety off on his M240 and triggered a short burst over the crowd's head. The warning shots had their intended effect. The people backed off.

To the north, another firefight broke out. The Mahdi ambushed the flank element from Charlie Company with small arms and RPGs. Now, surrounded by the staccato sounds of AKs and 240s, the scouts found themselves in the middle of an oasis in a neighborhood otherwise aflame with combat. It was a weird, eerie sensation, like being in the eye of a hurricane.

Behind the scout platoon, another crowd surged up an alley. Bumgardner, Mitts, and the LTC Hendrickson watched them with suspicion. Where they just curious? Or was this part of some Mahdi plan? Either way, the men held their weapons close and stayed ready for anything.

Something sizzled right over the platoon and exploded against one of the buildings on the south side of the street.

"*RPG!*" somebody shouted.

An engine roared. Chuck Mangus, who was manning the turret-mounted machine gun on Randy Mitts's Humvee, saw one of the Mahdi technicals that had chased them earlier sweep into an alley and barrel straight for the platoon. Mangus swung his turret to get his gun on target. The rig skidded to a halt. The militiamen in the bed were armed with machine guns and RPGs. One of the RPG men popped up over the cab and fired. Mangus saw the flash from the launcher. The rocket streaked right over his truck and exploded on the south side of the street.

Mangus went cyclic, tearing the pickup truck to shreds. The driver died instantly, so did his passenger. The RPG man was blown out of the bed by repeated impacts. He flopped to the ground, where Mangus hit him again and tore him apart.

The crowd behind the platoon parted. Two figures sprinted out from the crowd and ran behind a beat-up minibus parked on the side of Route Rogue.

Hendrickson saw them. The lead man carried an RPG. The trail one had a satchel full of rocket reloads. He flipped off his Beretta's safety and pulled the trigger. The full auto weapon sprayed nine-mil rounds downrange. The glorified Italian grease gun managed only to rip fresh holes in the nearby cars and walls.

The RPG man darted out from behind the minibus and triggered his weapon. To everyone there it looked as if he was aiming at Bumgardner. Tyson thought so, too, and in that split second, he thought he was a dead man. But the rocket deflected downward and exploded in the street fifty feet in front of the scouts. Bits of dirt and rocks and shrapnel flew in all directions. Smoke boiled from the impact site. Chunks of the roadbed pelted Tyson as he took a knee and drew a bead on the RPG gunner.

At the same moment, Mitts dashed behind a blue Chevy Suburban parked on the opposite side of the street. He opened through the vehicle's windows, shattering them with his first two shots. His third hit his target in the chest. Mangus also let fly with a long, raking burst. Bullet holes Swiss cheesed the minibus and probably struck the militiaman carrying the RPG reloads. Exactly which of the three Americans hit which of the two militiamen is unclear. In the chaos of such a moment, everyone remembers things a little differently. Mitts remembers everyone shooting at the same target, at least initially. But for Tyson, the moment was indelibly imprinted on his mind. He later recounted it, "I . . . instantly unloaded on that guy (the RPG gunner). I was on single shot but I remember firing so fast that my tracers looked like a red rope being sucked right into that guy's chest. I hit him with about half the magazine. Then he blew up."

The American counter-fire had probably touched off a grenade or an RPG reload somewhere on the Mahdi militiaman. The blast vaporized him instantly. When the smoke thinned, the Volunteers saw a charred black circle in the roadbed where he had been standing.

A pair of shoes smoldered in the middle of that charred circle.

Tyson reloaded and ordered his gunner to lay down some fire. Bullets began skipping off the road around them, but it still almost impossible to determine where the enemy was. Meanwhile, Bumgardner saw Trevor Ward trying to unjam his M4. The weapon had double fed, and he couldn't get it clear. Tyson ran over to him even as more AK rounds ricocheted off the road. When it became clear the M4 wasn't going to be functional any time soon, he ordered Ward back to their Humvee to get an M249 SAW.

Meanwhile, Hendrickson ordered Mitts to go retrieve the RPG launcher. He headed over to Bumgardner and explained what they needed to do. Tyson wanted support as they moved down the block, so he told Ward to get in the driver's seat of the Humvee and back it down the road after them. That way, his turret gunner could cover their movement.

Civilians still lingered in the area. Some were hunkered down in front of shopfronts. Others peered from alleyways. It was an eerie feeling, heading toward all those watching eyes. But together, the two Oregonians bounded down the street.

They hadn't gone far when a small truck suddenly appeared in an alleyway, speeding straight at Tyson. The driver evidently had no idea a firefight was going on, and seemed surprised to see an American soldier in the street ahead. Tyson spun to the left and saw the truck coming unchecked. He fired a single shot from about fifteen meters away and put the bullet through the windshield directly between the driver and the passenger. Message received. The driver slammed on the brakes, then threw the truck into reverse and backed out of the engagement area.

The diversion had slowed Tyson down, and Randy had not noticed. When Bumgardner turned to continue on his way, he saw Randy quite a distance ahead, moving alone as civilians watched from both sides of the street. Tyson sprinted to catch up with his friend.

They linked up, and together moved past the blackened circle where the RPG gunner had been. His shoes still smoldered in the street. They hadn't gone far when movement caught Tyson's eye. He glanced to his right and saw a terrified Iraqi woman clutching three small children, cowering in a storefront.

Tyson motioned to her that she should move farther into the shop. For a moment, she stared, eyes wide at him and his rifle, then she did what he wanted.

The two scouts reached the shattered bus. Beneath the vehicle, the loader lay facedown in a pool of blood, his clothes ripped and torn. The stench of burned flesh and hair lingered, mingled with the acrid reek of gunpowder and explosives.

The RPG launcher was nowhere in sight.

An AK cracked. The bullet snapped past Tyson. He and Randy

began searching the rooftops for the shooter. A moment later, another round ricocheted off the wall behind them. The two Americans hadn't seen where it had come from.

Tyson checked under the bus again. The loader hadn't moved, but the Oregonian couldn't be sure he was dead. He raised his rifle and was about to pull the trigger when the loader's eyes flew open. He looked right at Tyson, his face torn and covered in blood. With a shock, Tyson realized he was staring into the dying eyes of a teenage boy.

"Pleez, pleez don't kill me," he begged in English.

Tyson froze, staring down his weapon at the broken human under the bus as he pleaded for his life.

"Pleez. Help. Me," his forlorn voice, weak, in broken English, played across Tyson's ears.

Mitts saw all this happen from a few yards away and went cold. The Mahdi had been known to wear explosive vests, or detonate hand grenades when American troops approached them. All he could think of was his friend being blown to pieces before his eyes.

"Finish him, Bum," Mitts said.

Tyson held his weapon to his shoulder, but didn't fire.

"Pleez . . . am student . . ." the loader cried.

"Where's the RPG?" Randy demanded.

The loader cried,. "No RPG!"

"Kill him," Mitts said.

Another bullet cracked overhead and whined off the wall behind them. The unseen gunman still had them in his sights.

Tyson was a college student back in Eugene. Six months before, he'd been going to school and playing soldier once a month. Now he was staring down his sights at a kid who could have been a classmate.

Until this moment, Bumgardner had never known fear in combat. He'd seen battle as a team sport with guns. But as he stared at the horror in front of him, a raw and primal terror welled within him. It was not fear for his own life, however, but fear he would make the wrong decision, the consequences of which would last a lifetime.

His finger fluttered from the side of his M4 to the trigger.

"Pleez . . . ple . . ."

"No. I won't do it. I won't kill him," Bumgardner said.

He motioned to the kid under the bus and said, "Come to me."

With supreme effort, the Mahdi militiaman crawled from under the bus and somehow found the strength to stand up. He was little more than human wreckage. Blood poured from a dozen wounds around his face, head, shoulders, and chest. One arm dangled limply from shredded tendons. The boy looked down in horror and realized it was barely connected to his body. It swung like a bloody pendulum until he tried vainly to hold it in place with his left hand. But his left hand had been torn apart by shrapnel or bullets. Ruined flesh hung from shattered bones. He stood there, the full magnitude of what had happened to his body sinking in, and he began to scream.

Tyson looked on in horror. He heard himself reflexively say, "Dude, I don't think you're going to make it." Randy heard that and thought it was terrible thing to say. But in such an extreme moment, the mind reacts in unusual ways.

"Save me. Help me. Pleez, pleez," the teenage militiaman wailed.

He took a shambling, desperate step toward Tyson, but that was all he had left. He fell to his knees, his voice hoarse and fading as he started to beg Allah for salvation. His right arm swung free as he lifted his left hand beseechingly up to the Oregonian in front of him.

Tyson called Lt. Boyce and asked for a medic. Later, he said, "It was the only humane gesture I could offer him in a hopeless moment."

Lieutenant Boyce denied the request. The situation was just too chaotic, and the column was about to mount up and get out of there.

The dying kid lost his balance and collapsed, face-first in the street. Arm still outstretched, his hand fell atop Tyson's boot, leaving a smear of blood across it. He bled out in the gutter and died only a few seconds later. Tyson stared down at him, unsure what to do next. Then he remembered the mom and her children. Glancing over his shoulder, Tyson saw them watching him through the storefront's window.

Mitts heard Boyce's voice over his Motorola radio ordering them to come back to the vehicles. Mitts relayed the order to Tyson, whose gaze had returned to the kid who had just died at his feet. There was so much blood.

"Let's go, Bum."

As if in a dream, Tyson looked up at his friend. He'd come to Iraq to help students, not shoot them. A wave of pure anguish washed over him.

"Come on, Bum," Mitts said gently as he grabbed his shoulder.

Bullets still impacting around them, they moved back to their Humvees. As they did, Tyson ventured one last look. The loader, arm outstretched in death, lay in a crimson puddle by the fender of the shattered minibus. A pair of shoes smoldered in a charred circle in the street.

The shoes had not been empty.

CHAPTER TWENTY-FIVE
Red Mist

AUGUST 9, 2004
BAGHDAD
NOON

Keith Engle sat atop the Ministry of Interior, bored out of his mind. Months had passed since the torture scene had unfolded beneath them at this observation point. Since then, they'd seen almost no activity from the compound. He and Maries had been watching the Shia Uprising unfold around them, but had little ability to influence things from their perch.

He happened to be looking toward Sadr City when somebody started firing mortars at Patrol Base Volunteer. Engle saw the first launch and noted the Point of Origin (POO)—right on the edge of Route Pluto, the north-south highway that divided Sadr City from the rest of Baghdad. The enemy was mortaring their base several times a day, and there was nothing Keith or Kevin Maries could do about it from their vantage point. If only they could call in counterbattery fire, but the 39th Brigade would not allow that. The mortar teams used busy civilian neighborhoods, and smacking them with 105mm rounds would have devastated those areas. The civilian casualties would be high, and the cost of rebuilding the structures destroyed would fall to the American taxpayer. Engle grabbed the radio and called the launch in to the battalion operation center, thoroughly frustrated. It was all he could do.

The first mortar impacted on the American base. The civilian contractors working there scuttled for cover. Inside the scout platoon's barracks, the detonation roused Andy Hellman, the proud driver of the platoon's unarmed Rat Rig. Quiet, sometimes to a fault, Andy stayed on life's periphery, and moved through it as anonymously as possible. At parties, he was the guy in back watching everything, saying nothing. In battle, he always seemed to be a target, and he'd gotten the reputation as an RPG magnet. No matter, he strapped his gear on every day and went to work with a rock solid resolve that overcame all fear.

Curiously, he stepped out onto a second-floor veranda to see what was going on. Another scout, Sergeant George Gordon, soon joined him. As they observed the scene together, a second round exploded near the motor pool.

"Wow, that was pretty close," Gordon observed wryly.

The attack had caught Lieutenant Ross Boyce out in the open. He and Lieutenant Chris Boeholt, the battalion mortar platoon leader, had been walking back from the chow hall when the first round had landed. Now they ran through the incoming to get back to their men.

The third mortar struck midway between the motor pool and the scouts' barracks, sending up a thin column of smoke and dirt perhaps a hundred yards away. That was enough for Andy. "That's too close! Let's get back inside!"

The two Oregonians abandoned the veranda and went down the second-floor hallway, intending to get on the first floor. They could hear their medic, Mike Giordano, shouting something to some KBR employees who were outside and running for cover.

"That's right, run you fucking pussies!" they heard him yell in his irascible growl.

Vintage Giordi. Hellman stifled a laugh. He thought the world of the platoon's grouchy medic and his bah-humbug sense of humor.

The barracks convulsed. A flat, metallic burst of sound deafened Andy in the stairwell. Then a concussion wave slammed into Andy and nearly threw him off his feet. He stumbled down to the first floor.

Giordi lay sprawled on the ground a few feet from the open main door, covered in blood. Tendrils of smoke wafted through the room. Splinters of glass from shattered windows crunched underfoot as Hellman and Gordon rushed to their wounded medic.

Giordano had been hassling the contractors from the doorway of the barracks when a fourth 82mm mortar struck right in front of him. That he was even alive was a miracle.

"Check my eye!" Giordi growled.

"Your eye is fine," Gordon reported.

"Is my liver okay?" the medic demanded.

"You've been hit in the neck, Giordi."

Angry, seething with pain and fear, Giordano told Gordon how to treat his wound. More scouts and snipers emerged from their rooms to help out. Boyce and Boeholt arrived moments later. The sight of their medic roused everyone to fury. This mortaring shit had to stop.

A meat wagon arrived. The men lifted him into it, and he was sped first to the battalion's aid station, then to the Baghdad Combat Support Hospital. He had suffered a serious shrapnel wound to his neck and was lucky to be alive. Later, he was evacuated to Germany, then to Walter Reed Hospital in Maryland, where he barraged the doctors with demands to let him rejoin his platoon. It took months, but he finally talked the docs into it. When he returned to the scouts, he received a warm and hearty welcome.

But that was all in the future. In the meantime, the mortar attack had wounded two Volunteers. Enough was enough. Boyce and his men sat down to brainstorm ways they could put an end to them.

Boyce was not a Guardsman, but a regular army officer who'd been a general's aide at Fort Hood when Hendrickson promoted the scout platoon leader to a company command. The Volunteers were running very lean on officers at the time, and Boyce received an offer to take the platoon. The men greeted him with quiet skepticism at first, but he soon won them over with his willingness to learn, listen, and keep an open mind.

Together with Kevin Maries, Boyce developed a plan that was

both bold and fit within the narrow parameters of the current Rules of Engagement. They knew that Hendrickson faced a tough tactical situation, thanks to the cagey nature of the Mahdi Militia. The insurgents had discovered where the unit boundary was between the Volunteers and 2-5 Cav, which was assigned to Sadr City. The Mahdi promptly exploited the boundary by launching their mortar attacks on the Patrol Base Volunteer from inside 2-5's battle space. Had they just attacked from inside 2–162's area of operations, Hendrickson would have simply sent his Quick Reaction Force to chase down the mortar teams and kill them in the streets. Instead, the Oregonians couldn't get permission from 2-5 Cav to cross the unit boundary and hunt down the mortarmen with their motorized infantry platoons.

Lieutenant Boyce and Kevin Maries came up with a solution. Why not use the snipers to locate and kill the mortar teams with precision gunfire? The enemy had been lobbing rounds at their base from the same general area every day since the uprising began. If his scouts could find a tall building with a good view of western Sadr City, his snipers could take them out. That way, they wouldn't have to cross the unit boundary and run afoul of 2-5 Cav's commander or that battalion's own operations. With the sniper teams, they could stay in 2–162's own battle space and ambush the mortar teams from long range. If all went well, the Mahdi would never know what hit them.

Hendrickson, who had been impressed with the performance of the scout platoon all summer long, gave Boyce the green light. The twenty-six-year-old lieutenant went to work fleshing out the details with Maries and his squad leaders.

The main problem was manpower. With Gushwa hurt and the two outposts needing teams, Maries could only dedicate one team to the mission. Boyce would take enough men and firepower to protect the snipers and their Humvees, while the battalion would have a platoon of Humvee-mounted infantry ready to roll to their aid should they get in trouble. While no air support was available, 2–162's parent brigade, Arkansas's 39th Infantry, tasked a battery of heavy artillery to the scouts. Should they get into trouble, they'd have plenty of firepower at their disposal, plus ready backup only a few minutes away at Patrol Base Volunteer.

The plan was brilliant. Boyce had mobility, he had firepower, he had backup. Instead of using a single sniper team—more of an individualistic solution—the decision to use all the available men in the platoon would give them the firepower to tackle most threats should their hide site get compromised.

This was not a standard sniper employment; Boyce didn't pull it out of any tactical manual or book. But then again, no book has ever won a firefight.

Long after sunset, the platoon mounted up and slid through Patrol Base Volunteer's rear gate. They were going mortar hunting.

The platoon split up to search for a suitable overwatch position. Tyson Bumgardner led one patrol over to an abandoned amusement park by Martyr's Monument. They couldn't get a good vantage point from there, so Tyson and Buchholz climbed into a nearby Iraqi Police tower and observed Route Pluto for a few hours while the rest of the patrol pulled security for them on the street below.

The night was full of fireworks. Mahdi Militia teams kept launching rockets from Sadr City at the Green Zone, the administrative heart of the new government and Coalition forces. The Iraqi Police tower happened to be right under their flight path, and every few minutes one would buzz right overhead before exploding a few kilometers behind them in the blacked-out city.

From time to time, an AC-130 Spectre gunship would open fire from an orbit several thousand feet above Baghdad. Its massive firepower would lay waste to one of the rocket teams, but there always seemed to be more willing men ready to carry out the next launch.

As the night wore on, Tyson and Darren Buchholz decided to head back to the rest of the platoon. As they did, Bumgardner remembered an Iraqi Police checkpoint very close by at the Route Pluto entrance to Martyr's Monument. Three men manned that position, armed with two AKs and a Dragunov sniper rifle. They'd been told to expect the platoon, and they knew of their presence, but the patrol remained cautious as they passed close by it on their way back to Lieutenant Boyce.

When the scouts reunited, Randy Mitts told Boyce his patrol had found a great hide site in a neighborhood just north of Martyr's Monument. He led the way, and the scouts stashed their Humvees at the base of a skeletalized eleven-story skyscraper. A wall ran around the perimeter of the building, which provided perfect concealment for the platoon's rigs. Leaving behind a squad to protect the trucks, the rest of the scouts followed Lieutenant Boyce up into the skyscraper.

The war had not been kind to this building. Above the fourth floor, the fighting had torn away much of the outer wall, leaving the rooms within exposed to the outside. Scaffolding had been erected on the northeast side, a sign that the Iraqis were at least making some effort to reconstruct it. The higher they climbed, the more devastation they found on each floor. In some places, the interior walls had been removed by work crews who had also scattered construction supplies all over the place.

Ross Boyce set them up on the seventh floor, and the scouts settled down to take shifts on their weapons, eat, and sleep. They planned to be up there for several days, if necessary. Even in the darkness, they could tell this place had a prime view of the western edge of Sadr City and the neighborhood where Keith Engle had seen the mortar launches. A perfect ambush site. Now all they needed was an enemy to show up.

The hours of darkness passed slowly. The men grew exhausted. Some dozed. Others scanned the city below. Tyson went downstairs to grab some food from the Humvees. As he chatted with some of the other scouts down there, he remembered that it was his sister's birthday. For a moment, he wished he was at Volunteer so he could call her.

Around 0600, Lieutenant Boyce watched from the seventh floor as dawn broke over a city aflame. Eastern Baghdad had once again become a battleground. Rocket fire flared and distant muzzle flashes winked in the black streets below even as the sun crested the eastern horizon. The beauty of the red-orange dawn provided a stunning contrast with the skirmishes that seemed surreal to the Americans. At the same time, the sun blazing in their eyes made scanning Sadr City more difficult. Had it not been for the tactical situation, they would have found a hide that let them put the sun to their backs.

To Boyce's left, Darren "Buck" Buchholz lay catnapping beside his Barrett .50 caliber rifle. The platoon had acquired the semiauto version of the weapon, and already they'd found it their most deadly precision weapon. The Barrett stretches almost five feet long and weighs twenty-eight and a half pounds, making it as cumbersome as one of the platoon's M240 Bravo machine guns. The Barrett can hit targets over a mile away with a bullet traveling nearly twenty-eight hundred feet a second. The incredible velocity gives the round the ability to penetrate concrete and vehicular armor. Officially called the Special Applications Scoped Rifle, the Barrett is capable of knocking out vehicles and penetrating armor. A popular misconception holds that the weapon cannot be used against human targets under the Rules of Land Warfare—mainly due to the fact that it tends to cause people to explode when hit.

Buchholz was universally respected in the platoon for his dedication and refusal to quit. He spoke his mind and never held back his opinion to anyone regardless of rank. That blunt approach was refreshing, but not surprisingly it sometimes caused friction. If he was tough on those around him, nobody was harder on himself than "Buck," as the other scouts called him.

Darren was a native of Dallas, Oregon, a small rural community nestled at the base of the Coast Range. He grew up prowling the woods with a .22 that his dad had taught him to shoot. Just as he left high school, he started hunting deer and elk with his grandfather's pump-action .30-06. He later switched to a Steyr .30-06.

In December 1998, he joined the National Guard and was pulled into Bravo Company 2–162. He stayed with the unit for only nine months, before growing dissatisfied. He wanted to be more than a rifleman, and he wanted to find a way where he could make an impact within the battalion. Buchholz was a man imbued with a sense of service who always wanted to contribute. Not surprisingly, his attitude caught the attention of the scout platoon, and he received an invite to join. Maries pulled him into the sniper section not long after, and he graduated from the Little Rock schoolhouse in 2001.

Until sniper school, Darren's sense of perfectionism stemmed from a lack of self-confidence. He constantly criticized himself and never measured up in his own eyes. That came to a head in sniper school. Between the stress and the pressure, the PT and the technical work that demanded the utmost attention, Buchholz discovered the key to success for himself. No matter how tired, he had a knack for staying focused. At times, while others grew frazzled from exhaustion and the chaotic environments they were thrown into, Buck could stay calm and learned to trust his training. It all clicked one day in the field, and he knew he'd make it through, though half his classmates did not.

When he missed the August 6 firefight, he beat himself up for days. He raged at himself for not just sucking it up and rolling with his brothers. Never mind the fact that he couldn't walk. He'd started to spiral, and some of his old self-doubts returned. When this mission came up, he absolutely refused to be left behind. For him, it wasn't just an opportunity to avenge Giordi's loss, it was his chance at redemption.

While Darren slept, his new spotter, Joe Blon, kept watch on his scope. With Gushwa wounded and out of action, they'd be partnered up for a while. Blon was an unknown to Buck, and this would be their first mission together.

Downstairs, Tyson finished up his meal and rushed back to join Buck and the others. Along with Tyson's M240, the scouts had deployed two other machine guns, manned by Staff Sergeant Paul and PFC Albert. The gun Paul lay behind was the same one Nate Gushwa had used during the August 6 firefight. Both Tyson and PFC Albert's guns had only iron sites.

The snipers had set up their overwatch position in a half-built room on the northeast side of the building behind some of the scaffolding clinging to the exterior that they'd seen the night before. Iraqi construction crews had Sheetrocked one interior wall, and that became the dividing line between Tyson's M240 and the rest of the platoon. Buchholz had positioned himself next to the interior wall, with SSG Paul's machine gun and PFC Albert's deployed to his left. The rest of the men carried M4 carbines. Each scout on watch covered a specific sector of Sadr City. Through their optics, they'd seen considerable movement, but so far the targets they were stalking had eluded them.

The sun rose higher. Some of the men took a break from their observations to tear open MREs, and they scooted back deeper into the building to wolf down their breakfasts while others took their place on watch. The floor Boyce selected lacked outer walls on every side, which gave them a sweeping view of the city. With first light, it became clear to the scouts that the place hadn't been worked on in months, thanks to the escalating violence in the area. The floor was littered with debris, stacks of drywall, and other supplies. Most of the interior walls had yet to be framed. The men leaned against bare steel I-beams as they ate.

The morning dragged on. By 1100, the sound of gunfire echoed through the city as more battles broke out between patrolling American units and marauding bands of Mahdi fighters. Yet so far the neighborhood they were watching remained quiet. A few civilians went about their morning routines. It amazed the Volunteers how these Iraqis seemed to take the violence in stride. They made do under conditions most Americans would find impossible. Commuting to work under the constant threat of roadside bombs or getting caught in a crossfire between Mahdi RPG gunners and M1 tanks in traffic conditions worthy of Los Angeles had already claimed a lot of civilian lives.

Buchholz woke up and stretched. He sat up and leaned against the Sheetrocked wall far enough into the room to remain out of sight from the street below. Blon, his spotter, was on an M24, glassing the peaceful-looking neighborhood. He would take his place and give him a break in just a few more minutes.

Not far away, Sergeant Paul, who had been Gushwa's truck commander on August 6, stared intently through his binoculars.

He said, "Hey, Buck? I think we've got something."

The neighborhood was not as innocent as it first appeared.

Darren returned to his Barrett to have a look. Eight hundred yards away, a group of teenaged boys streamed from a house into the quiet street. A few of the boys carried tires, which they piled in an intersection and set afire. The scouts had seen this sort of thing before and knew these pyres functioned either as a rally point for other insurgent cells, or as a way to melt the street's asphalt so a bomb could be emplaced in the roadbed. Whatever the boys' intent, it telegraphed to the Americans that something bad was going to happen soon.

Boyce crawled over to watch the tire fire through his binoculars. Meanwhile, the other scouts assembled on the firing line. Tyson Bumgardner slipped behind his M240 Bravo machine gun. Its butt to his shoulder, he lay prone and watched the scene in the street over his weapon's iron sites.

A rash of gunfire swelled in the distance. A rocket-propelled grenade exploded. Somebody went cyclic on a machine gun. Brunch in Sadr City; the place was a zoo.

The Oregon snipers maintained their sharp watch on the streets. Suddenly, the men heard the hollow *thunk* of a mortar being fired. The round exploded near Patrol Base Volunteer. Nobody saw the tube.

The kids tossed a few more tires into their bonfire just as a white sedan sped around a corner and came into view. Buchholz and Paul tracked it to a ramshackle dwelling, where it stopped and the doors flew open. Four black-clad men jumped out and ran behind the house into the backyard. Buck kept his Barrett's scope on them.

The four men paused in the yard. One looked around then nodded to the others. Together, they lifted camouflaged sheets of plywood off the ground, revealing a shallow pit with an 82mm mortar nested inside. They jumped inside the pit and manned the weapon. There was a stack of ready ammunition at hand, and one of the men bent down, grabbed a round, and dropped it into the mouth of the tube. *Thunk!* The round arced over the city and exploded somewhere to the west of the platoon's position. The mortar had been preregistered to strike Patrol Base Volunteer. It was a cunning way to get off a few quick rounds before the Americans could locate their launch point and retaliate. They'd probably fire three or four more, then get back in their car and drive to another mortar pit to do the same thing.

It was time to spring the ambush. Boyce quickly assigned the men specific targets and told Buchholz to initiate. Once he fired the Barrett, the rest of the platoon would open up as well. They would smother the mortar teams with firepower in a matter of seconds. Quick, surgical, and deadly effective. With luck, nobody would even see how they died or where the Americans were hiding. The stand-off distance they had would make sure of that—at least for a while.

Boyce's plan to initiate with the Barrett made sense. Buchholz could take out a member of the mortar team with the first shot. It would not be an easy one to make. He had to factor in distance, elevation difference, wind, air temperature, humidity, and even the bullet's spin drift. To do it right required multiple, simultaneous calculations in his head. This is one of the reasons why there are two men per team. The spotter's job is to help with those calculations and even help dial in the shooter's scope. There are so many factors that need to be kept track of for a long-range shot, you really need two brains working together to be most effective.

Darren called to his spotter. No answer. He tried again. Nothing. He popped his head out of the scope long enough to look around. No sign of him. Where had he gone?

Kyle Trimble saw Buck by himself and moved over to spot for him. Using a pair of binoculars, the two men worked through the tactical and environmental issues. Buck got the range to their target. The first mortar tube was 625 yards away.

He dialed the range into his scope. Then he took a breath. It was time to take the shot. He let out half the air in his lungs before he pulled the trigger. The Barrett sounded like a howitzer in the semi-enclosed space of the building. The muzzle brake blew the weapon's gas exhaust ninety degrees to the right—directly into the Sheetrocked wall only a yard away. It sent a concussion wave rebounding off the wall that struck Darren so hard he thought somebody had kicked him in the head. It knocked him off the rifle and left him momentarily stunned.

He'd been so anxious to take the shot, he'd forgotten about the wall—and he'd forgotten to get his ear protection as well. Next to him, Trimble writhed. He'd been knocked flat as well. On the other side of the Sheetrock, perhaps four feet away, Tyson heard the Barrett thunder and felt the floor shudder from the muzzle blast and concussion wave.

Six hundred and twenty-five meters away, the Mahdi mortarman simply exploded. The other scouts saw him one instant, in the next there was nothing but a red mist settling in the air.

That Barrett is a fearsome beast. The ammunition it uses makes it even more destructive and terrifying. High Explosive Armor Piercing Incendiary, or HEAPI, is a jack-of-all-trades bullet that does a little bit of everything to whatever it hits. The outer shell is a mix of lead steel with a copper jacket. Inside the tip is the incendiary mixture, followed by the high explosive compound RX51-PETN. Behind that is a bullet within the bullet. This is the armor piercing part of the munition, made of tungsten carbide and capable of drilling through two-inch plates. When an HEAPI round strikes a target, it burns, explodes, and penetrates almost simultaneously. It'll stop vehicles, disable crew-served weapons, and cause human beings to disintegrate.

The rest of the platoon opened fire as Buck and Trimble snatched earplugs and slammed them home. Trimble moved over to help Bumgardner with the 240. He didn't have a spotter, and Kyle could see Tyson's bursts were falling short. Tyson had set his weapon's tangent for five hundred yards, and in the excitement had forgotten to adjust to seven hundred before he took his first shots. Before Kyle could settle in, Tyson adjusted fire and tracked the rest of the mortar team as they tried to escape. The Mahdi ran out into the front yard and tried to get into the sedan. Bum's 240 spat lead, and this time, he was right on target. His bullets tore into the car and left the men of the mortar team lying in bloody heaps around it.

Kyle brought his binos to his eyes just as Bum asked him to get him on another target. He didn't have to wait long: targets were boiling out into the street from everywhere.

A block away, the boys by the tire fire turned to see the ruined sedan and the dead men bleeding out into the asphalt. Instead of running away, they retrieved mortar ammunition from hidden stockpiles around the neighborhood and rushed them to concealed mortar positions.

Meanwhile, Darren rolled back onto his rifle and settled behind the scope. The scene on the street had changed in a matter of seconds. From the original two mortar crews, the neighborhood now swarmed with Mahdi Militiamen. They came rushing from houses and buildings all up and down the street. Darren glassed the area, watching dozens of armed insurgents running around seemingly at random. Everything was happening so quickly. Heads popped up. Vanished behind walls. Figures darted from one car to another. It was a target-rich environment, but in an overwhelming way. Trying to single an enemy out from the anthill-like circus below required intense focus and discipline.

Seventy yards up the street from the original mortar pit, Buchholz watched a number of Mahdi fighters bolt from what looked like a prefabricated you might find on a Stateside construction project. It was surrounded by a wall of tires, and he could make out several militiamen using them as cover.

Buchholz lased the tire wall. Seven hundred yards. He settled his reticle on an insurgent and fired. The HEAPI flew into the tire wall, blowing rubber in all directions. He fired again. His target still stood, and Darren had no idea where the HEAPI round had gone. He cursed himself and tried again. The Mahdi seemed unconcerned, which meant the .50 cal round had not impacted anywhere near him.

"What the hell? I'm not that bad of a shot," Darren said to himself.

It was a moment that underscored the importance of the two-man team approach to sniping. With so many enemy fighters in the open, Darren was dealing with an overwhelming environment. They were panicked, dashing in all directions. Unarmed kids were in the mix as well. Before settling on a target, Buchholz first had to positively identify the man as an enemy fighter. The only way to do that was to confirm whether that man carried a weapon or not. With the Mahdi moving around so fast through a neighborhood with plenty of walls, parked vehicles, buildings, and other concealment, this was no easy task.

After acquiring a target, Buck had to run the ballistic calculations alone. Change the scope settings, or "DOPE on the Scope," and assess the windage himself. When he missed, he had to figure out why and where his shot had gone so he could get on target. In the middle of a madhouse firefight, these complicated steps are best split between two men.

With Trimble gone, Buck was on his own. He pulled the trigger again. Missed again. Enraged, he suddenly realized why. He'd taken his first shot at 625 yards. Now he was trying to smoke-check a Mahdi militiaman at 700.

Through the ringing in his ears, he heard one of the other scouts shout, "Buck, you're low! You're low."

He didn't have time to redial the scope. He took his best guess, put the crosshairs a few mils above his target, and fired once more. The Mahdi Militiaman exploded.

The shot restored Buck's confidence. He swung the Barrett toward the prefab building just in time to see more men with guns emerging from it. Darren took them down one after another, then walked his fire through the prefab's thin walls until nobody else emerged.

He reloaded, paused, and took the time to put the proper DOPE on his scope. He dialed it in to eight hundred yards and went back to work on more distant targets now. His scope had a minute of angle for every hundred yards. At this range, if his aim was off by one inch, the error would be magnified eightfold and result in a missed target.

Buck didn't miss.

Several insurgents tried to take cover behind a cement mixer. Buchholz hit one with his Barrett. The bullet tore the man apart and sprayed the one next to him with gore. Stunned by what just happened, the man froze. Here was a case study of the Shock Factor at play. The sudden sight of his buddy blowing apart left the Mahdi fighter paralyzed. One minute the man had been running beside his friend, the next his feet melded to the asphalt as he stared at what the HEAPI round had done. His brain could not process that magnitude of trauma within the short time he had left.

He still hadn't moved when Trimble talked Tyson Bumgardner onto him. Tyson's 240 swept across the cement mixer, chewed up the wall behind it, and knocked the stricken militiaman out of his shoes.

Within moments, the street started to look like the set of an apocalyptic horror film, *The Walking Dead* without the zombies. Torn and bloody corpses lay sprawled in gruesome poses. Severed limbs and chunks of bodies littered the scene. A few wounded Mahdi mewled for help in Arabic.

Tyson pushed the 240 to its limits. He ran out of ammunition, called for more and began shouting at the enemy. When the barrel grew red-hot, he swapped it out with another and kept shooting. Brass cartridges bounced off the floor and fell into his shirt sleeves, badly burning his forearms. He never let up on the trigger.

Later, he recalled, "I remember hitting packs of Mahdi looking the wrong way, fully exposing themselves to our fire. I remember watching some of them explode and spray all over. Sometimes others would get caught by multiple ropes of machine gun fire from our converging tracers and get decimated."

Yet as fast as the scouts took them out, scores of Mahdi armed with AKs, machine guns, and rocket launchers joined the fight. At first, they had no idea the origins of the American fire. They shot back wildly in all directions. Some dove for cover if the incoming had been coming from the north instead of the southwest. This left them totally exposed, and they died without ever figuring out their mistake.

Kyle moved off to help SSG Paul, and Tyson swapped out barrels. Heaps of spent brass lay around his gun, and he took a second to sweep them out of his way with his forearms. In seconds, he returned to the fight, unleashing long bursts on the enemy below.

The scouts made the most of the chaos, killing the enemy with ruthless efficiency. Time and again, as their ranks were bloodied, the militiamen would freeze in terror. The Shock Factor at play once again. They died paralyzed with fright.

Somebody finally spotted the American position, thanks to the tracer bullets fired by the platoon's machine guns. At first, only a few stray rounds struck the skeletal building. One bullet pinged into an I-beam over Sergeant Bumgardner's head. Slowly, the incoming grew more accurate.

"We were already way above a maximum sustained rate of fire for the platoon," Bumgardner later said, "and in those split seconds I wasn't engaging, I was desperately looking for men to shoot because the incoming was getting heavier all the time. We were not panicked. We just understood our situation was very precarious."

The machine gunners tore through all their available belts, leaving the 240s surrounded by piping-hot brass shell casings. Buchholz aimed and fired his Barrett as quickly as possible, reloading every time he drained his ten-round magazine. Paul did the same. They finally had a target-rich environment, but they'd caught a tiger by the tail. There were so many targets that if they didn't kill or drive them off, the platoon could be in for some serious trouble.

Lieutenant Boyce grabbed his radio and called for an artillery-fire mission. When he gave the coordinates, the Arkansas brigade balked at the idea of dropping howitzer shells on such a densely populated Baghdad neighborhood. Not only would the civilian casualties be high, but the Americans would have to pay the surviving homeowners for the damage the shells inflicted on their domiciles. The Arkansans said no to both. Without the firepower, Boyce's men would have to deal with the threat on their own.

The Mahdi fighters were slowly getting organized now. Most had taken cover behind cars, walls, and the corners of the dilapidated houses in the area. Brave ones would pop up every few seconds to send a few bullets at the Americans. Though Paul, Bumgardner, Albert, and Buchholz had killed most of the mortar crews, new insurgents had back filled them, reinforcing those positions. They were in the pits now, dropping rounds into tubes. The snipers went to work taking them out as the machine gunners swept the streets.

The engagement area originally consisted of about a block and a half of west Sadr City. Now, as more insurgents arrived, Boyce could see muzzle flashes all over the neighborhood. The platoon started taking flanking fire from the right as even more fighters joined the fray. But unlike my situation in Somalia back in 1993 when we had a pair of Super Cobra gunships on our shoulders, the Guardsmen couldn't get their promised backup.

Even without help, they elected to fight it out.

With the machine guns almost out of ammunition, Sergeant Randy Mitts scampered down the half-completed stairwell to grab more from the Humvees parked behind the building. At the trucks, he joined Andy Hellman, who had been guarding the rigs. Mitts told him what he needed. Together, they began grabbing ammo boxes. Just as they got to work, a mortar round exploded inside the skyscraper's perimeter. The shrapnel splash laced the building, tearing apart scaffolding and showering the Humvees with debris.

Arms loaded with eight boxes—sixteen hundred rounds of 7.62mm belted ammo, the two scouts sprinted back upstairs to get the machine guns back into the fight. When they arrived, the amount of incoming fire had swelled significantly. Most everyone had flattened themselves against the floorboards to present as small a target as possible.

Bum saw them coming and shouted to Randy to bring him his body armor. He'd left his Kevlar vest in a room deeper inside the building, and had been in the fight without protection from Buck's first shot.

Boyce kept trying to get more firepower from brigade, but that was a lost cause. He radioed Patrol Base Volunteer and reported the situation. A platoon of New York National Guardsmen attached to 2–162 was standing by, and Lieutenant Colonel Hendrickson ordered them to Boyce's aid. As they launched through Patrol Base Volunteer's back gate, the Mahdi slowly gained the upper hand on the scouts. Sheer weight of numbers gave them fire superiority.

Buchholz's Barrett roared again and again. The horrifying effects of his weapon scattered body parts and gore as his bullets blew humans to fragments. Often, such scenes would break an enemy's will to resist. In this case, the opposite happened. The more victims Buchholz's rifle claimed, the more enraged and determined the insurgent militia became.

A deeper report echoed from the streets above the din of full-auto AK-47 bursts. The snipers recognized it right away as a Dragunov, a Soviet-built scoped rifle used by enemy snipers. It seemed to be coming from the right flank, but none of the men could locate the shooter.

An enemy sniper is the worst foe an American sniper can face. Trained for stealth, accuracy, concealment, and patience, they can pin, disrupt, shock, and kill just as effectively as our men can. This is why they automatically become our highest priority targets when encountered on the battlefield.

Whoever had the Dragunov was good. He had located and maneuvered on the Oregon snipers, then found a concealed position on the platoon's flank. Though forced by the battlefield geography to shoot from a lower elevation than his targets, which gave him a difficult shot, his bullets kept coming uncomfortably close to Boyce's men.

The scouts searched frantically for his hide, but could not see a telltale muzzle flash or brief flare of sunlight reflecting off a scope.

All they could do was keep low and pray that the guy on the other end would make a mistake. He was too good to make a mistake. Despite their efforts, the scouts failed to locate the enemy sniper. Tyson thought that the shooter must have been near the Iraqi Police checkpoint at Martyr's Monument. That made him remember the Dragunov they'd seen there.

Could the shooter have been an Iraqi cop? It was possible; they knew the scouts were there. But there was no way to be confirm that suspicion. A rocket-propelled grenade exploded a story below them. The building shook from the impact. Machine guns raked the partially finished ceiling overhead. If this got any worse, they could be pinned and trapped in place. The Mahdi might even assault the building, overrunning the small detachment below guarding the platoon's vehicles. The scouts needed the New York boys, but the inexperienced lieutenant leading that platoon got lost in Baghdad's mazelike streets. Boyce tried to talk him to the building, but that only seemed to confuse him more. The situation was growing desperate.

Bumgardner reloaded his 240 machine gun with a fresh belt given to him by Mitts and Hellman. With Kyle helping Paul, Tyson asked Andy to spot for him. Hellman moved beside him just as the Dragunov boomed; its bullet slammed into an I-beam next to Andy. He dropped to a knee and returned fire with his carbine, kneeling beside Bumgardner's left shoulder. The enemy sniper fired again, this time narrowly missing Kyle Trimble.

Bits of ceiling tiles and other debris rained down on the platoon as bullets and rockets swept the building. Without artillery or air support and with their reinforcements roaming around lost somewhere to the west, Boyce could either withdraw or stick it out. Withdrawing under such heavy incoming fire seemed a ticket to disaster. The platoon would be exposed while the men sprinted down the open stairwell, and they would not be able to keep much suppressing fire on the Mahdi as they pulled out.

Boyce didn't want to make that play unless he had no other alternative. They'd stick it out and hope that the New Yorkers would turn the tide back in their favor. If they showed up.

Meanwhile, the platoon needed every man in the fight to try and wrest fire superiority back from the Mahdi. Lieutenant Boyce knelt beside Sergeant Paul and pulled another M24 to his shoulder. Though not a qualified sniper, Boyce had trained extensively on both the M24 and the Barrett since joining the platoon. Sergeant Maries and the other snipers had tutored him well. On the ranges back at Fort Hood, he'd demonstrated uncanny marksmanship.

Through the scope, he could see Mahdi militiamen, dressed all in black with green arm or headbands bounding through the neighborhood below. He settled his scope on the prefab building seven hundred yards away. He dialed in the range, adjusted for the slight summer breeze, and glassed the ramshackle compound. An RPG man stepped out of the prefab, catching Boyce's attention. He slid his crosshairs over the man. Finger on the trigger, he began to put pressure on it.

He hesitated.

Though Boyce came from a military family, he had no intention of making a career out of the Army. He'd joined to do his part for his country, and he'd wanted the infantry because it was the one arm that all other elements of the service supported. Yet he was a gentle human being with a deep streak of altruism and compassion. He yearned to go to medical school and become a surgeon.

Now, instead of saving lives, he was about to take one.

He pulled the trigger. His bullet knocked the RPG man off his feet.

He racked the bolt. Aimed again. Sick at heart, but knowing he had no other choice, he squeezed again. With every rack of the bolt, Boyce realized how much he did not want this life. Trapped by the dire circumstances, he killed, and killed again.

The Dragunov roared. Its bullet creased Bumgardner's helmet, tore off the mount for his night vision goggles and struck Andy Hellman's right knee. It exited sideways, leaving the wound a near-perfect impression of a 7.62mm bullet in profile.

Bumgardner flung himself protectively on top of Hellman until Sergeant Mitts and Sergeant Ash came over to help. Together, they dragged him clear of the firing line at the edge of the building.

"I'm sorry, sir! I'm sorry!" Hellman kept shouting to Boyce, who was watching the scene from the platoon's far left. He was in intense pain, alternating between crying out, swearing, and trying to talk to the guys around him.

The scouts tore open Hellman's pant leg and went to work bandaging the wound. It was well cauterized by the bullet and wasn't bleeding much. "Looks like you'll need a new hinge," somebody said.

Tyson started dressing the bullet hole. He saw the look on Andy's face and tried to keep him loose. "Fucking hell, Andy, you're always trying to get out of everything, aren't ya?"

Hellman, despite the pain the wound inflicted, wanted this documented. "Grab my camera! Take a picture of this thing!"

Seconds later, he went into shock.

"We gotta get outa here," he suddenly babbled, "we gotta go. We need to go. We gotta go." He began shaking violently.

The New York platoon still had not shown up. With Hellman wounded, Boyce knew he had to pull the platoon out. They'd have to do it fast. Without the machine guns and the sniper rifles keeping the insurgents down, they were sure to get hit with a ferocious volume of fire.

He ordered everyone back to the Humvees. Trevor Ward helped Hellman to the stairwell as Mitts, Bumgardner, Paul, and Buchholz covered them. Hellman insisted on tackling the stairs alone, though his friends hovered nearby in case he faltered.

To cover the withdrawal, Tyson ran back to his 240 and sent the last of his ammunition into the enemy below. As he ran out, he began to secure his gear. Ash came up and helped him even as a hail of Mahdi machine gun fire laced the room.

When the last man disappeared down the stairs, Bumgardner stood up, hefting Andy's M4 as Ash slung the machine gun over his shoulder. Then he motioned to Mitts that it was time to leave. Just as they reached the landing, they heard the Barrett roar. The floor quivered. Buchholz was still in the fight.

The two scouts ducked low and went to get him. It turned out he never heard Lieutenant Boyce give the order to displace. He'd opened fire at the start of the engagement without earplugs, and now he was stone deaf, thanks to the Barrett's thunderous report.

Mitts grabbed Buchholz's shoulder and pointed at the stairwell. The sniper looked around in surprise at first, then understood what had happened. He still had work to do though. He'd moved his sector of fire out to a thousand yards by this time. The street no longer teemed with confused enemy. They'd taken cover to return fire, making them significantly more difficult to identify and take out.

An insurgent armed with an AK suddenly bolted across the street. Buck tracked him. A thousand yards away, the man moved laterally from right to left. Buchholz had seconds to calculate how to hit him and what technique to use. For such shots, there are two methods of hitting a running man. The first is the tracking shot and is used when you don't know where the man is going. The key is to know how much lead you'll need at the range you're shooting from, a calculation every sniper practices in training until he learns exactly how many mils he needs to lead the enemy. It is a time consuming process that requires a lot of documentation in the sniper's notebook to perfect. But in combat, that knowledge is the difference between life and death.

The other technique that can be used in this situation is called the ambush. Here the sniper guesses, or knows, where his target is running to and then picks a point somewhere in front of him. He waits until the enemy fighter reaches his mil lead in the scope, then pulls the trigger.

Buchholz didn't have time for the ambush technique. He tracked the running militiaman, drew the scope in front of him until he had the lead just right. He fired as the man made it almost halfway across the street.

The shot was low. It caught the man in the hip and blew him in half. Randy Mitts had been watching and he was astonished at the shot. "Holy crap, Buck!" he shouted.

Enough was enough. They had to leave. Buchholz's body armor, helmet, and pack lay scattered on the floor nearby. As the enemy fire intensified even more now that the Americans weren't fighting back, he scurried around to gather all his gear. Finally, Kevlar on, IBA strapped tight, and the rest of his stuff jammed hastily into his assault pack, he signaled he was good to go.

He got up and moved with Bumgardner for the stairs.

"Hold up," Mitts said. He'd glanced over his shoulder and had seen a Mahdi Militiaman break cover. Exactly how far away he was will probably never be known for sure. Buchholz estimated he was eight hundred yards away. Bumgardner later estimated about six hundred. Mitts put the range around four hundred. Whatever the actual distance, it was a long shot for an ACOG-equipped short-barreled M4. Randy shouldered the weapon. All the training, all the muscle memory developed over years of field exercises kicked in with that one snap-shot. Tyson and Buck watched the man crumple to the pavement. It was the most amazing feat of marksmanship they'd ever seen. Randy smiled as they shouted at him, then shrugged it off like it was all in a day's work. The three of them ran downstairs together, the last ones out of the building.

At the base of the stairs, the men loaded Hellman into one of the waiting Humvees. When Mitts, Buchholz, and Bumgardner reached the ground floor, the platoon piled into their rigs while under mortar fire and sped back to Patrol Base Volunteer.

The battalion's medical staff saw right away that Hellman needed surgery. They called for a MEDEVAC, and a few moments later, a Blackhawk swung onto final approach.

As the chopper landed, the scouts ran to their barracks and grabbed an oversized American flag Hellman kept in his room. It was strictly forbidden to fly it in the open, especially now that Paul Bremer's Coalition Provisional Authority had turned Iraq over to a temporary Iraqi government. But this one moment, that rule was forgotten.

As Hellman was carried to the Blackhawk, the scouts stood on the roof of their barracks, waving Old Glory furiously in the noontime Iraqi sun.

Back in the shrapnel-scarred scout barracks, where the windows had not yet been replaced, Buchholz ignored the growing pain in his head. He had been so severely concussed by the initial pull of his Barrett's trigger that he was slurring his words and having a difficult time keeping his balance as he walked around. Yet before he went to see the medic, he wanted an answer. Where had Joe Blon been during the fight?

He found his spotter and demanded to know where he'd gone. Blon muttered, "I went to the roof to get a better view."

That stank, and Blon knew it. A spotter's place is next to his shooter.

"Did you get anyone?" Buchholz asked, his temper flaring.

"I dunno. I think so," Blon replied.

Buck seized the man's M24 and opened the bolt. It was clean and well oiled. Blon hadn't fired a single round.

Darren looked Blon in the eyes and said, "You are dead to me."

He turned and walked out of the room. Buchholz could hold his head up. He'd come through in the clutch. There would be no thoughts of redemption in his mind ever again.

Buck went down to the battalion aid station and got checked out. Concussion be damned. In a day or two, he'd be ready to roll again.

It had been a hell of a week. On the western edge of Sadr City, Boyce's men had killed at least twenty-two Mahdi Militiamen and wounded more than thirty. The mortar attacks that had plagued Patrol Base Volunteer diminished after that. It was quite an accomplishment for such a small number of men, one that exemplified what a couple of sniper teams could achieve if properly employed. Thanks to Lieutenant Colonel Hendrickson, they had the opportunity to do what we snipers do best. They located, closed with, and destroyed the enemy with long-range, precision fire that minimized civilian casualties.

When things went wrong and the promised support did not arrive, the platoon didn't panic. Far from it. They maintained the discipline needed to stay in the fight until there was no other choice but to break contact and get away. By the time they left, this handful of Americans had been fighting well over a hundred Mahdi insurgents. That they returned home with only one man wounded was a testament to their professionalism and coolness under fire.

CHAPTER TWENTY-SIX
Baghdad 911

Following the August 10, 2004, ambush, the Mahdi Militia continued to launch attacks all over east and northeast Bahgdad. While the main part of the battalion continued to fight it out in the streets of the capital, two platoons joined the 1st Cavalry Division's counterattack in Najaf. The city had been taken over by the Mahdi Militia, and through the first three weeks of August, a combined Iraqi National Guard–U.S. Marine and 1st Cavalry Division assault led to intense building-to-building fighting in that holy city. It would take most of the month to finally subdue the Mahdi Militia and wrest control of the Iman Ali Shrine away from al-Sadr's most fanatical devotees.

As the violence escalated, Lieutenant Colonel Hendrickson let the scout platoon try ever more daring operations. The snipers had proven themselves to be reliant, proactive, and intelligent, and Hendrickson trusted them to use their talents in ways some battalion commanders would never have dreamed of allowing.

The sniper section began inserting into hide sites around northeast Baghdad in hopes of picking off bomb-laying militiamen. This led to one of those unexpected combat moments for Darren Buchholz when, after taking over a civilian's house, they discovered the youngest daughter in the family was very, very pregnant. The Volunteers treated her deferentially and made sure she was well taken care of, but her presence worried them from the outset. The family was sequestered into one room on the first floor, then the men went about setting up overwatch positions inside the house.

Sniper Specialist Jim Schmorde booby-trapped the yard with claymore mines in case they were detected and the enemy assaulted their position. The doors were barricaded, the windows covered. They set up three-hundred-sixty-degree security and took shifts behind their optics.

They settled in for a long week overwatching Route Pluto, the main north-south highway in their section of the capital. Once emplaced in a hide site, the scouts would provide a quick reaction force, but otherwise no American unit would come close to it, lest they give the location away. Should they be attacked, the five snipers in the house would have to hold out for at least fifteen minutes before the scouts could ride to their rescue.

A few days into the mission, the pregnant girl began to show signs of distress. The family wanted to get her to the doctor. Buchholz, afraid that letting them leave would blow their hide site, refused. They tried to make her as comfortable as possible, but the situation deteriorated. The girl began to sob. The family begged Darren to let them leave. He refused.

A day dragged by. The girl showed real signs of distress. Buchholz began to worry that they might end up having to deliver a baby prematurely. One afternoon, the family's doctor came to the house to check on the girl. The father pleaded with Darren to let him in as he knocked on the front door.

Here was a moment Darren never expected to encounter. He had to balance the military needs of the mission with the realities inside the house. They were there to help make the lives of everyday Iraqis better. Denying a pregnant woman medical care was not the way to achieve that. Yet every day Americans, Iraqi troops, and civilians were dying on Route Pluto. Stopping the bomb layers was sure to save countless lives.

Buchholz refused to let the doctor in. The pregnant girl broke down again. The family despaired. Her condition worsened until Buchholz could not in good conscience let her suffer any longer. He let the family take her to their doc. As they left, the Volunteers hastily packed their gear and called the rest of the scout platoon for extraction. The mission was a wash, and the snipers would never be able to use that hide again.

Other missions proved highly successful. One day the battalion received a tip identifying the hiding place of an enemy financier whose cell was responsible for the deaths of forty Iraqi National Guardsmen. Earlier in the deployment, such intel would come in and it would take the battalion considerable time to get approval up the chain of command to lay on a raid. Ninety percent of the time, the raids came up empty.

This time Lieutenant Boyce wanted to do things differently. His men were already locked and cocked, and he knew the financier could bug out to another safe house at any time. He approached Hendrickson and told him the urgency of the situation. Hendrickson gave him the green light to go hit the hideout.

First, he arranged to have a UAV deployed to scope the financier's lair, which was a used car lot. Using the real-time feed, the scout platoon was briefed and they planned the raid on the fly based on the UAV's imagery. It took another ten minutes to brief Hendrickson on how they planned to take the car lot down. He approved. The men loaded up and rolled out.

It took forty minutes from the time they received the intel to get the Humvees on the road. The platoon encircled the lot and sent in an entry team. Being short on bodies, several of the snipers filled positions in the stack that went through the door. Nate Gushwa, back in action despite continued issues with his August 6 wound, later recalled, "I spent almost as much time with the entry team as the number two man in the stack as I did in hide sites." It was a testament to the section's versatility that the snipers could step into an assault role so seamlessly.

The scouts kicked the door in, swarmed inside, and found the financier and a pile of money. Both were scooped up and hauled back to Patrol Base Volunteer in what became the model for future raids. Less than two hours after getting the tip, they'd been able to take down the target. It was so impressive that Major General Peter Chiarelli, commander of the 1st Cavalry Division, called Hendrickson to personally congratulate him on the operation.

At the end of August, Hendrickson ordered Delta Company, 2–162, to raid a large warehouse complex smack in the middle of the August 6, 2004, free-fire zone. The warehouses had been used as a staging base for the Mahdi Militia cells that had attacked the Volunteers and the Arkansans from the 39th Brigade. Take down the warehouses, remove any weapons or supplies inside, and the Oregonians figured they could put a dent in the enemy's ability to operate in Zones 22 and 50.

Delta Company would provide both the entry teams and set up an inner perimeter around the warehouses. To keep civilians and any enemy reinforcements from interfering with the operation, an outer cordon would also be established at key intersections around the complex. Hendrickson still had a platoon of 2/7 Cav's Bradleys, and he tasked them with setting up the outer cordon.

The snipers were to provide overwatch for the operation on the outer cordon. Buchholz, Nate Gushwa (who had recently returned to action despite constant pain in his neck, arms, and hands), and Keith Engle received the assignment.

Given that the battalion had been attacked almost every time they went into Zone 22 throughout the month, Hendrickson asked for, and received, Kiowa scout helicopter air support. The 1st Cavalry Division's aviation brigade was spread thin, so the Kiowas could only remain on station for a short time. After that, the Volunteers would either have to get out of dodge or make do without an eye in the sky.

The battalion launched the raid on August 30. The enemy had been tipped off. When Delta Company surrounded the warehouses, which took up a full city block, the entry teams found very little war matériel.

As the search continued, the enemy began moving around on the perimeter. Every time a militiaman appeared, a Kiowa would sweep overhead to investigate. The terrorist would go to ground and wait until the beat of the American helicopter's rotors grew distant again. Then he'd pop up to maneuver through the urban jungle toward the American perimenter.

As the operation continued, the enemy grew bold. The Bradleys started to take small-arms fire. Mortars began to land. Delta Company's commander urged his men to move faster, get the search over with so the whole force could pull out. But the warehouses were a maze of subdivided rooms and bays, filled with all sorts of random boxes, crates, and junk. Lieutenant Brandon Ditto, the platoon leader in charge of the entry team, could not rush this. His men worked methodically to check every nook and cranny.

In the meantime, the Kiowas were needed elsewhere. When they pulled off the target area, the Mahdi seized the moment. On the south side of the perimeter, two Bradleys covered an intersection next to a repair and truck depot used by the Iraqi Ministry of Transportation. On the other side of the MOT compound were blocks of multilevel apartment buildings with a school several hundred yards away.

Urban fighting in some ways is a lot like combat in natural terrain. The high ground becomes crucial in either environment. Hills and mountaintops have been scenes of key battles throughout history, and in Baghdad, tall buildings served the same function as hills. The Mahdi had learned this the hard way in Najaf and firefights in Sadr City. This time, while elements moved in the street, other militiamen flowed into the apartments and found shooting positions in windows and on rooftops. The MOT vehicle compound became the fight's no-man's-land, like a big mini-fortress just waiting for one side to occupy it. The problem was, getting to it was sure to draw fire no matter which side attempted it.

The level of incoming swelled. The Brads battled back with their 25mm auto cannon. Rocket-propelled grenades struck the street around the tracks. Much of the warehouses remained to be cleared, so this was only going to get worse.

The Brads needed the snipers on the high ground. The MOT compound included a tall building in the middle of its truck park.

Buchholz took his team, supported by a dismounted squad of cav troopers, and dashed through the firefight to the Ministry of Transportation's front gate. When they reached it, the Americans realized they had no way to breach it. The gate was heavy, thick metal and well reinforced. A small sliding peephole door sat in the middle of it. That gave Buchholz an idea. He pounded on the gate with one fist until, at length, the peephole door slid open and a pair of eyes appeared.

"U.S. Army! We need to come in," Buchholz said.

Nate Gushwa, who was standing next to Darren, heard a voice say in broken English, "Go away!"

The peephole slapped shut. Darren and Nate exchanged a glance. In the middle of a firefight, they were having a Wizard of Oz moment.

Darren pounded on the door again. The peephole opened. The same eyes reappeared.

"What you want?" the voice asked.

"We are coming inside. Let us in," Buck said.

"No."

"Yes, we are."

Bullets cracked and whined, an RPG exploded in the street by a Bradley. The situation bordered on the ridiculous.

The eyes tracked across the Americans. Between bursts of gunfire, the Iraqi said, "We cannot guarantee your safety."

"Open the fucking gate right now."

The gate swung open. The Iraqi stared at the Americans as they flowed through it and entered the truck park. There was no time to search the courtyard, so they decided to clear the building and use part of the dismounted Bradley squad to pull security for the snipers.

They stacked up on the door and entered the main building, weapons at the ready. On the first floor they found medical supplies and bloody bandages. The Mahdi had been using the Ministry of Transportation's facility as a casualty evacuation point earlier in the fight.

Hyperalert now, the men headed upstairs ready for anything. Moving in pairs, they cleared the next floor, finding American currency and grenades. No bad guys.

They finished clearing the building and Buck took Keith up to the roof. Nate set himself up one floor down using a window that overlooked both a series of apartments and the school. He settled down behind his M24 and stuck his eye to his scope.

The Mahdi were everywhere, darting from alley to alley, firing at the Bradleys from windows and rooftops. There was no time for deliberate calculations; Nate had to use Kentucky windage to get his M24 on target.

About six hundred yards away, a militiaman broke cover carrying an AK-47. Nate happened to have the scope trained on that section of the street when he made his move. He tracked the enemy, but before he could take the shot, the man reached the school, pulled open a door, and plunged inside.

Nate saw him through a tinted plate-glass window as he moved into a room.

The day had become a furnace—a hundred thirty-five degrees in the sun. The heat meant the M24's bullet would travel farther with less resistance, affecting its drop. No wind meant Nate would not have to compensate for it. Still, at six hundred yards, hitting the enemy through a window presented serious shooting challenges that he had not yet been exposed to in training or in a real-world situation.

This kind of shot is something our Marine Corps shooters first get exposed to in advanced school, then in greater depth in urban sniper school. Glass affects the trajectory and behavior of a bullet significantly. Without understanding that dynamic, it is easy to miss when shooting through a window, even at close range. The type of glass, its thickness, and how it will react to a bullet strike also play a significant role in such a shot.

Nate was dealing with one of the most complex scenarios a sniper can encounter. Six hundred yards is a tough shot under any circumstances, but this young sniper was also firing from an elevated position. Had the target been in the open, Nate would have had to change his point of aim to counter the height difference. When shooting down at a target, the bullet will travel high, so the aim point has to be below center mass. Exactly where to aim is based on the elevation difference and distance to the target. This is the "dangle of the angle," and it is an exceptionally difficult calculation to make on the fly. As a result, we use cheat sheets for such shots.

In Nate's case, he had to fire through glass on top of figuring the dangle of the angle. The elevation distance ensured that the bullet would not strike the pane directly head-on. Instead, it would be coming in at an angle, creating a whole different set of variables as to where the bullet would actually go.

Normally, when shooting through glass without any elevation difference, the bullet will break high and to the right. At six hundred yards, if Nate had aimed at the man's chest center mass, the bullet would have hit the pane, deflected upwards and caught the target in the shoulder. In a situation like that, the sniper will aim a little lower and to the left to compensate.

Now, with elevation changes, the ballistics invert. With the rifle above the target shooting down at him, the bullet fired will strike the pane of glass and deflect low and to the left, catching the target on the right side of his body. In this case, if Nate aimed center mass, his bullet would strike the Mahdi militiaman in the right side between his ribs and hip.

The type of glass plays a role in such a shot as well. Thick, double-paned, or shatterproof glass will affect a bullet differently than a single pane. Will the glass shatter, or will the bullet pierce it and leave only a hole surrounded by spiderweb cracks? In each case, the ballistics are different. We're trained in advanced and urban sniper schools to recognize the type of glass and estimate its thickness, then compensate for what that material will do to our rounds. If we guess the type of material wrong, we'll miss. Glass that shatters deflects the bullet in a myriad of little ways. Glass that doesn't shatter slows the bullet down more as it penetrates, which increases the rate of drop.

Bottom line: this is one of the most difficult shots a sniper can make.

Nate had been shooting his entire life. Every sniper brings a set of intangibles to the table. Our schools hone those natural skills, develops those talents. Sometimes, as in my case, those skills and talents are discovered. Unlike Nate, I had never fired a weapon before I joined the Marine Corps. The Corps taught me everything I knew. Nate Gushwa was the exact opposite: he'd spent almost his entire life with a rifle in hand, honing his skills. Those days spent in the woods, or in his backyard refining his talents gave him the knack to shoot anything well. The Army and Guard trained him, brought him to new levels of skill and knowledge, which fine-tuned his native intuition.

In that moment, those instincts nurtured since childhood took hold of Gushwa. He remembered his grandfather's most important lesson: take a few calming breaths before pulling the trigger.

Inside the room, the militiaman paused to peer outside. He wasn't moving anymore. He probably assumed he was safe now that he had ducked inside the school.

The Oregon deadeye breathed out, in, out again. His body relaxed. He set the crosshairs just a hair high, then fired.

"Nate! Get up here!" Buchholz called from the roof.

Gushwa had time only to see through his scope the hole in the plate-glass window his bullet had made. It seemed to be on target, but he couldn't see the Mahdi fighter any longer. Had he hit the man? Or had he missed and caused him to dive away from the window? Nate had no way to know, and no time to observe and find out.

He picked up his M24 and dashed upstairs. When he burst onto the roof, the scene unfolding there made him stop in his tracks. Engle was hunkered down behind the Barrett .50 cal, which he'd laid atop the waist-high parapet that defined the roof's perimeter. Flanking him on either side was a fire team of Bradley dismounts, all of whom were hunkered down beneath the parapet, out of the line of fire.

Bullets cracked overhead, ricocheted off the building and whined in random directions. Buchholz stood totally erect, his M4 to his shoulder, walking back and forth, his upper body exposed to the Mahdi. The enemy was pouring it on trying to bring the big Oregonian down. He'd pause every few steps, take a shot, then move again to find another target. He was growling and cursing, blasting away at the enemy without any regard to his safety. He seemed oblivious to the bullets whipping past him.

Buchholz had an ACOG four-power scope on his M4. Each time he paused to fire his carbine, he'd face the enemy. Anyone who has ever shot a rifle from the standing position knows how difficult it is to do it accurately. If prone is the easiest, standing is the most challenging, and the way the Army trains its soldiers to shoot this way is very different from most civilian marksmanship classes. Instead of standing with your shoulder pointed downrange, shooting from a profile stance, our warriors learn to put their chests toward their target and lean slightly forward. This method was developed to maximize the safety of our men. Shooting in profile exposes the soldier's ribs and side to enemy bullets. Our body armor does not cover these areas, just the back, chest, and stomach. Some have adaptors that protect the neck, shoulders, and groin, but most infantrymen and snipers don't wear those accessories as they are cumbersome and heavy. But firing with our front to the enemy gives us the full protection of our body armor.

Most of us had to learn this method of shooting while in the service, and it takes some men a lot of time to break their old civilian habits.

Nate took a knee and watched his friend pop off another round. "He looked like Conan the Barbarian playing whack-a-mole with an M4," Gushwa later recalled. "For God's sake, Buck, get behind cover!" he'd told him.

Darren ignored him and kept shooting. Just then a captain who had been in the Bradley with them appeared on the roof. He had come along on the mission as an observer and was not part of the 2-7's platoon attached to the Oregonians. "Hey, I need to take some photos for my research project," he shouted over the gunfire. Buch-holz impatiently waved him forward. The man crouched, camera in hand, and moved up beside Buchholz. He peered over the parapet, snapped a few photos, and went white as a South Dakota winter.

Buck smoke-checked another Mahdi. Suddenly, an RPG swooshed right between him and the captain. The heat of the weapon and the total shock of the near miss caused the captain to flop flat on his back. Staring skyward, he lay there as Buchholz pulled his eye out of his scope to regard him.

"Ya got enough photos yet, sir?" Buchholz deadpanned.

The captain stammered, "Uh, yeah. I'm good."

He crawled off the roof and disappeared downstairs.

A few of the 2–7 dismounts began popping up over the parapet to add their firepower to the fight. Nate moved to the parapet, too. Darren tried to contact Lieutenant Colonel Hendrickson on the sec-tion's secure radio to give him a status report, but the device malfunc-tioned. With the amount of incoming growing, Buck didn't have time for fussy technology. He stowed the radio and knelt beside Gushwa and Engle. In the apartments and street, there were more targets than bullets. Just like August 10.

Several RPG teams maneuvered on the Bradley. Hendrickson was standing near the track when they launched their rockets. The sudden barrage scored several near misses and convinced the 2-7 crew to back their Bradley out of the immediate line of fire. The 25mm spewed flame. Down the street, the cannon shells killed an RPG man, then set fire to the car he'd been using for cover. A moment later, the Brad had repositioned to a less vulnerable spot out of the intersec-tion.

When the track disappeared from the Mahdi Militia's immediate field of view, they shifted their fire to the snipers and the dismounts on the roof of the MOT building. The parapet was swept with a storm of bullets and incoming RPGs.

The dismounts left to return to their Bradley. Buchholz, Engle, and Gushwa refused to leave. Darren spotted an RPG launch in the street, called it out to Nate, who settled his scope on the militiaman's position. He was using a loophole in a concrete wall as a firing slit for his launcher. Gushwa got the range: one hundred twenty-five yards. The loophole was only a few feet high and perhaps eighteen inches wide. The RPG man reloaded, then stuck his weapon through the loophole. Nate drilled him before he could shoot again.

Below them, the car the Bradley had hit now blazed from bumper to bumper. Black smoke filled the street and boiled hundreds of feet upwards.

Three men stole out of an alley and jumped into a blue minivan—one carried an RPG, another hefted an AK. Buchholz called it out. The three snipers concentrated on it. Keith got off one shot with the Barrett .50 cal. His HEAPI round struck the back of the van. Seconds later, Buck shot the driver. The other two bailed out and ran inside a nearby building.

Over the din of the firefight, the snipers heard a wailing siren. It seemed to be growing nearer. Looking around, Nate spotted an Iraqi fire truck speeding toward them.

The Baghdad fire department had arrived. Apparently, somebody had dialed 911.

The firemen drove straight through the middle of the battle, totally oblivious to the bullets and rockets flying around them. They stopped near the burning car the Bradley had hit, pulled out their hoses, and set to work extinguishing the blaze.

On the roof, Gushwa's jaw dropped. Buck turned to him and said, "Is that really happening?"

The Mahdi incoming never slackened. As the firemen doused the car with long streams of water, the fight continued. Keith spotted an AK-47 appear in a window in one of the apartments. Buchholz saw it, too, and knocked the man down with a single snap-shot. Moments later, Nate watched a Mahdi militiaman run into the street five hundred yards away. He called it out, and Buchholz pinned the man with his ACOG's reticle. He triggered a shot, but was low. The bullet struck the man in the leg. He staggered under the impact, but didn't lose his footing. The Oregonians watched as he limped the last few yards to cover.

The car, now good and soaked by the firemen, sizzled and steamed in the street. The Mahdi grew cautious. Fewer exposed themselves in the street, choosing instead to pop around corners to let off a few rounds before ducking out of harm's way. By now, it was mid-afternoon and the day's hundred-thirty-five-degree heat was punishing the snipers, who had no overhead protection from the sun. Nate, bathed in sweat, began to get dizzy. He slid under the parapet and peeled off his body armor as he sucked water from his Camelbak.

"We need to call for ammo resupply," Buck said to Nate.

"Roger," Nate did a quick count. He had borrowed Kevin Maries's M24 for this mission and had brought forty rounds with him. He was down to just a handful of 7.62, with no M4.

Buck and Keith were in the same boat. They wouldn't be able to stay on the rooftop much longer if they didn't get resupplied.

Nate keyed his radio handset and called the BC. He explained their situation and asked for ammo.

Hendrickson replied, "Try to shoot less. We're getting ready to unass."

Buck and Keith heard this and turned to Nate. "Really? Shoot less? You gotta be shitting me."

Fortunately, back at the warehouses, Lieutenant Ditto's men finished the search at last. They'd found very little inside the structures, though it was clear from leftover trash that the Mahdi had been using them as staging bases. Ditto and his men mounted up. Lieutenant Colonel Hendrickson gave the word to pull out.

The snipers broke contact, dashed downstairs and through the Wizard of Oz door to a waiting Bradley. Back at Patrol Base Volunteer, LTC Hendrickson angrily demanded to know why his snipers hadn't been giving him contact reports and status updates. When Buck described the hornet's nest they'd found themselves in on the MOT's roof, all was forgiven.

●   ●   ●

Not long after the warehouse raid, Buchholz and Gushwa took part in another sweep through the same area. This time, the battalion went to go clear the school on the other side of the Ministry of Transportation's motor pool facility. During the search, the Volunteers found a room bathed in blood. At first there was talk that they'd found a Mahdi torture chamber. Then Nate and Buck went to take a look. They walked in to find dried blood all over the floor and wall. The heavy, double-paned, shatterproof window in the room held a single 7.62mm bullet hole. As Nate peered at it, he saw the MOT building in the background. This was the room he'd seen the Madhi militiaman run into during the warehouse scrap. That was his bullet hole. Until that moment, he hadn't known if he'd made the shot. Now, as he stood there with Buchholz, it was clear that he had, and the amount of blood suggested the target probably had not made it.

Only a handful of snipers could have made that shot.

Over the next four weeks, the battalion lost three more men killed in action. Two died in a roadside bomb attack north of Baghdad, while the third, Specialist David Johnson, died in northeast Baghdad in another blast while on a resupply run.

Yet just as quickly as the Second Shia Uprising began that summer, it came to an end that fall. October was dead calm in Zones 22 and 50. November saw a major series of attacks launched by Sunni insurgents reinforced by a cadre of al-Qaida, but the Shia militias never again posed a serious threat to 2–162. A few scattered firefights with the Mahdi Militia remained to be fought in December and January, but the days of massed attacks ended with the warehouse raid.

Lieutenant Colonel Hendrickson took his battalion home in March 2005. During the year the Volunteers had been in combat, they had suffered nine killed and over eighty wounded in action. Over ten percent of his citizen-soldiers had become casualties while struggling to bring stability in Iraq. It was the most difficult and battle-torn deployment the Oregon National Guard had experienced since fighting across the Pacific with General Douglas MacArthur in World War II.

The snipers came home with dozens of confirmed kills, but that is not what they remember. They take pride in the lives they saved at the Ministry of Interior in June 2004. They take pride in stopping the mortar attacks and the friendly casualties they incurred. Who knows how many lives they saved with their August 10 ambush.

Most importantly, Staff Sergeant Maries brought everyone home. Despite rocket attacks, firefights, roadside bombs, and urban ambushes, Nate Gushwa was the only one from the sniper section to be wounded in action, though there were several men from the scout platoon who were hit, including Andy Hellman, Randy Mitts, and Giordi.

Of his section's performance in Baghdad, Kevin later said, "Nate and Buck—they were the best sniper team I had. I could always count on them to get the job done, and they need credit for that."

Ten years later, Tyson Bumgardner looked back on the deployment and summed things up: "Most of us had families with a military hero in them. We all read the literature voraciously, we knew our unit's unique history. We wanted the fight more than most. I think our scout/snipers were able to survive so many close fights with relatively few casualties because of our solid leadership . . . our aggression, discipline, and training. We thought of ourselves specially picked—and Oregon men are expected to never quit any fight. Ever."

Six months after returning to Oregon, Hurricane Katrina devastated the Gulf Coast. The governor of Louisiana appealed to Oregon for help. The 41st Brigade mobilized, and within a week deployed to New Orleans to put an end to the violence and looting there. Hendrickson took three hundred fifty men, veterans of the Baghdad firefights, into the Big Easy with him.

In a neighborhood that once had been home to eighty thousand Americans, the Volunteers found precisely seven holdouts. Here at home, they patrolled the trash-strewn streets and felt nothing but revulsion for the sights they witnessed. Block after block had been devastated by looters and vandals. Gang wars had broken out. The cops had gone rogue and the Volunteers caught them looting businesses and private homes. They encountered bullet-riddled corpses in mini-markets and gas stations, suicides closeted in waterlogged houses. One patrol encountered a corpse whose groin was being eaten by a stray dog. On another, the men escorted a distraught young man searching for his grandmother. Upon entering her home, they found her corpse draped across an upright piano. When the levees broke and the floodwaters hit her neighborhood, she'd been knocked off her feet by the first wave and slammed into a wall. She fell, dead, atop her beloved piano, her corpse rotting in the stifling humidity of late-summer Louisiana.

Running water did not exist in the city. Neither did power. The men slept on concrete walkways and on the steps of the chapel at the New Orleans Baptist Seminary. They took whores' baths, ate MREs, and endured swarms of chiggers, mosquitoes, and other insects every night as they bunked down. None of the men grew used to the stench of the dead city. It permeated their filthy uniforms, lingered in their nostrils, and even the gentle breeze and occasional summer showers offered no respite from the charnel house smell.

Baghdad had not been as bad as this. Said Keith Engle later, "That an American city smelled worse than Baghdad was . . . unbelievable."

Morale in the battalion was tested to the limits. The men had just picked up their civilian lives when they were thrust into this new nightmare. Some of the wives refused to believe they were even in the city, and at least two moved out while the Volunteers were gone. Many of the men, including Tyson Bumgardner, were scheduled to start college in the fall. The New Orleans deployment wrought havoc with those plans.

The cost of this deployment to his men was not lost on Lieutenant Colonel Hendrickson. Within a week, he began to send the student-soldiers within his battalion home so they could make the start of the term at the University of Oregon and Oregon State. Others with family hardships soon joined them. The battalion's footprint shrank until a kernel of one hundred fifty devoted men remained.

Through it all, the sniper section shined. During an early patrol, Specialist Jim Schmorde took one of the battalion's few thermal sights with him. While moving along a raised railroad embankment at night, he spotted a heat signature in a neighborhood that had been particularly hard hit by the floodwaters. After studying it, he was convinced he'd found somebody. Was it a looter? One of the gang-bangers known to be in the area who were shooting at passing rescue crews?

The next morning, the scout platoon went to find out. Using boats scrounged from the area, they motored across opaque black water filmed with rainbow slicks of oil. Schmorde led the search ef-fort to the block where he'd seen the signature. The water there was still at least six feet deep. In places, the flood line reached the eaves of the one-story buildings.

They maneuvered from house to house, unsure of what they would encounter, but ready for anything. At last, as they knocked on one waterlogged front door, they heard a muffled and weak cry for help. Using crowbars, they broke into the house and found a dying eighty-nine-year-old woman. She'd been trapped inside her house for almost two weeks. When the floodwaters receded, they left her doors so swollen that she did not have the strength to open them. Same with her windows. Her rescuers eased her and her wheelchair into one of their boats and returned to the high ground where Patrol Base Volunteer, New Orleans, had been established. There, an ambulance sped her away to Belle Chase Hospital, leaving her wheelchair aban-doned in the middle of Chef Menteur Boulevard.

She survived only because Jim Schmorde had brought a thermal sight on patrol with him. As in Baghdad, here at home the Oregon snipers saved lives.

At the end of September 2005, the last of the Volunteers returned home. Staff Sergeant Maries left the battalion soon after and joined an aviation unit. Buchholz left the Guard, but his desire to make a difference burned inside him. Six months after leaving the Guard, he found himself in a meaningless, dead-end job drawing a paycheck. It was a hollow existence for the man who always wanted to do more for his country and community. After a client yelled at him for an inconsequential error, he walked out and never looked back. He became a police officer in Independence, a small town just outside of his native Dallas. He was accepted onto the county SWAT team and served with distinction before moving on to the Salem Police Department. He continues to patrol the state capital today.

Nate Gushwa was medically retired from the Guard as a result of his wounds. He settled back in his hometown on the coast and rejoined the construction company he'd worked for prior to 9/11. He went to school and is a draftsman today.

He lives with the lingering effects of his wounds every day. The wire that clotheslined him on Route Hamms did permanent nerve damage to his neck. Sneezing for him is an agony. The sudden spasms it causes sends shock waves of nerve pain through his neck, arms, and hands. At times, his fingers tremble uncontrollably.

His refusal to leave the sniper section after he was wounded made things worse for him. Wearing his Kevlar helmet and body armor ensured that his tendons never healed properly. Scar tissue built up over the nerve bundles in the back of his neck. Over the years, the scar tissue has continued to build up and can be seen on X-rays. There's no surgical option for Nate, so he lives with these constant reminders of his time in Baghdad.

Keith Engle returned home and went to sniper school. He took the section back to Iraq when 2–162 deployed for a second time in 2009. It was a very different place by then. The streets weren't filled with Mahdi Militia, the civil war between the Sunni and Shia that had begun at the end of their 2004–2005 deployment had mostly subsided. The battalion ran convoy operations, guarded bases, and chafed at the inactivity, boredom, and separation from their families. Engle lives with his family on the southern Oregon coast and remains in the National Guard today.

The 2–162 snipers still get together whenever they can. They hunt with their sons. On those trips, Nate and Darren use customized Remington 700 rifles built by Daryl Holland specially for them. At night, over drinks, they'll sometimes speak of their firefights and gut-check moments in Baghdad. In their most serious moments, they grow bitter and angry over what happened at the MOI. For all they accomplished that year in Iraq, the pall cast by June 29, 2004, and the discovery of the torture compound has left them with unanswered questions. Who gave the order for the scouts to withdraw? Who was responsible for the unit inflicting the torture?

But most of all: what happened to the men who were not released? Those thirty-three men the scouts could not save. No matter where the snipers will go in their lives, those tortured, battered men are never far from their thoughts.

If only they could have done more.

It is the lament of soldiers and snipers whose sense of duty, honor, and service are embedded in their DNA.

EPILOGUE

America has always had a schizophrenic relationship with her snipers. On one hand, precision shooting is coded into our national DNA. To survive in the New World once required a combination of rugged individuality and the ability to use a rifle effectively. Shooting was not a recreational activity, it was a matter of life and death. It was a crucial life skill men took pride in and shared with their sons. Rifles became precious heirlooms, passed down from one generation to the next as a sacred American rite of passage. In battle, our sharpshooters played a key role in securing our nation's independence at such places as Saratoga and Cowpens. They also saved the young republic more than once, most notably at New Orleans in 1815.

As warfare evolved through the nineteenth century, sharpshooters remained an important component of the American experience in the Civil War and the Indian Wars, but there developed a sense that there was something odious about such tactics. Sniping violated another deep-seated American value, one of sportsmanship and fair play. That revulsion contributed to the Army's refusal to establish a permanent sniper corps in peacetime. That lead to a lot of hard lessons in World War I and II, when poorly trained American snipers went up against crack German and Japanese shooters who were better equipped.

The Army's riflemen came to consider snipers a necessary evil. When pinned down by enemy shooters, they called for our own snipers to help clear the way. At the same time, they looked with disdain upon those who carried scopes atop their M1903s, considering them little more than killers.

Legendary war correspondent Ernie Pyle perhaps summed it up best in *Brave Men:* "Sniping, as far as I know, is recognized as a legitimate means of warfare. And yet there is something sneaking about it that outrages American sense of fairness."

The importance of sniping was recognized most clearly in the Marine Corps, which established three stateside schools dedicated to the craft. Yet even within the Corps, it was a necessary wartime evil. Soon after VJ day, the schools were closed down and the minting of new shooters came to an end.

The same thing happened after every war. In the heat of battle, the call for snipers was heard from every fighting front. In peacetime, their bastard stepchildren status ensured they were the first element of the military cut as budgets withered.

That prejudice against snipers cost a lot of American lives in the twentieth century as our enemies remained far more advanced in this realm than we were. Only after Vietnam did we finally learn the lesson. Both the Corps and the Army established dedicated, and permanent, sniper schools. The craft was taught, but often money for our specialized equipment languished. American snipers often bought their own gear and ammunition to compensate for their government's penny-pinching.

The War on Terror changed the American sniper's status within the military, and our society. Time after time on these new battlefields, shooters proved their worth as agents of death and protectors of life. Countless American soldiers and Marines returned home to their loved ones because of the expert work of America's snipers. As combat shaped and revised our tactics, our shooters grew to be the most skilled and experienced on the planet. Not since the earliest days of our nation have our snipers played such a transformational role on our battlefields. Their prowess and achievements have led to a renewed golden age for our small, elite corps of warriors, unseen since the days of the Messenger of Death standing high atop the ramparts defending the Big Easy.

And yet, with peace almost upon us as our forces draw down in Afghanistan, America's snipers fear for the future. While new weapons and technologies that will make them even more effective on the battlefield are just now coming into service, the Army and Marine Corps face massive budget cuts in the years to come. If history is any guide, that does not bode well for our battlefield sentinels. The shortsided mistakes that followed World War I and World War II are being repeated, and unless Marine and Army snipers gain powerful advocates in Washington, their specialty may again disappear, or at least be imperiled. Should that happen, the next time America's warriors are called to battle, they will be thrown into the fray without these angels on their shoulders.

Every shooter who has ever looked through a scope at America's enemies knows the tragedies that will follow should we fall into the trap of our historical mistakes. The Shock Factor isn't just about dominating a battlefield, killing the enemy or destroying him psychologically. It is about protecting our own. Without the men behind the scopes, the soldiers in the street will be forever vulnerable. That is the great lesson of the War on Terror, and every sniper prays our nation takes that lesson to heart.

ACKNOWLEDGMENTS

JACK COUGHLIN:

This book was written as a testament for all snipers who have served our nation. John and I are grateful to every shooter interviewed for this book. Your time, energy, and memories made this book possible, and we hope as you read our words you feel like we've done justice to your achievements on the battlefield.

JOHN BRUNING:

In May 2008, I was fortunate to function as an OPFOR "sniper" for Alpha Company, 2–162 Infantry during a National Guard field exercise at Goshen, Oregon. I remember very clearly being hunkered down under a pine tree on a slope overlooking a makeshift village by the Lane County dump, observing 2nd Platoon as they worked. Trying to simulate a react-to-sniper drill was tricky at best, and there was clearly no way to create the Shock Factor that makes snipers so valuable in battle. Yet the drill left a deep impression on me. I looked through the scope at men I knew well, most were good friends, and one by one, I pulled the trigger and called their names to the Observer Controller functioning as the referee for the exercise. As each man went down, and the platoon took cover and countered my presence,

I gained a glimpse of how vulnerable our warriors are to a concealed, trained shooter. The importance of having such men protecting my friends as they went about their missions was driven home to me, and I left with a great appreciation for those who carry scopes into combat.

So when I had the chance to work with Jack Coughlin on a book about such men, I jumped at the chance. I had just come home from Afghanistan, where I'd been an embedded writer with elements of the Oregon National Guard and the 3rd Combat Aviation Brigate, 3rd ID, and wanted a new project that had value and meaning to me. When our agent, Jim Hornfischer, suggested we team up on *Shock Factor*, I was all in.

Working with Jack was a tremendous professional experience, and he has become a valued friend. Thank you, Jack, for everything.

To Charlie Spicer—it has been a great pleasure to work with you and the team at St. Martin's. Your patience as our snipers came and went on overseas deployments was much appreciated, and the final result is very much a product of the great team we all became. Thank you for taking a chance on me, I am grateful for the opportunity. April, your tireless work and patience have been much appreciated. The book is much better for your efforts on our behalf. Thank you, and thanks to the rest of the team at St. Martin's who made *Shock Factor* a labor of love.

Much of *Shock Factor* was written in my library in Independence. My daughter, Renee, made sure I was taken care of through many long nights. I would find notes on my laptop, treats on my desk. At odd hours of the night, she would get up and check on me to see how I was doing. Later, after Renee went through brain surgery, she spent six weeks with me day and night as she recovered from her operation. I've never had so much fun working, Cricket, than when you were hanging out with me. Thank you for all the motivation and the care. You're an amazing young woman.

Both Renee and Ed joined a rifle team soon after I started writing *Shock Factor* with Jack. As a result, Ed was fascinated with the stories we were developing, and sharing chapters with him became one of the rituals that defined much of the book's progress. Thank you, Ed; your love and support have been pivotal.

To Jenn, it didn't turn out the way we thought it would, but your friendship and love have always been a vital part of my life. Thank you for all the countless things you've done for me as I've worked to develop this crazy career of mine. Our children will go far in life, no doubt because of the passion, care, and devotion you've given to them. Just know, I will always appreciate all that you have given me.

Kevin Maries was the first military sniper I ever met. Kevin, you are a marvel, and your friendship means more to me than I can ever express. We may go months or even years without seeing each other, but I always know you're there. Thank you for everything you've done for me.

Dan, Tyson, Randy, Darren, and Nate—you guys are the best. Thanks for all your time and effort; I hope you feel like we've done the sniper section justice here. And guys, thank you for letting me be a small part of the battalion's training operations from 2007–2013. Those are weekends I'll never forget, and my appreciation for everything you all accomplished was reinforced by those experiences.

To Jason and Adam, new friends made through this book—thank you for everything. Adam, I'm still listening to that song you told me about! Jason, I hope we can link up in New York at your restaurant some day; I'm really looking forward to that.

Chris Kyle, though you'll never read these words, it was a great privilege to get to know you a little bit back in the fall of 2011. When we talked about your mission to kill or capture Thomas Tucker's abductors, this book became personal to me. Thomas was an Oregonian. I met one of his cousins in a restaurant in Independence a short time after he'd been killed. The pain of his loss was evident, so being able to write about the justice exacted on those responsible for that pain made *Shock Factor* more a crusade than just a book for me. Thank you for sharing those memories.

Jim Hornfischer—what can I say? You've been a friend, a rock, a man who transformed my life in 2006, then transformed it again after I came home from Afghanistan. Your efforts, your honesty, and your integrity in a business that Stephen King once called a "Tiger Pit" is utterly unique. Thank you for all that you have done for me and my family—and one of these days we really need to have a beer, damnit!

Allison—your support and faith in my writing has never wavered. Even after I returned home unsure of the way forward, feeling lost and questioning the course of my career, you've been there to remind me why I've been put here in the first place. It wasn't for fluffy kitten stories. Honoring those who served with the best words I can find is more than a profession, it is for me almost a monastic calling. You made sure I never lost sight of that again. Thank you for reminding me who I am and will always be. And when the sadness and pain of loss that surrounds what I do seems overwhelming, you are there with warmth and humor to lift me back up. Thank you for so many gifts so selflessly shared over these many years.

Lastly, Taylor Marks: I carry your spirit with me through every day, every decision. I've lived with your sense of adventure, your strength and courage as my guide every day since the war took you from us. My family will never forget.

INDEX